T

Stevan E. Hobfoll

Tribalism

The Evolutionary Origins of Fear Politics

palgrave
macmillan

Stevan E. Hobfoll
Department of Behaviorial Sciences
Rush University Medical Center
Chicago, IL, USA

ISBN 978-3-319-78404-5   ISBN 978-3-319-78405-2   (eBook)
https://doi.org/10.1007/978-3-319-78405-2

Library of Congress Control Number: 2018939905

This Palgrave Macmillan imprint is published by the registered company Springer International Publishing AG part of Springer Nature.
The registered company address is: Gewerbestrasse 11, 6330 Cham, Switzerland

PRAISE FOR TRIBALISM: THE EVOLUTIONARY ORIGINS OF FEAR POLITICS

"Who among us has not been concerned, even frightened, by daily exposure to the significant and growing divides among those who inhabit this globe? In his usual thorough, well documented, and candid manner, Stevan Hobfoll helps us understand the varied derivative domains, the evolution, and the current manifestations of these divisions. Grounded in these factors, he also provides a road-map toward healthier ways to live with our neighbors. This book will make readers think and question. Hopefully, it will also, be a call to action in service of finding our shared humanity."

—Brian W. Flynn, Ed.D., *Rear Admiral & Assistant Surgeon General, USPHS, Ret.*

"In this profoundly illuminating book, leading psychologist Stevan Hobfoll explores the tribal thinking that threatens to tear whole nations apart. He explains how our evolutionary tribal capacities are being manipulated and how to renew the battle against these harmful processes. It is an essential book for our times that changes how we see ourselves and will have broad social and political impact."

—Stevan Weine M.D., *Professor of Psychiatry & Director of Global Medicine, University of Illinois at Chicago College of Medicine. Author of* When History is a Nightmare *and* Testimony after Catastrophe

"Hobfoll's decades of influential theoretical and empirical psychological scholarship, alongside his years of international military experience during both war and peace, cast an unprecedented and riveting lens to one of the most vexing topics of the 21st century... immensely readable, this brilliant and mesmerizing volume will be of interest to social and behavioral scientists, medical and military scholars, as well as anyone who seeks to be intellectually challenged..."

—Roxanne Cohen Silver, Ph.D.

To Dr. Ivonne Hobfoll, my partner and greatest supporter for these many years, and our world journey. It took courage to marry me!

ACKNOWLEDGMENTS

There are always many people to thank in the production of such a book. Dr. Thomas Deutsch quickly and insightfully read every chapter and made formative comments. Another colleague and friend who chooses to be anonymous was also instrumental and gave brilliant comments on each chapter. Alexandra Fischer, Dr. Kenleigh Rodem Foreman, Dr. Teresa Lillis, and Katie Rim helped edit, check references, and proof-read thoughtfully and offered many insights and gently raised issues of errors and lack of clarity. The Palgrave Macmillan team, including Kyra Saniewski, Rachel Daniel, and Mary Al-Sayed, was great to work with and always supportive. Susan Schulman was an early champion of the book and rich in ideas and insight.

Of course, the work and everything said in it is my responsibility and not of their making.

CONTENTS

LIST OF FIGURES

LIST OF IMAGES

CHAPTER 1

The Primitive Self and the Power of Catastrophic Threat

When Mexico sends its people, they're not sending their best....
They're sending people that have lots of problems, and they're
bringing those problems with us. They're bringing drugs. They're
bringing crime. They're rapists. *(Donald Trump in a speech
announcing his presidential candidacy [1])*
The black-haired Jewish youth lies in wait for hours on end,
satanically glaring at and spying on the unsuspicious girl whom he
plans to seduce, adulterating her blood and removing her from the
bosom of her own people. The Jew uses every possible means to
undermine the racial foundations of a subjugated people. *(Adolph
Hitler, Mein Kampf [2])*

There is no message more powerful, primal, or primitive than the evoca-
tion of the need to protect the family and "tribe." We are genetically
primed and culturally shaped to alert, defend, and aggress, and even to
sacrifice the self in the service of that protection. In fact, the alert, defend,
and aggress system is primary and fundamental to how humans are biologically built, emotionally primed and cognitively programmed. This
extends to the protection of our way of life and the fundamental elements
of those things we hold most dear—the protective response against
threats to our freedom, our nation, our land. The provocation of outsiders raping our women is one of the most primitive and basic of these

© The Author(s) 2018
S. E. Hobfoll, *Tribalism*,
https://Doi.org/10.1007/978-3-319-78405-2_1

threats. Rape invalidates the blood line, as the progeny of such an act may not be ours, and the loss of our women or our children translates to the end of the tribe.

Seen this way, the warning of the threat of attack by the "evil other" is a base warning to our built-in, hard-wired protective response system. It appeals to a primal need to protect the tribe and the family from the evil predator, the "other" who, once identified, must be destroyed. Humans are imbued with a deep intellect and the ability to think and process complex information in a rational manner. Even deep emotions can be reasonably understood and evaluated, arriving at fair and balanced conclusions. However, our rational thought and the processing of complex information are very much forebrain activities, relating to what are termed our "executive brain functions," and is the last portion of the developed human brain in evolutionary time.

More basically, and more substantively, humans are protective animals with deeper brain structures that are more primitive and equally part of our origins, playing a major regulatory role determining how our brains and bodies function. Fight and flight are reflexive responses, and the fight-flight response is nested in deep, more primitive brain structures that developed for survival. Our responses to threat of the self, the family, our loved ones and the tribes to which we belong alert the brain and body to concentrate, act without thought, and ignore the vagaries of sound argument and compassionate consideration that might delay the need to rapidly and decisively respond. They cue hormones, blood, and muscles, and signal tribal affiliation behavior for mobilization of the protective response system.

1.1   WE ARE PRIMED TO BE ALERT AND READY TO REACT TO A DANGEROUS WORLD

Our modern, cultured self is a rather recent evolution in human existence. Any semblance of what we call culture consists of no more than perhaps 20,000 years of our history, when the first towns were formed near the Sea of Galilee during the Last Glacial Maximum. Our biology and our brain had over 2 million years of time to develop prior to this, and during this entire period, and for the most part until a few hundred years ago, the instinct to protect and survive was central to existence.

It is only recently that the threat of attack and loss due to famine, war, criminal violence, and disease was not essential parts of human life. Our built-in sensitivity to loss and threat is a response to our need to defend against disease, attack from neighboring tribes and wandering bands, and internal violence within the group. We are of course aware of the threat of disease prior to more modern public health and medical intervention, principally the introduction of soap, clean water, and penicillin. More surprisingly, the murder rate in Medieval Europe was dramatically higher than today, with scholars reporting rates as much as 30 times higher than modern Europe, including acts of terrorism [3].

We decry the upswing of "modern" violence in the U.S., longing for the "good old days." In fact, U.S. rates of homicide in colonial times were many times higher than today. The presence of increasing law and order structures in the form of better laws and better policing, and the reduction of poverty, resulted in a drop in homicide from the colonial period, which saw homicide rates of greater than 25 per 100,000 of population, compared to recent national rates below 5 per 100,000, a fivefold decrease [4]. Put in other terms, the rates of homicide nationally from 1700 until the Civil War were appreciably higher than the murder rate in New York City in 2015 of below 4 per 100,000 [5]. In fact, homicide rates today are markedly lower than in the early twentieth century in the U.S. [6]. Clearly, our news media portrays us as living in a dangerous world, but this state of affairs is better than in nearly any prior period.

Because of the saliency and consistency of ongoing, monumental threat throughout human development, we do not need to scratch humans deeply to bring the primitive, protective, and aggressive self to the fore. As an illustration of how close our primitive self is to the surface, we witness how aggressive affiliative behaviors are acted out on the playing field of often violent competitive sports, where teams are followed with a dedication akin to nationalism, and fans dress in tribal colors, carry team flags, and scream for blood. In Europe, fan behavior has actually blended with White supremacy nationalism, in a dangerous mix.

The game of soccer (what the rest of the world calls football) evolved in medieval times, involving hundreds of players in what is sometimes referred to as "mob football." In these pitched battles, rival villages and towns watched a form of controlled warfare to decide disputes over land, personal arguments, and rights of commerce [7]. Fast forward to 2015, soccer violence has escalated, as economic and national tensions rose. Fans, dressed in tribal-like colors and face painting, ripped out seats in Belgrade, Serbia, and attacked rival Parizan, injuring dozens of police in a bloody melee, hurling lighted flares and metal objects using military-like tactics [8]. Brazilian fans have murdered offending referees and players [9].

Any quick minimization of this as only a phenomenon of overzealous sports enthusiasts, and not related to political process, is quickly dispelled when one understands that the attacks are often perpetrated by White supremacist groups, and that they are intimately linked with "[r]acism, anti-Semitism, and xenophobia...[which] are becoming...widespread" [among these fans], according to Moshe Kanto, president of the European Jewish Congress [10].

1.2   OUR BRAINS RESPOND TO EXAGGERATED MESSAGING OF LOSS AND DOOM

The most effective way to add fervor, strength, and resolve to any political or social argument is to invoke the specter of loss and doom. The hyperbole of threat, and particularly existential threat, is the most powerful fuel of action. Framing in black and white, not shades of gray, is both the means and the terminus for attracting any audiences' attention, whether at the doctor's clinic, in the courtroom, or in the world of politics. Reasonableness and carefully weighed argument does not sell newspapers, does not keep the viewer from the remote control, and does not attract donors' dollars.

Only if the enemy is committed and perceived as capable of destroying us can we advocate, as did presidential candidate Ted Cruz in December 2015, "*If I am elected president, we will utterly destroy ISIS.... We will carpet bomb them into oblivion. I don't know if sand can glow in the dark, but we're going to find out!*" [11]. As carpet bombing is aimed at obliterating human life of civilians, of leveling whole cities, and is an ineffective strategy for undermining military capability of an enemy, we can understand that the true purpose of such bloodthirsty political diatribe is meant to excite some powerful and primitive force experienced by a large segment of the population. It is what they want to hear.

This primitive response is more universally experienced when there are real threats of terrorism, whose purpose is to create a sense of terror far disproportionate to its actual danger. We only require the hint of threat to alert our protective systems. For evolutionary purposes, our brains developed to be loss sensitive [12]. The loss of a tooth, of several females of productive age, of two hunters in the tribe, of a source of water, all threatened end of life, end of the tribe, and an end of our progeny. In contrast, the brain barely recognizes gain. It was not possible for our ancestors to make more than temporary gains during our evolutionary period of development. Indeed, the sole purpose of gain was itself to protect against future loss. This primitive and basic element of our brain shapes our emotions, how we organize our attachment to others, our seeking protection and safety, and the very way we form our cultures and governments. It is therefore a highly effective strategy to speak in terms of extremes and the extremis of threat and annihilation.

Hence, Obama is not just someone we deeply disagree with; his political agenda has been the "worst in U.S. history" and he is a threat to us no less than communism, Hitler, and ISIS. Indeed, if we go further, and we link President Obama to terrorism as he himself is a Muslim, and then we argue that Muslims are our enemy who we must annihilate, then we must annihilate President Obama. He is not just someone that the right deeply disagrees with, he is not an American, he is part of the Muslim world that plan our destruction, and the worst president in history.

1.3   GUNS AND VIOLENCE AS AN OBVIOUS OUTGROWTH OF THE PRIMITIVE PROTECTIVE SELF

The same argument of extreme, with a basis in impending doom, is set forth by the gun lobby. We require, they argue, an armed populace to defend against ultimate threat. But to energize this argument, they must make our government and its leadership suspect. Government itself, and recently our own FBI, must be seen as either already conspiring to take away our liberty, or likely to take such action. For again, if that threat is only theoretical, far-off, or unlikely, then there is little energy in the defense of Second Amendment rights to bear arms. They must be the Nazi Gestapo and the Soviet Secret Police. Ironically, those who take this route sow the seeds for fascism by so doing. This is vividly portrayed in recent attempts by Fox News, using Trump surrogates to discredit the FBI and the Justice Department as they investigate Russian meddling, and potential conspiracy by the Trump team in the last election.

The FBI has become America's secret police. Secret surveillance, wiretapping, intimidation, harassment, and threats. It's like the old KGB that comes for you in the dark of the night banging through your door...the FBI is a shadow government. [13]

The stench coming out of the Justice Department and FBI is like that of a third world country. Well, it's time to take them out in cuffs. [14]

6 S. E. HOBFOLL

If this need to demonize is not understood, then those from more liberal camps, or even the reasonable political center, cannot understand why
the gun lobby will not accept restrictions on automatic weapons and see
this as an infringement of their rights. Those not familiar with weapons
might think a handgun or hunting rifle is sufficient for any private citizen.
But those are wholly inadequate against the weapons of war that a government might bring against us.

To stand up against a government, already infiltrated in their minds by
Nazi Gestapo and Soviet KGB, requires an assault weapon. An AK-47
(Kalashnikov) or an M-16 effectively fires 100 rounds per minute, and gun
advocates would like to have the maximum 100-round drum magazine
available. Only if you understand the nature of the threat they feel as real,
can you appreciate that they still feel insecure without the assault rifle's
available grenade-launching capabilities. Such weapons have no purpose in
hunting, unless you are hunting terrorists, and are all the more necessary
if your government is perceived as having the near-term potential to act
against you. Such weapons have no purpose in hunting, unless the fear is
of the Mexican rapists and murderers that Donald Trump claims are pouring across our borders. Such weapons have no purpose in hunting, unless
your fear is of Blacks rising against Whites in a race war.

In his chaotic speech at a recent NRA national meeting, the conservative talk show host, Glen Beck, projected a giant image of a Nazi character
in a "Sieg Heil" salute as the enemy of gun owners' rights and the right to
bear weapons. But the image was of New York City Mayor Michael
Bloomberg, himself a Jew, who had the audacity to promote gun safety
[15]. Similarly, NRA leader Wayne LaPierre promotes the right to buy
any, including automatic weapons, as necessary for our survival in the face
of "riots, terrorist gangs, and lone criminals…the threat of Latin American
drug gangs…and civil unrest" [16]. His writing is infused with racial over-
tones. He responds, as he likely truly and deeply believes, that "it's not
paranoia to buy a gun. It's survival." Survival means survival of the self
when facing a criminal, but the energy of his words is only empowered
when he evokes survival of "our way of life," "America," and places imminent threat as immediate, and not some vague distant possibility.

We must take people at their words. LaPierre knows guns and knows
that for reasons of ease of access and maneuverability a full-length or even
a short breach automatic weapon is not best for the tight quarters of protecting one's home. He is advocating for the private ownership of weapons of war. They are called "assault rifles" for the obvious reason that they

are weapons of tactical assault. His messaging is meant to alert the tribe to the imminence of the threat from the "Black hoard" that is ready to erupt at any moment.

The invoking of the image of survival is inherent in our conceptualization of the ultimate evil of Nazism. The survival drum is beaten constantly not only by extremists, but by mainstream political figures. Mike Huckabee has been a conservative evangelical candidate for president in several recent electoral cycles and appears more grandfatherly than hateful. But he warned during his role as a Fox News host in April 2013 that Obama was plotting to use gun confiscation to create a Nazi-style regime [17]. When Ted Nugent, a member of the NRA board and someone who has no national political stature, compares Obama to a Nazi, it can be more easily dismissed, but when sweet, compassionate, and deeply Christian Mike Huckabee evokes these images, it must be seen as a mainstream fear as Huckabee received tens of millions of votes in his presidential bids.

1.4   THE STORM OF TERRORISM AND THE PRIMITIVE RESPONSE

The purpose of terrorism is to create a sense of terror and fear, far disproportionate to the actual destruction caused by the violent act itself. The term we use, calling it *terrorism*, is likewise exploited to justify our response to it. In a strict definition, terrorism is political violence brought to innocent civilian targets. However, we are no less likely to call it terrorism when the target is against the USS *Cole*, a powerful nuclear-armed guided missile destroyer (12th of October 2000 in the port of Aden, Yemen). We still call it terrorism when the attack is the deadly 1983 Beirut truck bombing of the barracks of the 1st Battalion 8th Marines, killing 241 American Servicemen. And there is no rule of war that combatants when they are off-guard are out of bounds.

Before I am accused of supporting terrorism, let me set the record straight that as a former officer of the Israel Defense Forces and in many civilian roles that I have filled I am dedicated to stopping terrorism, and I would and have supported ultimate force in doing so. I am pretty hawkish on the topic. Rather, my point is that we use the word terrorism to raise the fear factor and rally a united response. I personally am equally motivated to merely defend those I love and the nations and people I support against violent acts of war, traditional or nontraditional. But for politics to stir the masses, we need the concept of terror, and the enemy needs the concept of freedom fighter, preserver of liberty, defender of the Holy Koran, or our "Christian way of life."

Terrorism evokes terror, and we respond to the apparent randomness of the threat. Global news also sells newspapers and air time for advertisers, priming the pump of terrorist threat. In this way news sources serve as the public relations department of terrorist organizations, getting their message of fear out far better than the terrorists alone could ever manage through their internet capacities. In fact, terrorist organizations often strike on Friday so that the news and photos of the terrorist events remain unfiltered until Monday, as journalists move to a more part-time pace over the week end. In this way, terrorist organizations utilize the media in a sophisticated manner. They rely on the internet for direct communication, motivating adherents, and planning. They use public news broadcasting to project their message of violent threat and this is central to their success in projecting their image of power.

The attacks of terrorist organizations are designed to frighten the population, assert their power, and disrupt life. Their attacks are planned to create the most vivid and disturbing visual images. Israel has long experienced the brunt of such attacks, with Passover celebratory Seders, public buses, shopping malls, and night clubs being the target for bloody suicide bombings. It is the images of torn flesh, screaming women and children, and shaking cameras that project the chaos and terror that terrorists hope will punish their enemy. The softer the target, the harder the impact, so they aim violence at the most vulnerable elements of society. Filmed beheadings and executions are well-thought-out and orchestrated in the theater of violence they script for broadcast in 24-hour news around the world.

A central element of the fear evoked by terrorism is that it can occur anywhere, and often targets civilians in their everyday human endeavors. The horror of the September 11th attack on the New York World Trade Center brought the war of terrorism home to Americans. Europeans remained more complacent, even amidst endless warning of a large radicalized Jihadist element living in their midst.

That complacency ended abruptly in 2015 when Paris was rocked by the Charlie Hebdo attack, killing 11 journalists for the crime of cartooning the Prophet Mohammad. Not yet fully heeding the warning, all doubt evaporated for the French on Friday, November 13, 2015, when coordinated terrorist attacks struck Paris and the northern suburb of Saint-Denis. Beginning at 9:20 pm on date night, a time of fun, and dancing and laughter, when young people should fear nothing worse than failing to find a desirable romantic partner, ISEL terrorists murdered 130 people, seriously wounding another 368 people in a multi-site attack on innocent civilian targets. It was intentional that they chose a time of laughter and everyday celebration.

Ironically, during my time in Paris just prior to the Charlie Hebdo attacks, lecturing on terrorism as an American who also holds an Israeli passport I found that most young Parisians were anti-Israel and had bought into a rather anti-Semitic view of the Middle East that they shared with the terrorists. In most of my talks it was clear that my audience sided with the terrorists against Israel and indeed most voiced the opinion that Israel was the terrorist organization. I was advised to hide my Israeli identity, and to not mention that I was Jewish (especially by French Jews) for fear of not just isolated reprisal by Muslim extremists, but because of the overt, shared hostile view among the general public, especially young people, toward Israel. But this is small irony, as these young people became victims because they were French and because destruction of their freedom, their joy of living in a world where women are not covered, would serve as a testimony to the power of ISEL and their disturbed version of Koranic law and principles. And terrorism works.

Americans', and now Europeans', fear of terrorism is far disproportionate to the threat in any rational sense. Examining preventable diseases and injury-related deaths in the U.S., figures from the Centers for Disease Control and Prevention indicate that yearly deaths due to heart disease are estimated at around 633,000, nearly 80,000 people die yearly due to diabetes, and over 38,000 die yearly due to liver disease and cirrhosis [18]. For 2015 the U.S. National Highway Traffic Safety Administration reported 10,265 U.S. road deaths with confirmed blood alcohol level of 0.08 [19]. Thirty-six percent of those killed were not the intoxicated driver. By comparison, from 2001 to 2013, which included September 11th, over 406,000 people died by firearms on U.S. soil, compared to 3030 people killed by terrorism [20]. Subtracting the large tragic number of victims who died when the World Trade Center was attacked on September 11th, "only" 424 individuals were killed by terrorist acts on U.S. soil, since that date. Although these statistics are somewhat in arrears due to the time it takes to officially accumulate statistics, the general trends still effectively hold. The chance of Americans or Europeans being killed or injured during a terrorist attack is less than slight. Each loss of life is devastating, but terrorism is not a likely threat.

As humans we must always manage risk probability. Getting into a car is typically the most dangerous thing civilians do. But we do not fear our cars and seldom change our behavior to avoid travelling in a car. Clearly if you should be fearful of something it is driving in a car, alcohol, obesity, or the gun in your own home, not terrorism. Words matter because they reach into deeper brain structures and elicit primitive levels of fear that are disproportionate to any reality. It is hard to rally the public to the fear of cows or lightning, even if the CDC reports that cows and lightning yearly kill more Americans than Islamic terrorists. Cows and lightning do not have the billion-dollar modern news empire working at their behest, and we are not hard-wired to fear them as we are the "evil other."

1.5   WHO ARE THE TERRORISTS ANYWAY?

It is also instructive to look at who the terrorists are, as to make ourselves safe we need to know from what direction the threat is coming. The conservative right has clearly painted much of the Muslim world as suspect. Both leading Republican presidential candidates Ted Cruz and Donald Trump insinuated that Muslim Americans were also not to be trusted, promoting internal surveillance of Muslims living in the U.S. Despite clear and overwhelming evidence that such events never occurred, and unable to produce the film records he claims he saw, Donald Trump insisted…

There were people that were cheering on the other side of New Jersey, where you have large Arab populations. They were cheering as the World Trade Center came down. … There were people over in New Jersey that were watching it, a heavy Arab population, that were cheering as the buildings came down. [21]

By such means, the threat of the outsider is manipulated by political opportunists who pump public fear, evoking the dual image of the foreign enemy and the enemy in our own midst. As President, Trump has continued by forwarding fake videos depicting Muslim violence against Christians. In this manner, President Trump has promoted hatred in a way that is reminiscent of Fascist pre-WWII Europe. Indeed, the videos were originally posted by Britain First, a far-right ultranationalist political group [22]. This group is so far out of the political mainstream that it was deregistered as a political party by Britain's Electoral Commission [23].

The facts regarding the actual sources of terrorism would be surprising to most Americans. Since September 11, 2001, nearly twice as many people have been killed by White supremacists, and anti-governmental fanatics and other non-Muslims in the U.S. than by radical Muslims [24]. By championing the idea that there is a war on Whites and a war on Christianity, politicians are ideologically arming terrorism in the U.S. Governor Rick Perry, when running for election in 2012, promised that if he was elected he would "end Obama's war on religion" [25]. Bobby Jindal, the presidential candidate and governor of Louisiana, warned that "the American people, whether they know it or not, are mired in a silent war" against "a group of like-minded [liberal] elites, determined to transform the country from a land sustained by faith into a land where faith is silenced, privatized, and circumscribed" [26]. Such language clearly insights "patriots" to act against the aggressor, only the aggressor is America itself, or at least liberal America and its government.

Once again we see the use of the language of war and the ultimate enemy to exhort the passions of the brain regions related to tribal survival. On July 10, 2015 in the publication Red State, the leading conservative news and opinion blog, the author writes "But make no mistake – *the aims of secularists in America are the same as those of Islamic terrorists in the Middle East and elsewhere: to drive Christianity out of public life*" [27]. This writer is not voicing an extremist position, as he is essentially echoing presidential candidate Ted Cruz who has repeatedly stated that there is a war on religious freedom and Christianity in particular. To a gathering of 2500 at the Iowa Events Center on August 21, 2015, Cruz spoke powerfully from the podium, "There is a war on faith in America today, in our lifetime....Did we ever imagine that in the land of the free and home of the brave, we would be witnessing our government persecute its citizens for their faith?" [28].

It is this language of threat to our founding principles, the principles that generations have shed their blood to preserve that rallies political votes, because it evokes the passion of war and sacrifice on the tribal level. It motivates voters to make it to the polls, to vote for Christian leaning, conservative candidates. But it is also a rallying cry for violence that mirrors the language used by Jihadists about the "West and the American Satin in its Israel helpmate." Just as in Islam, there are four ways for believers to fulfill their Jihadist obligations:

1) with faith in the heart, 2) by preaching and proselytizing, 3) by good deeds, and 4) by confronting unbelievers with the sword. [29]

Islam, like all world religions, is a religion of peace, but violence is called for when the religion and those of the religion are attacked, when war is made on them, as radical Muslims believe is occurring. Thus, extremists worldwide use the argument of black vs. white, good vs. evil, us vs. them, and that you must choose "our side" "our tribe," or you are among the evildoers of the other side.

> *O ummah [community] of Islam, indeed the world today has been divided into two camps and two trenches, with no third camp present: The camp of Islam and faith, and the camp of kufr (disbelief) and hypocrisy—the camp of the Muslims and the mujahidin everywhere, and the camp of the Jews, the crusaders, their allies, and with them the rest of the nations and religions of kufr, all being led by America and Russia, and being mobilized by the Jews.* (Abu Bakr al-Baghdadi, leader of ISIS [30])

Substituting the words of Conservative politicians of the right is a simple exercise that illustrates their use of these same structures for their call to arms.

> **Fellow Christians**, indeed the world today has been divided into two camps and two trenches, with no third camp present: The camp of **Christianity and faith**, and the camp of **secularism, liberalism** and hypocrisy—the camp of righteous **Christians** everywhere, and the camp of the **liberal secularism** led by the **liberal left**. (insertions mine)

And with such powerful language, reasonable Christians are incensed and rally to the polls, less reasonable Christians turn to far-right talk radio and develop wild conspiracy theories, and extremist Christians blow up buildings and attack Black churches. But each of these groups claims the illegitimacy of the elected liberal, secular government that is argued by mainstream political leaders.

1.6   ADD THE INGREDIENT OF EXISTENTIAL THREAT TO ANYTHING AND…VOILA INSTANT PRIMITIVE RESPONDING

It might appear obvious that the primitive, protective self is a closely wired response to the threat of violence, terrorism and war. But the depth of the threat narrative, like a magic poison elixir, can be applied as an ingredient to virtually anything to produce the dynamics of the response to ultimate threat. Our brains are so alert to such threat messages that once flavored with existential threats, little else rational is processed. Attention, argument, and behavior rally around the threat theme and support it because of the essential biology of survival. In fact, in a natural response, the brain begins to filter out non-threat messaging as dangerous because they avert attention from the required protective response.

Ted Cruz, in September 2013 from the floor of the U.S. Senate, said, *"If you go to the 1940s, Nazi Germany. Look, we saw in Britain, Neville Chamberlain, who told the British people, 'Accept the Nazis. Yes, they'll dominate the continent of Europe but that's not our problem. Let's appease them'"* [31]. You would imagine he was responding to Obama's lack of response to terrorism, or Europeans not taking action to protect Israel, or even abortion, which for many is akin to murder. But, he was relating to the Affordable Care Act, Obamacare. In this way, the Affordable Care Act becomes Nazism, Obama becomes Hitler, and any who fail to make an ultimate sacrifice against it, become cowards. Further, their act as cowards drives us to the precipice of what, overspending, making medical care more intrusive by government? No, it takes us to the precipice of ultimate evil and the end of days.

From the beginning, opponents' view of Obamacare was that it would destroy the country, making it an ultimate existential threat, as to destroy the country is to destroy who we are and all we cherish. How this will occur is seldom explained, and now many years after its inception, no apocalypse has occurred. True, Obamacare is not a perfect program, but even major corporations are fairly comfortable with how it has played out. Obamacare increases taxes, switching costs that were largely occurring anyway to the tax base. And one can appreciate the conservative viewpoint both against large government and higher taxes, but it is not an ultimate threat. It is a much smaller program than social security, Medicare, or public schools. So, it is neither ultimate in size nor impact. So, the rhetoric of destruction and end of America is a clarion call that they know will rally the troops, as troops are willing to go to war against ultimate evils. And of course, many conservatives are also against public education and the Environmental Protection Agency.

Christian Evangelists are largely against Obamacare (and the EPA for that matter). Is it somehow a threat to Christianity? In fact, Obamacare has seen the extension of medical care to millions of formerly uninsured individuals, bringing them the miracle and succor of modern medicine. Is this not the most Christian of acts? Even if costs were higher, is this not the Christian thing to do? And indeed, economists have consistently found that health care spending costs have slowed to record lows, since the Affordable Care Act was introduced. There has been a sizable drop in the nation's uninsured, millions receiving regular access to medical care for the first time. Older children remain medically protected among the middle class, a sizable percentage of these being the children of Evangelical Christians, along with all of our adult children, as parents can keep their children on their health insurance until age 26. So again, the Affordable Care Act seems to be consistent with Judeo-Christian values (as it is to the values of all the world's major religions).

For centuries, the Church and Christianity has spent greatly and disproportionately to heal the sick. Hospitals throughout the world have been and still are largely sponsored by Christian charity. So, perhaps it is the provisions of Obamacare for contraception and abortion, but these are matters of health policy that can and are largely enforced through any medical insurance, that must meet federal law and nondiscrimination. One can even see the rationale behind the argument that the Bible speaks to freedom, and the Affordable Care Act limits some freedoms by enforcing certain choices. But so do many laws, and certainly many major laws.

So, what becomes apparent is that the Evangelical abhorrence to the Affordable Care Act is more about their being right-wing Republicans than any Christian group. And then when they choose Donald Trump over Ted Cruz and Marco Rubio, and indeed a much more Christian-practicing Hillary Clinton or Barack Obama, it would appear that it is Obama and Clinton they hope to defeat, and not the evil of Obamacare. In this manner, this desire to defeat the Democrats is a desire to defeat ultimate evil, or logic just cannot become this twisted. Otherwise they would be fighting to preserve the universality of Obamacare, and remove the offending religious infringements, not the entire ending of Obamacare. They would be offering clear, workable proposals to keep millions of children and families insured and speaking to those very Christian aspects of Obamacare. But the Evangelical right is silent on these issues.

Obama "the dictator" is another ultimate argument where the magic ingredients of infusing any issue with survival and ultimate doom are applied as they refer to "Dictator Barack Hussein Obama." Rep. Robert Pittenger stated in response to President Obama's executive order on guns in January 2016 that "legislation is passed by Congress. It's not passed by monarch" [32]. We are a democracy and this makes the image of the totalitarian dictator abhorrent to us, a reason to rise up and overthrow a false government. We do not want a president who rules us, but one who shares power with the Congress.

But the courts have not struck down these "dictatorial executive orders," the point being that legal authority has preserved his use of Executive Authority, consistent with the constitution. So perhaps what is meant is that Obama is just dictating too much, and a real president would be less executive. Luckily, executive orders are numbered and have been since the Federal Register Act in 1936. Franklin Roosevelt, likely due to the exigencies of war, tops the list with 3721 Executive Orders. Barack Obama has issued the fewest Executive Orders of any modern president per term, and they number under 250, through March 2016. Ronald Reagan far exceeded Barack Obama with 381, and George W. Bush ended his presidency with 291 [33]. As Fig. 1.1 shows, President Obama was the least dictatorial of presidents, but the call for our freedom against the great dictator, the ultimate threat to our freedom and way of life has been made and the call to our patriot spirit has been made...damage done.

What we must instead conclude is that those who in mainstream politics charged him with the punishable crime of being a dictator, merely

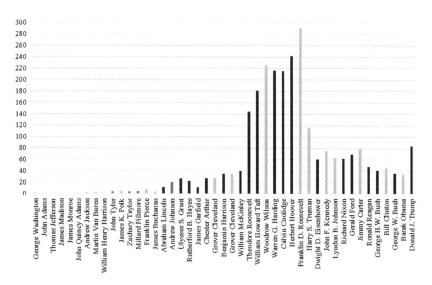

Fig. 1.1   Executive orders per year in office. (Adapted from Kristen Bialik, *Pew Research Center* [33])

meant that they did not like his politics. But arguing mere political differ-ences does not evoke any of the rancor, disdain, and hatred that these poli-ticians desire to fuel the defeat of a government which they do not even recognize as legitimate. The Muslim, noncitizen, falsely elected, commu-nist president is also a dictator...words of revolution, not political activ-ism. As the poster which popular right-wing radio host Alex Jones encourages you to download and place in public places and Facebook, the dictator must be stopped [34]. Extremist of course, but his radio show has up to 2 million listeners per week, more than Rush Limbaugh and Glenn Beck combined (Image 1.1) [35].

Once the Nazi metaphor is raised, to argue in favor of the target, is to argue in favor of tyranny and ultimate evil. Conservative, evangelical presi-dential candidate Ben Carson assigned the Nazi framework to nearly every aspect of political opposition. In August 2015 on the TV show *Nevada Newsmakers*, Carson compared Planned Parenthood to Nazi liquidation genocide.

I certainly see a connection in the sense that Margaret Sanger, their founder, and people like Adolf Hitler ... felt there were certain people who were superior and certain people who were inferior. And the way that you strengthen the soci-ety was to enhance superior ones and eliminate the inferior ones. [36]

Image 1.1   InfoWars.com's "Stop Dictator Obama" contest [34]

In the broadest terms, Ben Carson extends the Nazi metaphor to all of those who sit on the opposite side of government. As quoted on the conservative web site Breitbart.com, Carson states that "the current state of our government and institutions are very much like Nazi Germany": *"You had the government using its tools to intimidate the population. We now live in a society where people are afraid to say what they actually believe"* [37]. He [Carson] blames in particular political correctness and government intimidation for the state of today's Nazi-like reality.

Nor is this tool of infusing any issue with existential threat and the assignment of the evil of Nazism only used by Republicans against Democrats or by the far right against the left. The use of fear messaging that alerts the brain's built-in responses of deep fear and survival reaction can be effectively added to nearly any argument. It is a language that is used as a weapon of politics amongst the right as they justify their position and attack the position of their political competition within their own conservative faction of the Republication party.

On April 10, 2016, on NBC's *Meet the Press*, Donald Trump's convention manager Paul Manafort said of conservative presidential candidate Ted Cruz, "You go to these county conventions, and you see the tactics, Gestapo tactics, the scorched-earth tactics" because "they are not playing by the rules" [38]. So, "not playing by the rules" constitutes Gestapo tactics and the life-threatening scorched-earth policy. The German Secret State Police, the Geheime Statspolizei (Gestapo for short) were the personification of the evil of Nazism. The utterance of their very name struck the deepest chord of fear. They had the power of arrest, interrogation, and incarceration, often summarily executing any perceived enemy of the Nazi regime. With terrifying authority, they descended on the home and workplace abducting Jews, communists, labor leaders, gypsies, and Christians. Their tools were terror, liquidation, starvation, summary execution, confiscation of property and theft of cultural treasures. They performed as supervisors in the death camps. To use the Gestapo metaphor is abhorrent, but it is a powerful rallying cry if politicians choose to rely on the politics of fear to rally their supporters and delegitimize their opposition.

1.7   THE SEARCH FOR OUR HUMANITY

How we react to those who oppose us is always a tightrope walk when deeply felt issues are being addressed. Terrorism, war, abortion, and even conservative versus liberal politics raise many difficult questions. Even determining our direct response to terrorism itself draws the best and worst of our reasoning.

Responding to terrorist attacks in Israel, Rabbi David Stav, national-religious chairman of the orthodox Tzohar rabbinical association, stated that a terrorist who is injured and no longer posing an immediate danger must not be harmed further. *"In these days in which the blood is boiling... it is important to preserve our moral superiority; [we must] not harm those involved in murderous acts who have already been neutralized and do not represent a threat,"* he ruled [39]. But Safed Chief Rabbi Shmuel Eliyahu stated unequivocally that *"[i]t is forbidden to leave a murderer alive ... Jewish law is clear... there are courts that can avenge blood and there are individuals who can avenge blood"* [39]. Another prominent Israeli religious authority, Rabbi Ben-Tzion Mutzafi, laid his interpretation of Jewish law out in no uncertain terms, *"It is commanded to take hold of his head and hit it against the ground until there is no longer any life in it"* [39].

Addressing and combating extremist ideology in word and deed is perhaps the greatest, most defining struggle of our generation. How we counter extremist ideology will likely be the meter on which our success as a civilized society will be judged by the lens of history. If everything is argued in the extreme and all who oppose us in political life are delegitimized and cast as tainted by ultimate evil, we lose the proportionality that is required for political discussion, and to know when discussion should legitimately end and violent defense of the self, family, and nation begin. Losing this proportionality is as old as the bible, and you may choose which bible you are referring to. For Torah, Old Testament, an "eye for an eye," had nothing whatsoever to do with taking another's eye in revenge, no matter how often it is misused. It is a tract that details the financial obligation incurred toward one's neighbor if you are responsible for the loss of his eye. But our desire for revenge, to protect through all means possible, is hard-wired in our deep brain and easily brought to the surface of any issue that we feel passionate about. All we need is to portray the opposition as rapists, murderers, or dictators who will steal our freedom. Label them Nazis, terrorists, or fascists, and we elicit the primitive response system of rally, defend, and aggress, allowing no sanctuary. Our passions are found in the same deep, early formed regions of our brain, and essential for our survival as a species. The human response to words, and sticks, and stones is deeply ingrained in our fundamental, evolutionarily developed biology, and easily signaled and brought to the surface.

REFERENCES

1. The Washington Post. (2015, June 16). Full text: Donald Trump announces presidential bid. *The Washington Post*. Retrieved September 20, 2017, from https://www.washingtonpost.com/news/post-politics/wp/2015/06/16/full-text-donald-trump-announces-a-presidential-bid/?utm_term=.28651ffda224

2. Hitler, A., & Murphy, J. V. (1981). *Mein Kampf.* London: Hurst and Blackett.

3. Eisner, M. (2003). Long-term historical trends in violent crime. *Crime and Justice, 30*, 83–142.

4. Fischer, C. (2010, June 16). *A crime puzzle: Violent crime declines in America*. Berkeley Blog: Politics and Law. Retrieved September 20, 2017, from http://blogs.berkeley.edu/2010/06/16/a-crime-puzzle-violent-crime-declines-in-america/

5. DeStefano, A. M. (2017, January 3). NYC homicide stats comparable to '60s; other crimes down as well. *Newsday*. Retrieved September 20, 2017, from https://www.newsday.com/news/new-york/nyc-homicide-stats-comparable-to-60s-other-crimes-down-as-well-1.12858407

6. Dunning, E. (1999). *Sport matters: Sociological studies of sport, violence and civilisation*. London: Routledge.

7. Todd, O. (2015, April 25). Violent scenes at derby between Red Star Belgrade and Partizan Belgrade delays game and leaves 35 police officers injured. *Mail Online*. Retrieved September 20, 2017, from http://www.dailymail.co.uk/sport/football/article-3055654/Violent-scenes-derby-Red-Star-Belgrade-Partizan-Belgrade-delays-game-leaves-35-police-officers-injured.html

8. CBC News. (2013, July 7). Soccer fans stone, decapitate referee in Brazil. *CBC News*. Retrieved from http://www.cbc.ca/news/world/soccer-fans-stone-decapitate-referee-in-brazil-1.1398879

9. Young, J. (2014, May 28). Soccer's deadliest fans: The troubles world of Brazil's 'organizadas'. *Rolling Stone*. Retrieved September 22, 2017, from http://www.rollingstone.com/culture/news/soccers-deadliest-fans-the-troubled-world-of-brazils-organizadas-20140528

10. Bendavid, N. (2015, April 29). Soccer violence escalates in Europe. *The Wall Street Journal*. Retrieved September 22, 2017, from https://www.wsj.com/articles/soccer-violence-escalates-in-europe-1430308902

11. Glueck, K. (2015, December 5). Cruz pledges relentless bombing to destroy ISIL. *Politico*. Retrieved September 20, 2017, from http://www.politico.com/story/2015/12/cruz-isil-bombing-216454

12. Tom, S., Fox, C., Trepel, C., & Poldrack, R. (2007). The neural basis of loss aversion in decision-making under risk. *Science, 315*(5811), 515–518.

13. Jarrett, G. (2017, December 6). *Hannity*. (S. Hannity, Interviewer).

14. Pirro, J. (2017, December 9). *Fox News*.

15. Walshe, S. (2013, May 7). Glenn Beck offends Jews by depicting Mayor Bloomberg in Nazi-style salute. *ABC News*. Retrieved September 22, 2017, from http://abcnews.go.com/Politics/jewish-leaders-glenn-beck-apology-comparing-bloomberg-hitler/story?id=19119684

16. LaPierre, W. (2013, February 13). Stand and fight. *The Daily Caller*. Retrieved September 22, 2017, from http://dailycaller.com/2013/02/13/stand-and-fight/

17. Shen, A. (2013, April 3). Mike Huckabee: Obama may be planning to grab guns and launch a Nazi-like dictatorship. *Think Progress*. Retrieved September 22, 2017, from https://thinkprogress.org/mike-huckabee-obama-may-be-planning-to-grab-guns-and-launch-a-nazi-like-dictatorship-63e4950effa6/

18. Centers for Disease Control and Prevention. (2017). *Leading causes of death*. Centers for Disease Control and Prevention. Retrieved September 22, 2017, from https://www.cdc.gov/nchs/fastats/leading-causes-of-death.htm

19. National Highway and Traffic Safety Administration. (2015, December). *Alcohol-impaired driving*. National Highway and Traffic Safety Administration. Retrieved September 22, 2017, from https://crashstats.nhtsa.dot.gov/Api/Public/ViewPublication/812231

20. Jones, J., & Bowen, E. (2015, December 30). American deaths in terrorism vs. gun violence in one graph. *CNN*. Retrieved September 20, 2017, from http://www.cnn.com/2016/10/03/us/terrorism-gun-violence/index.html

21. CBS News. (2015, November 22). Trump claims thousands in Jersey City cheered 9/11 terrorist attacks. *CBS News*. Retrieved September 22, 2017, from https://www.cbsnews.com/news/trump-claims-thousands-in-jersey-city-cheered-911-terrorist-attacks/

22. Landers, E., & Masters, J. (2017, November 30). Trump retweets anti-Muslim videos. *CNN Politics*. Retrieved December 18, 2017, from http://www.cnn.com/2017/11/29/politics/donald-trump-retweet-jayda-fransen/index.html

23. Smith-Spark, L. (2017, November 29). Britain First, the far-right anti-Muslim group retweeted by Trump. *CNN*. Retrieved December 18, 2017, from http://www.cnn.com/2017/11/29/europe/uk-politics-britain-first-trump/index.html

24. Bukay, D. (2006). The religious foundations of suicide bombings: Islamist ideology. *The Middle East Quarterly, 13*(4), 27–36.

25. Blake, A. (2011, December 7). Rick Perry ad condemns Obama's 'war on religion'. *The Washington Post*. Retrieved February 8, 2018, from https://www.washingtonpost.com/blogs/the-fix/post/rick-perry-ad-condemns-obamas-war-on-religion/2011/12/07/gIQAZHpZcO_blog.html?utm_term=.d1eca71e0e08

26. Miller, J. (2014, May 10). Bobby Jindal: Government waging "silent war" on religious freedom. *CBS News*. Retrieved February 8, 2018, from https://www.cbsnews.com/news/bobby-jindal-government-waging-silent-war-on-religious-freedom/
27. Red State. (2015, July 20). A war on Christianity? Surely, You Jest.... *Red State*. Retrieved February 8, 2018, from https://www.redstate.com/diary/davenj1/2015/07/10/war-christianity-surely-jest/
28. Margolin, E. (2015, August 21). Cruz warns of 'war on faith' at religious freedom rally. *MSNBC*. Retrieved February 8, 2018, from http://www.msnbc.com/msnbc/ted-cruz-warns-war-faith-religious-freedom-rally
29. Shane, S. (2015, June 24). Homegrown extremists tied to deadlier toll than Jihadists in U.S. since 9/11. *The New York Times*. Retrieved September 22, 2017, from https://www.nytimes.com/2015/06/25/us/tally-of-attacks-in-us-challenges-perceptions-of-top-terror-threat.html
30. SITE Intelligence Group. (2014, July 1). *Islamic State leader Abu Bakr al-Baghdadi encourages emigration, worldwide action.* SITE Intelligence Group. Retrieved September 22, 2017, from https://news.siteintelgroup.com/Jihadist-News/islamic-state-leader-abu-bakr-al-baghdadi-encourages-emigration-worldwide-action.html
31. Wing, N. (2013, September 25). Ted Cruz takes Nazis, the moon, pro wrestling, and children's books to Senate floor speech. *Huffington Post*. Retrieved September 22, 2017, from https://www.huffingtonpost.com/2013/09/24/obamacare-ted-cruz_n_3984245.html
32. Gordon, G., & Off, G. (2016, January 6). N.C. Republicans sharply criticize Obama's gun-control measures. *McClatchy DC Bureau*. Retrieved February 8, 2018, from http://www.mcclatchydc.com/news/politics-government/congress/article53377870.html
33. Bialik, K. (2017, January 23). Obama issued fewer executive orders on average than any president since Cleveland. *Pew Research*. Retrieved September 22, 2017, from http://www.pewresearch.org/fact-tank/2017/01/23/obama-executive-orders/
34. InfoWars. (2012, June 18). Explosive activism: Stop dictator Obama contest. *InfoWars*. Retrieved September 22, 2017, from https://www.infowars.com/explosive-activism-stop-obama-dictator-contest/
35. Blakeslee, N. (2010, March). *Alex Jones is about to explode*. *Texas Monthly*. Retrieved September 22, 2017, from https://www.texasmonthly.com/politics/alex-jones-is-about-to-explode/
36. Phillips, A. (2015, October 9). Ben Carson: The biggest fan of Nazi metaphors in politics. *The Washington Post*. Retrieved February 8, 2018, from https://www.washingtonpost.com/news/the-fix/wp/2015/10/09/ben-carson-the-biggest-fan-of-nazi-metaphors-in-politics/?utm_term=.160392df5355

37. Breitbart TV. (2014, March 12). Exclusive – Dr. Ben Carson: Our government is like 'Nazi Germany'. *Breitbart TV.* Retrieved September 22, 2017, from http://www.breitbart.com/video/2014/03/12/exclusive-dr-ben-carson-our-government-is-like-nazi-germany/
38. Manafort, P. (2016, April 10). *Meet the Press.* (C. Todd, Interviewer) NBC.
39. Sharon, J. (2015, October 15). Rabbis in conflict over whether to kill wounded terrorists. *The Jerusalem Post.* Retrieved October 3, 2017, from http://www.jpost.com/Israel-News/Rabbis-in-conflict-over-whether-to-kill-wounded-terrorists-426051

CHAPTER 2

Threat and the Tribal Self

Asa McCoy, a Union soldier, came home after discharge in 1865 and was hunted down and murdered by a Confederate local militia with members of the Hatfield family. Thirteen years later, Randolph McCoy claimed that a pig possessed by Floyd Hatfield was really his. Not appreciating the judge's verdict, two McCoy brothers killed the offending Hatfield who testified in the case. Next, like Romeo and Juliet, Roseanna McCoy ran off with Johnse Hatfield, leading to kidnappings of the betrothed by her family and further violence. The feud reached its peak with the 1888 New Year's Eve Massacre on Randolph McCoy's cabin, where his two children were murdered and his wife beaten and left for dead. The final feud trial was in 1901, 36 years after the original event. [1]
Farida was captured by ISIS fighters after ISIS overcame Kuchu, a Yazidi village of 2,000 near the Sinjar Mountains in northern Iraq. Together with 80 other Yazidi girls and young women, she reports being taken to the ISIS slave auction where men would buy and take away two or three girls each. She recalls the men joking about how they would abuse her and about their sexual prowess. The men from her village had been already separated and executed. Farida, only 19, and other girls much younger were raped, beaten and starved. They were kept as sexual slaves, rewards to ISIS leaders first and foremost and secondarily to ISIS fighters. The ISIS justification is clear and simple. The Yazdi are non-Muslim and murder of the men and sexual subjugation of their young women is justified by ISIS perverted interpretation of Islamic law. [2]

© The Author(s) 2018
S. E. Hobfoll, *Tribalism*,
https://doi.org/10.1007/978-3-319-78405-2_2

2.1   BEHAVIORAL GENETICS AND THE PRESERVATION OF THE TRIBE

Our behavioral genetic predisposition to tightly affiliate with the tribe also leads us rather repeatedly to the feuds of the type described in the Hatfields and McCoys. Our tribal strength and social bonding help explain the otherwise bewildering human capacity for annihilation and sexual exploitation of others who we label as foreigners, infidels, immigrants, and abortionists. Our predisposition to assert our tribal honor is tied to behaviors as different as the widespread practice of honor killings among Muslims, and the high murder rate by Southern White males in the U.S. Our behavioral genetic programming as humans and how we behave in groups has much to do with the Sunni and Shia split that has resulted in Islamic wars since the death of the Prophet Muhammad in 632. Coming to terms with our tribal behavior requires an understanding of the context in which most of human evolution occurred. Our genetic heritage and our reaction to threat and loss of those things we value deeply lead us to Tea Parties, both the social kind and the political kind. We are primed to prevent, defend, and react to loss of that which we love, and we love our own honor deeply.

Putting all this together, we understand why the tribe is such a fundamental biological grouping. Said another way, I am biologically not an individual, but rather I am biologically clan or tribe. This clan or tribe must be protected, preserved, and advanced, and this leads to several key behavioral pressures.[1] From the earliest cave evidence of our species, human evolutionary development occurred in the context of families and tribes. Already in the human remains found at Terra Amata, France, our ancestors 400,000 years ago were living in groups, with collections of families seeking the survival, protection, and sustenance that the tribe could provide. Our several hundred thousand years of existence in small tribes means that our genetics are built around survival within this powerful social arrangement.

We are not genetically built for living alone. Our tendency to form strong social groups is one of the most fundamental adaptive aspects of human survival. Those humans whose genes disposed them to solitude would have never survived in the harsh environmental landscape with animals many times fiercer and stronger than humans, times of scarcity of food sources, or other warring tribes. Evolutionary pressures led to adaptions toward being cooperative, following group norms, being loyal, and being open to sharing resources. At the same time, they signal our fear of outsiders and strong in-group versus out-group applications of our human nature.

To gain insight into how context shaped us, we need to know a couple of the rules of Darwinian evolution, and there are several key Darwinian principles that are often misunderstood.

First, survival of the fittest does not mean survival of the fittest individual. Instead it means survival of the genes possessed by groups that *share a common genetics that has some advantage* in spreading their genes in the gene pool versus others' genes. The genes of a single powerful lone wolf in a pack will be diluted in time by the genetics of other members of the pack. But, if a *kind* of wolf occurs that has some advantage in survival, and there are many of this *kind*, their kind will increasingly dominate the genetics of the pack, and then the region.

Second, I do not need to myself have many progeny or indeed have any progeny survive to be the fittest. Rather, those who share my genetics need to have many progeny. This extends not only to my brothers and sisters and their children, but to those in my clan or tribe, as we share a swath of common genes. Anything that I can do to give an advantage to those who share my genes is to my advantage in ensuring that *my kinds of genes* predominate.

Third, evolutionary psychology teaches us that humans are not slaves to their behavioral genetics. Rather our behavioral genetics prime us to act or behave in certain ways and to different degrees for different behaviors [3]. Some of our behavioral genetics keep us on a tight leash of possible behaviors. The behaviors related to obtaining food and response against aggression are rather automatic and hard-wired. We will seek food when hungry and we will counter-aggress or flee when attacked. Our sexual behavior and seeking sexual contact and fulfillment is mid-wired. Men have a tendency to act in a dominant fashion to women and to "push" for sex, and this appears to be in the mid-wired range. This does not mean that there is a defense of rape, or of male dominance, because our genetics pushed us to rape or to act in a dominating way to women. But there is a push in this direction, as we can see by how multi-culturally common male dominance behavior is. We also have genetic predispositions as a species that are soft-wired, or on what can be called a long leash. Long leash genetic behaviors allow for great human variability. So, universally humans seek a God and spirituality, affiliate in families or something that resembles a family, and sing and dance and experience joy in singing and dancing. All these are in our behavioral genetics, and evolutionary psychology helps us understand this genetic push that influences but does not determine our behavior.

Fourth, many of our behaviorally programmed predispositions have to do with the push to affiliate in tribes. Much of what we call culture is a complex outgrowth of this behavioral set of predispositions. They are clearly strongly expressed in the human genome, and they tend to fall between the soft, long leash set of behaviors and the mid-wired, moderately leashed set of behaviors. How do we know this? Like all Darwinian evidence we work backwards. If (1) the behavior or trait is universally or near universally expressed, if (2) the expression has common characteristics, and if (3) it occurs despite pressure to suppress it, it is genetically primed. Tigers act like tigers, bears act like bears, and humans affiliate in certain common fashions. How do we know if this array of genetic predispositions is in the range of soft-wired to mid-wired? We know this because family and group behavior has broad variation and can be suppressed by cultural strictures as the evolutionary psychologist David Buss has emphasized [4]. That is not to say that such suppression comes easily or is iron-clad. Genetic push of aggression often wins the day over our rules, sanctions, and pressures against violence.

A few more examples of our tribal programmed behaviors will clarify this complex concept and how nuanced and finely tuned our behavioral genetics programming is expressed. Mothers became genetically primed to be dedicated to their infants and children in a hard bond that is universal. Fathers' genetics lead them to be somewhat dedicated to their infants and children. They strive to protect and nurture their families, but the rate of paternal abandonment is far more common than maternal abandonment. They are also built to hunt and defend, and if required to aggress. If fathers were as tied as mothers to their children, they could not depart on the long hunt or risk death in tribal warfare.

Other complex behaviors illustrate how deeply ingrained tribal and family behavioral genetics are. In almost all cultures incest is abhorrent. Men and women will fight ferociously to protect their children, but less so for the children of others. Men and women will fight to protect children of their tribe, but will attack and murder children of "opposing" tribes. Many cultures exist where men have multiple wives, but hardly any exist where women have multiple husbands. Rape within the tribe is abhorrent and retribution for rape is often violent. Attacking and raping neighboring women is not only common, it likely has a genetic basis in that it spreads one group's genetics over another's.

Tribal behavior and preserving the tribe likewise result in certain customs, practices, and laws. The primacy and preservation of honor is a striking example of this tribal element of our genetics. Under a widely practiced Islamic law, family honor after a death brought on even by accident by another family can only be repaired with spilling of revenge blood. In Albania this law called Kanun was outlawed by communist rule but revived in the post-communist era. More than 2500 modern family feuds have occurred, resulting in hundreds of deaths and sending families into hiding [5]. In many Muslim regions of the world, honor killings occur over land, rape, adultery, homosexuality, and accidental death. Note that all of these constitute threats to the tribe because the tribe needs its land and resources, must know whose progeny are whose, and must procreate. Cover-ups make it difficult to estimate how common honor killings are, but the United Nations estimated that 5000 women are victims of honor killings each year, and women's advocacy groups have estimated a much larger number approaching 20,000 honor killings of women yearly [6]. Even in the United Kingdom, acid attacks, mutilations, and honor beatings have been recently reported as widespread by groups who brought these cultural practices with them [7].

Often those in the West imagine that such primal tribal behavior is entirely unlike how they live. People in the West, and those parts of the world settled by Europeans, see themselves as individuals, acting as independent agents. At the same time, given the pervasive nature of the threat landscape in politics, we increasingly aggregate and defend our political parties with Democrats and Republicans, liberals and conservatives, Evangelicals and secularists, caught in the concrete of their views and unable to seek compromise. We believe ourselves to be highly rational individuals, but act more tribally and irrationally each day, with tribal extremism overtaking politics, moving from what was the fringes to the guiding center. We are led by a president who is bent on exploiting those divisions, and accentuating a worldview in which working-class Whites are pitted against liberals, the political swamp, the free press, Blacks, Mexicans, feminism, and anything else that happens to get in the way of his tribal movement. As both Americans and Europeans have begun to recognize, tribalism and fear politics is not limited to the Middle East, Africa, or the Balkans. When we are threatened, or can be led to believe we are threatened, our tribal tendencies predominate.

2.2   WHAT ELICITS STRONG GROUP BEHAVIOR?

Group affiliation behavior is a natural human tendency. But we can also see that much of modern society, worldwide, is more individualized. This more primitive level of our genetic programming is expressed with greater salience when under threat. This threat can be real, but perceived threat, if consistent and presented with authority, can elicit strong affiliative behavior and the fortress mentality of guard and counter-attack.

We can see how threat and loss produce a mentality of "us against them" in the battle lines drawn between the police across the U.S. and African Americans as expressed in "Black Lives Matter." Both sides feel hunted, violated, and vulnerable. Both sides feel a profound sense of loss of esteem and humiliation. Not minimizing the real issues at the basis of this conflict, the war of words transforms rapidly into a war of violence with increased police violence towards Blacks and Blacks responding with accelerating militancy. The lone gunman who ambushed and killed 5 police officers in Dallas on July 7, 2016, acted in the extreme, but he was responding to a week of fatal police shootings of Black men in Minnesota and Louisiana, on a day of a peaceful march protesting this police violence. It is notable that the gunman, 25-year-old Micah Johnson, was apparently acting alone, but inspired by the New Black Panther Party website, which not unlike ISIS websites, promotes a tribal mentality and encourages Blacks to kill Whites and Jews [8].

Such fear-mongering is as old as politics itself, but it is made more facile and powerful through the use of modern media of radio, television and the internet. The then new introduction of radio allowed the broadcast of Mussolini's and Hitler's hate messaging into families' living rooms in Italy and Germany. In the U.S., the virulent anti-Semitic diatribes of Father Charles Coughlin during the 1930s were broadcast weekly to tens of millions of Americans. With Americans reeling and threatened by the Great Depression and looming war in Europe, his message was clear and widely applauded: *"When we get through with the Jews in America, they'll think the treatment they received in Germany was nothing."* [9] He was the hero of the "Christian Front," who responded to his call for a "crusade against the anti-Christian forces of the Red Revolution," and make no mistake he saw Roosevelt and the Democrats as leaders of this war on Christianity. The Christian Front was raided and shut down by the FBI in 1940, amidst a plot to murder Jews, communists, and U.S. Congressmen. But despite overwhelming evidence, the all-White jurors proved sympathetic to the defendants and they were set free [9].

In their highly sophisticated internet recruiting video, *There Is No Life Without Jihad*, ISIS spreads the message of Jihad emphasizing that they are together, that they are fighting to protect Muslim children and women from their being disgraced by the West and enemies within the Arab world. The young Jihadist men are seen in heroic filming, sitting together as comrades. "Oh you who believes, answer the call of what gives you life. And what gives you life is Jihad," says the passionate, calm, young man [10].

The handsome armed fighters first talk about how they are together from all over the world. They speak of their success, and speak from their heart of their success against the enemies of Islam wherever they may be. We have come, he says, "only to make Allah's word true." The men are seen smiling in groups, clearly enjoying being together. Another young man tells how before he read the Koran and took on Jihad he was nothing. To fight until there is not "fitnah" [disbelief and worshiping of others along with Allah]. Allah, he says, "does not need you, you need Allah, and to sacrifice for him." If you sacrifice for Allah you will receive 700 times what you give. He states that he knows that in the West you feel depressed. And that if you come to Jihad with ISIS you will be happy and welcomed. He tells his global audience that if you come "you will feel the happiness we feel." Another young man from Australia speaks of Palestinians killed by Israelis. In Fallajah, he says, our women were disgraced and "are giving birth to deformed babies." He takes the Koran from his pocket and speaks of the need to live by His (Allah's) rules.

The video challenges the listener's manhood in this world and place in the afterlife in the next. When it comes to Jihad there are two kinds of people, states the young fighter, "Those who will find every excuse to not come to Jihad and those who will make every excuse to fight Jihad." Another young man from Britain, so armed with weapons that he can barely sit, chastises the listener for living in comfort. He warns that your resurrection will come where you have lived, communicating a strong message of shame. You are in comfort, "while your brothers are giving their blood...and living in trucks." As a fighter you will not even feel death. It will be no more than an insect sting, he says. A Muslim child will be showed killed before you (when you will face Allah) and you will be asked where you were protecting him [11].

Now listen to the words of Newt Gingrich, former member of Congress and one of the principal architects of the politics of hatred and fear-mongering brought into the modern mainstream.

The left-wing Democrats will represent the party of total hedonism, total exhibitionism, total bizarreness, total weirdness, and the total right to cripple innocent people in the name of letting hooligans loose. [12]

These people [Democrats] are sick. They are so consumed by their own power, by a Mussolini-like ego, that their willingness to run over normal human beings and to destroy honest institutions is unending. [13]

I think one of the great problems we have in the Republican party is that we don't encourage you to be nasty. We encourage you to be neat, obedient, and loyal and faithful and all those Boy Scout words. [14]

Are the language and tools of hatred so different in responding to the Jihadist threat, when Donald Trump, the top Republican vote getter for President at the time, and the man destined to become the 45th president, stated he would "bomb the s*** out of them" [15] and increase use of torture [16], because water-boarding is not effective enough? He told stories of using bullets dipped in pigs' blood to humiliate them [17]. He repeatedly states as president that "Islam hates us." "There is an unbelievable hatred of us—anybody." [18] He called for a complete shutdown of Muslims entering the U.S., a statement so extreme that prime minister of Israel, Netanyahu, came out against such a policy, breaking the usual respectful silence of foreign leaders during the election process. Where experts estimate about 100,000 Jihadist fighters in the world, Trump claims that he estimates that 250–300 million Muslims are militant and ready to go to war against us [19]. Trump went on to state the following:

"According to Pew Research, among others, there is great hatred towards Americans by large segments of the Muslim population. Most recently, a poll from the Center for Security Policy released data showing '25% of those polled agreed that violence against Americans here in the United States is justified as a part of the global jihad'." [20]

What the survey had in fact found was that about 25 percent of Muslims sometimes condone violence in some instances against those who defile or attack Islam. There was no hint of their supporting or being ready to go to war against the West. This is fear-mongering, and Trump supporters appear thrilled by it. In a survey reported in the *NY Daily News* on December 18, 2015, 41 percent of likely Trump voters were in favor of bombing Agrabah [21]. Disney Studios would be incensed, as Agrabah is the fictional Arab city in the Disney film *Aladdin*!

When asked by journalist Jake Tapper on CNN's *State of the Union* whether he would condemn support by former Ku Klux Klan Grand Wizard

David Duke, the KKK and White supremacists, Donald Trump repeatedly stated that he had no knowledge of them and could not condemn them. Tapper repeatedly gave him chances to state his condemnation of these purveyors of racism, anti-Semitism, and violence. Trump's response,

I don't know anything about what you're even talking about with white supremacy or white supremacists, he said. So I don't know. I don't know—did he endorse me, or what's going on? Because I know nothing about David Duke; I know nothing about white supremacists. [22]

The messages are clear. Muslims are our enemy, and this pertains to all Muslims being suspect. Only the proviso, "I suspect some are good people," is used as a qualifier [22]. But, White supremacists and the KKK, according to Trump, can only be condemned with careful scrutiny.

As president it should come as no surprise that Trump retweeted staged (read fake) virulent anti-Muslim videos that were reminiscent of the Nazi's chief propagandist films of Jews taking advantage of Aryan girls. If this sounds like an exaggeration, just read the titles of the three videos. "Muslim migrants beats up Dutch boy on crutches!" "Muslim destroys a statue of Virgin Mary!" and "Islamist mob pushes teenage boy off roof and beats him to death!" [23].

2.3   WE FEAR THE STRANGER AND THE STRANGER AMONG US

There is a link between familiarity and liberalism and between separateness and conservatism. If you live near other people, you are likely to be a Democrat. If your neighbors are distant you are likely to be a Republican. From deep in our genetic core, the familiar becomes friend and the stranger is suspect. But our deepest fears seem to be evoked by the stranger among us, those that live nearby but are kept at a distance nonetheless.

An arm-chair demographer David Troy looked at the relationship in the U.S. between population density and voting. As may be seen in Fig. 2.1, those in lower density regions of the U.S. had a strong tendency to favor Mitt Romney in the 2012 election. Even stronger was the tendency for those in areas of about 800–1000 people per square mile to favor Barack Obama. In fact, the only major U.S. cities that voted Republican in the 2012 presidential election were Phoenix, Oklahoma City, Fort Worth, and Salt Lake City. Even in conservative leaning states,

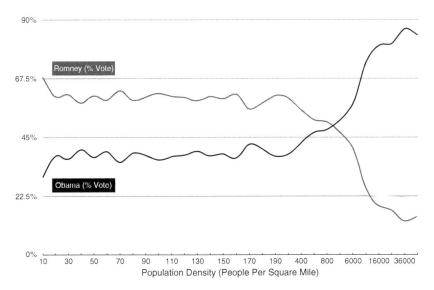

Fig. 2.1 Population density versus 2012 election results. (Courtesy of Dave Troy [24])

the urban areas lean left, including Atlanta, Indianapolis, New Orleans, Birmingham, Tucson, Little Rock, Charleston (SC), Austin, Dallas, and Houston [24].

Do unto your neighbor before he does it to you, seems to be connected to having had less contact with neighbors of different color, religion, and stripe. Those who have less contact with others unlike them in the U.S. are more likely to be in favor of isolationism, on one hand, and military intervention on the other. They are more anti-Muslim, anti-Mexican, anti-Semitic, and racist. They are more in favor of the use of torture and more anti-gay.

Our tribalism also responds to the stimulus of the stranger in our midst, the near enemy and not the enemy from afar. So, Whites in Wyoming are not going to have much to say about Blacks in the U.S. because they are highly unlikely to be exposed to Blacks. Our primal tribalism can be evoked through media, but the near enemy is more compelling. The ten most racist states in the U.S. were calculated based on racist terms on Twitter and representation of KKK organizations [25]. They were:

1. Texas
2. Mississippi

3. Georgia
4. Alabama
5. North Carolina
6. Tennessee
7. Arkansas
8. Louisiana
9. Florida
10. Illinois (rural Illinois making the difference)

Using a similar methodology of Google searches, researchers found that searching for the N-word revealed the most concentrated racist cluster along the spine of the Appalachians, going from Georgia in the South to up-state New York and southern Vermont [26]. So, although the ten most racist states are mainly Southern, racism follows a trek north following the rule of low population density and having nearby African Americans.

So, how can we explain the distrust and even hatred of Muslims in regions with few Muslims? Republicans, living with no contact with Muslims for the main are nevertheless more than twice as likely to be deeply concerned about Islamic extremism in the U.S. (54 percent very concerned), versus Democrats who are much more likely to have some contact with Muslims (24 percent very concerned) [27]. This fear of Muslims, even where none are around, is promulgated by constant news broadcasts on conservative media messaging that Muslim extremists are everywhere and plotting against our very way of life. These conservative areas are much more likely to already be incensed by what they see as a war on Christianity, which President Trump has continued to promulgate. So, the "hidden Muslim" amongst us or ready to invade us becomes an accessible target.

A 2013 Carnegie Mellon University study found that in states that went Republican in the 2012 presidential election, Muslim job candidates were eight times less likely to receive a job call back than a Christian job candidate. In Democratic leaning states there was no difference in callbacks from employers based on Muslim versus Christian leaning profiles. In North Carolina 40 percent of poll responders believed that Islam should not be allowed in the U.S., and another 20 percent were unsure. Fully 72 percent thought a Muslim should not be allowed to be president of the U.S. [28]. Calling themselves Patriots and Tea Partyers, they appear unaware that the first words of the First Amendment are "Congress shall make no law respecting an establishment of religion, or prohibiting the free exercise thereof;" unless of course it is infringing on their religion.

2.4   AS THREAT INCREASES THE TRIBE BECOMES ESSENTIAL, AND OFTEN DEADLY

Humans have an amazing capacity to live in mixed communities in harmony—that is until they don't. This transition from gentle neighbor to actor of genocide illustrates how fragile civilized culture is and how quickly it can degrade into powerful tribal animosity.

Few examples of this are as poignant as the former Yugoslavia [29]. Prior to 1992, Bosnia was populated by a mixture of ethnic groups. This is a region with a rich and complex history. Roman Catholic Croats and Orthodox Christian Serbs had been divided in the split of the Roman Empire in the fourth century, dividing the Balkans essentially down the middle. The regions Muslim origins stemmed back from the advance of Islam into the West by the Ottomans in the mid- to late-fifteenth century. The Ottoman victory at the Battle of Kosovo Polje in 1389 resulted both in an infusion of Muslims and conversion of local populations to Islam. Bosnia and Herzegovina remained attached to the Ottoman Empire until 1831, when the population rose up against Ottoman rule. It was formally brought into the West under the rule of the Austria-Hungarian Empire in 1908. And believe me, this is the region's history told in its simplest form.

Throughout this history, the three groups lived together, often intermarried, and shared their lives. But the tribal nature of their existence was always just below the surface. Elections and political parties were separated by their ethnic affiliation and violence did erupt in several periods. During World War I, which by the way began with the assassination of the Austrian archduke by a Bosnian Serb nationalist, ethnic groups were divided with the Serbs fighting alongside England, France and the U.S. During World War II, many Croat nationalists and Muslim Bosniaks supported the Nazi invaders, and participated in the death camps where Jews, Roma, and hundreds of thousands of Serbs were murdered. One of the only non-German Waffen-SS divisions (the dreaded armed wing of the Nazi party) was the 13th Mountain Division comprised of Bosnian Muslims with some Catholic Croat officers.

In April 1992, the government of the Yugoslav republic of Bosnia-Herzegovina declared its independence from Yugoslavia, and the iron fist of Tito, who had controlled Yugoslavia since World War II until 1980, was removed. It did not take long for former ethnic rivals to reassert old hatreds and to enact revenge for past wrongs. In the years that followed, Bosnian Serb militias, backed by the Serb-dominated Yugoslav army, killed over 100,000 people, most of whom were Bosnian Muslims. The Bosnian genocide and the ethnic cleansing campaign was committed by Bosnian Serbs at Srebrenica and Žepa most brutally and more widely by the Army of the Republika Srpsska during the 1992–1995 Bosnian War in the former Yugoslavia. Bosnian Serbs targeted Muslim Bosniaks and Bosnian Croats in unspeakable acts of murder, rape, torture, beatings and robbery. The intent appeared to be a combination of deeply expressed hatred and a desire to remove people (cleanse) from their land [30].

Clearly there is more than behavioral genetics at work here. But the clinging to one's tribe of origin is a central aspect of this story. Power, money, and control are all at work, but the messaging is the same as that being promulgated by ISIS in 2016. It is "us against them" and we must be true to our brothers and sisters that share a common heritage, religion, and ethnicity. The hallmarks of modern progressive society are equity, safety, ethnic minority and women's rights, and openness to dialogue and differences of opinion. We promote religious tolerance and equality, with no religion standing over another. We think in terms of equality on economic as well as religious planes, even if this is an ideal. As the primitive self emerges, only safety seems to remain and then only for those with good standing within the tribe. However advanced our culture, we never seem far from this primitive self.

It would be easy to look to the places that we consider culturally primitive in the East and Africa or religiously stuck in Medieval times such as the case of "the Troubles" that for decades plagued Northern Ireland. But, culture is not what would be correctly labeled as primitive in the sense that I propose. Cultures East and West, African and Asian are rich in traditions. The rules of correct behavior in Africa and the Far East are far more respectful and honor-based than those in the West. So, as I will assert often, the biological, primitive origins of our behavior are shared for all humans and not far below the surface.

As we look across history and cultures, it appears to be the threat of loss of personal, social, or material resources that activates the deeper brain behavioral genetic push. We can live in relative harmony when resources related to survival are not threatened or substantively lost. But even the whiff of threat of loss, awakens our deeper protective genetic makeup.

2.4.1   Red Bloody Summer: Chicago 1919

During World War I, there was a great migration of African Americans from the rural South to the urban North and places like Chicago. The factories, work houses and stock yards of Chicago had great need for Black labor during the war. African Americans had moved from the Deep South, Georgia, Mississippi and Alabama, to Chicago, increasing Chicago's Black population markedly. In 1900 African Americans constituted only about 1 percent of Chicago's population. During the war years, the African American population of Chicago expanded to about 109,000. African American men had also joined the Army as soldiers and served courageously in Europe, and in 1919 they were coming home, and expected improved rights and opportunities upon their return.

With White men also returning home and the war economy winding down, housing and labor became suddenly highly competitive. Arkansas journalists wrote about a planned uprising by Blacks, an uprising "aimed at the general slaughter of White people." [31] Pre-war Chicago was known for racial tolerance, but in 1917 the Chicago Real Estate Board established a policy of segregation, mapping out the White and Black enclaves. Major newspapers in Chicago joined in reporting trumped up charges of crime by Blacks and many papers spoke of rape by Blacks of White women.

The powder keg of the Red Bloody Summer was set off when a young Black man was stoned and killed for the "crime" of entering a "Whites Only" beach on the city's south side Douglas community on July 27, 1919. White gangs comprised mostly of ethnic Irish whose jobs and neighborhoods were most threatened by the Great Black Migration entered Black neighborhoods in the following week committing murder and arson. Rioters barricaded streets to prevent firefighters from responding. About 1000 individuals, mostly African Americans, were left homeless by the fires. In total 23 African Americans and 15 Whites were killed, as African Americans did act to defend themselves. Many more were prevented from going to work, and refused entry into the Union Stock Yards. The police force was largely Irish Catholic and did little to intervene to protect the Black community.

The attacks by Whites against Blacks had actually been planned for weeks, and were only quelled when the Governor of Illinois Frank Lowden authorized deployment of the 11th Illinois Infantry Regiment and machine gun company, along with the 1st, 2nd, and 3rd reserve militias. Along with about 3500 soldiers, the Cook County Sherriff deputized between 1000 and 2000 ex-soldiers to restore the peace. The reserves and militia guarded the city's Black Belt, and the city arranged for emergency provisions to provide Black residents fresh food and water and clothing. There were many instances of White courage and solidarity for Blacks as well. Whites brought food, clothing and necessities to the military line and passed them to African Americans for distribution to the besieged population. The meat packing plants arranged delivery of pay to arranged points in the city so that Black workers could obtain their pay, even though the packing plants were locked tight [32, 33].

This history of ethnic and racial divisiveness is made all the more revealing by the then headlines of the *Chicago Tribune*. The *Tribune* was a Republican-affiliated, Protestant-owned newspaper, representing the Republican Protestant community and deeply suspicious of Irish Catholics. The *Tribune* was no friend of African Americans, but they also had a long-held aversion for Catholic Irish, and largely blamed them for the riots. Recalling an earlier *Tribune* article published in 1855, "Who does not know that the most depraved, debased, worthless and irredeemable drunkards and sots which curse the community are Irish Catholics?" [34] As written in the 1898 *Chicago Post*, "Scratch a convict or a pauper and the chances are that you tickle the skin of an Irish Catholic...made a criminal or a pauper, in a word, a savage, as he was born." [35]

2.4.2   Rage at the Tribal Enemy

On December 7, 1941, at 7:48 a.m. 353 fighter planes and bombers of Imperial Japan were launched from six undetected aircraft carriers against the U.S. base in Pearl Harbor, Hawaii. By the end of the attack, 2403 Americans were killed and 1178 others were wounded. The U.S lost 4 battleships, 3 destroyers, and several other ships, along with 188 aircraft. On the following day, the U.S. declared war on Japan.

Fear, anger, and rage is an emotional trilogy that accompany threat. As perceived threat increases, human fear becomes magnified, and our biological adaptive systems actually seek to accelerate the fear in order to ensure a mobilized and alert defense. In an evolutionary sense it would be suicidal to avoid the threat and adaptive to focus on the threat, and even to exaggerate it. This leads, in turn, to the emotions of anger and rage and a call to action.

As I will go into in greater detail in a later chapter, logic might appear to be an adaptive route, but logic requires a cool head and thoughtfulness. Cool heads under fire are rare and that is why good generals are rare and must keep above the firefight. Instead, humans look for all the details about the threat they can muster, and any argument against action is quickly dismissed.

Racism against Japanese on the West Coast of the U.S. was already widespread before Pearl Harbor. Following the Japanese Meiji Restoration, just after the U.S. Civil War, until 1924, when the U.S. essentially closed its gates to immigration from Europe and Asia, about 180,000 Japanese immigrated to the U.S. mainland. Many anti-Japanese groups formed during this period, against what they termed the "Yellow Peril," including the Japanese, Exclusion League, The California Joint Immigration Committee, and the Native Sons of the Golden West. Not allowed to set up shop in White areas, "Japan towns" sprouted up in Los Angeles, San Francisco, and Seattle (Image 2.1).

Image 2.1   Anti-Japanese sentiment in the U.S. during World War II [36]

With the war imminent, President Roosevelt ordered the Office of Naval Intelligence and the FBI to investigate the threat from Japanese Americans living on the West Coast and Hawaii, led by Curtis Munson. The commission's report determined that the threat from the Japanese was "nonexistent." Indeed, his report submitted in November 1941, a month prior to Pearl Harbor, "certified a remarkable, even extraordinary degree of loyalty among this generally suspect ethnic group." [37]

But hatred and fear of the stranger in our midst is a powerful tribal force. An editorial in the *Los Angeles Times* read as follows:

> *A viper is nonetheless a viper wherever the egg is hatched.... So, a Japanese American born of Japanese parents, nurtured upon Japanese traditions, living in a transplanted Japanese atmosphere... notwithstanding his nominal brand of accidental citizenship almost inevitably and with the rarest exceptions grows up to be a Japanese, and not an American.... Thus, while it might cause injustice to a few to treat them all as potential enemies, I cannot escape the conclusion... that such treatment... should be accorded to each and all of them while we are at war with their race.* [38]

This extreme editorial is fully consistent with the policy that was enacted through Executive Presidential Order 9066. The Japanese were robbed of their homes and businesses and mirroring the early deportation of Jews in Europe, were herded into detention camps in the interior of the U.S. at distances of greater than 100 miles from the Coast. The racist intent was blatant, as the edicts included individuals of part-Japanese ancestry up to one-sixteenth ancestry, the standard used in the South historically for Blacks. The Nazis only designated non-Aryan as one-eight Jewish.

Given such discrimination and treatment, it would be easy to imagine young Japanese Americans turning their back on their adopted country. But the tribal tendency to coalesce and prove itself took another form. Some 20,000 Nisei (2nd generation) Japanese men volunteered for what became the 442nd Regimental Combat Team. The 442nd clawed its way up Italy in the most vicious fighting against the entrenched Nazi war machine. The Allied's Italian Campaign was the first major thrust into Europe, so the Germans were fully prepared and fully fortified. The 442nd became the single most decorated military unit in U.S. history. Twenty-one members of this relatively small force were awarded the Medal of Honor, the nation's highest award. They fought with a tenacity unparalleled, as indicated by their shedding so much blood in combat as to be nicknamed the "Purple Heart Battalion." They were used as piercing troops, flung against the Germans, and often with blatant disregard for their lives.

The Nisei men of I and K Companies of the 442nd were sent to save a cut-off U.S. battalion behind the heavily entrenched German line between Rambervillers and Biffonataine, France. In an uphill charge the Nisei attacked up the steep slope knowing that few could survive. Their charge broke the German defenses, rescuing the cut off battalion. When placed in formation after the battle, of the original 400 men, only 18 men of K Company and 8 men of I Company stood in formation. The tribe had proven its courage and resolve, its willingness to die for the greater tribe to which they declared allegiance.

2.5   ARE WE RECREATING AN ETHNO-RELIGIOUS DIVIDE IN OUR RED STATE BLUE STATE POLITICS?

Since the rise of militant language of Newt Gingrich as Speaker of House of Representatives, from 1995 to 1999, and the explosion of political extremist right wing radio, the U.S. has been increasingly divided between Red and Blue States. The differences are made more divisive as they are portrayed as a war of patriots against those who would destroy the U.S., as that is whom patriots fight. Our violence is as of yet contained in relative terms. But our language is borrowed from the playbook of those who were willing to risk violence and we risk violence by following in their path. We have left the reasonableness of the conservative icon Ronald Reagan. Reagan raised taxes on multiple occasions to keep deficits from looming out of control. He helped expand Medicare and Medicaid, much larger programs than the Affordable Care Act, and championed by Democrats at that time. Wrote Ronald Reagan of compromise,

When I began entering into the give and take of legislative bargaining in Sacramento, a lot of the most radical conservatives who had supported me during the election didn't like it. "Compromise" was a dirty word to them and they wouldn't face the fact that we couldn't get all of what we wanted today. They wanted all or nothing and they wanted it all at once. If you don't get it all, some said, don't take anything.

I'd learned while negotiating union contracts that you seldom got everything you asked for. And I agreed with FDR, who said in 1933: "I have no expectations of making a hit every time I come to bat." What I seek is the highest possible batting average.

If you got seventy-five or eighty percent of what you were asking for, I say, you take it and fight for the rest later, and that's what I told these radical conservatives who never got used to it. [39]

Certainly we have witnessed more tribal fear tactics from the extreme right in recent years, but the left is not immune to the process when tribal politics emerge. Supporters of Senator Bernie Sanders, who ran a taught campaign against Secretary Hillary Clinton, emphasized the tribal code words of being a "movement," and of being a "movement betrayed" by the Democratic Party. "Movement Betrayed" is an anger-evoking message to the tribe. They celebrated Sanders' wins with cheers and dancing. But, when losses occurred, they were met with threats of violence toward party leaders, sexual threats against female party leaders, and threats of resolve to violence should they not win. Just as with candidate Trump stating that his constituents' anger is well justified, Sanders sidestepped condemnation of such ugly violence.

Sanders' supporters communicated about Nevada Chairwoman of the Democratic Party, Roberta Lange [40].

"This is a citizen of the United States of America and I just wanted to let you know that I think people like you should be hung in a public execution to show this world that we won't stand for this sort of corruption, …I don't know what kind of money they are paying to you, but I don't know how you sleep at night. You are a sick, twisted piece of s— and I hope you burn for this! …. You cowardless b—,running off the stage! I hope people find you."

Another text message read: *"We know where you live… where your kids go to school/grandkids. We have everything on you."* [40]

The lessons of history teach us that we live in harmony on a tight-wire in a careful balancing act. We thrive together when we find common links and bridges. However, we do not share resources easily and threat, loss, and survival realities and even the words that signal threat, loss and survival speak to a deeper evolutionary biology of who we are.

As a child of six, I remember going from Chicago 80 miles north to Lake Geneva Wisconsin. My parents told me "Don't act Jewish, they are only recently allowing Jews in." I thought it had something to do with not ordering a kosher hot dog, the only meat my parents allowed me to eat out of the home. I was so blond that I was more likely to be mistaken for a Swedish youth than a Jew, but there was still great suspicion of the Jewish "other" in 1950s America.

2.6   Tribalism Just Below the Surface

Our evolutionary origins create a tribal capacity that is not obvious because we assume that our behavior is rationale. There is no signal to the brain that you are acting this way because you are hungry, because you are threatened, or because you are in love. As the saying goes, "love is blind," meaning that it takes over your rational thought processes.

We tend in particular to see other cultures as tribal, especially when we look to Africa and the Middle East, and partially because they represent themselves as tribal. As I have argued, tribalism is not just found in the Arab world, however. We see it in our clinging to political parties, to sports teams, and to our often passionate and sometimes violent religious fervor. We do not see the tribalism in plain view because we see ourselves as individuals, and falsely interpret our behavior as thoughtful and rational. Our emotionally based "thinking" feels no different from our rational thought processing. We occasionally allow ourselves to see our biologically driven self in our sexual behavior, where we will sometimes admit that our sexual lust overtakes our thoughtfulness. We can also see our irrational self override our rational processes when passionate love is thwarted or betrayed. Simply put, how many people have you seen behave rationally amidst divorce? Indeed, when it is us caught up in divorce, we typically delude ourselves in thinking that we are rational and only our spouse or former spouse is to blame, irrational, destructive, and stubborn.

As we have explored in this chapter, when humans are not in circumstances where the valence of loss and threat is high, our more rational selves are activated, and this means the engagement of our forebrains, the most complex, late arriver in our evolutionary development. Our capacity to problem solve is very much forebrain involving the most recent evolutionary capacities of our brain's development. The great apes do show considerable cognitive ability, but it is at the level of perhaps a human toddler. According to the social brain hypothesis, set forth by British anthropologist Robin Dunbar, human intelligence made rapid advances to solve the labyrinth of challenges inherent in cooperation in tribal groups of about 150 [41]. Our intelligence as a species surged forward to meet the needs of complex cooperation, social systems and social exchange at this tribal level. Our advanced brain developed rapidly and greatly to engender the capabilities of empathy, insight, and the ability to step back from a problem and consider its many facets. Humans have the unique ability to think in the abstract and to bring such thought back to the practical.

The demands of rational thought add further complexity when people need to work together, and think as a team, rather than as individuals. Make no mistake, that much or our advanced brain capacity is for social dominance, but it is dominance through social exchange, social skillfulness, and social bonding [42]. *Moreover, it is critical to point out that our genetic template for social interactions stopped evolving at the tribal level of group size of more or less 150 people* [43]. *We simply apply that genetic template to politics, religion, work, and our views of the "other."*

When our personal, social, or material resources are threatened in ways that challenge survival or even our way of life, humans' tribal capacities are signaled and become prominent in orchestrating our thinking and behavior. This begins with the "fight and flight" response, which must be rapid, "shoot from the hip," "all out," instantaneous, and instinctual. Once engaged, the body hardly allocates resources to the forebrain, as the large muscle groups (legs, arms) and the "aggress and defend" response requires all our energetic resources. Brain and digestion can wait, as fight and flight take precedence.

After the initial "fight or flight" reaction, what passes for rational thought must continue to pass through a set of biases that allow little room for the shades of gray of measured logic, as long as the prism of threat and loss are in place. And, as I have developed previously, that survival drive extends to survival of the culture and set of beliefs. Only humans, unlike any other animal, organize around and are willing to make sacrifices for the abstract divisions within which humans aggregate. Only humans develop devotion and willingness to sacrifice and fully defend abstract notions of culture, be they the fight for freedom, the fight for communism, the fight for the fatherland, the fight for Christianity, or the fight for Islam.

2.7   WE LIVE IN TRIBAL TIMES

We are clearly at a time when White, Evangelical Christians feel threatened. White men are clearly voting in a way that indicates that they feel betrayed and undermined. Conservative Americans believe that the Affordable Care Act is a major thrust to deny them their freedom and liberty. Although we have killed many thousand times more Muslims than Muslims have killed Americans, Americans feel that Islam is an imminent threat to them. We seek to pray to one God, but choose to do so without anyone that does not look like us, have the color of our skin, or our ethnic heritage sitting in prayer with us. We even divide our churches based on political ideology.

When catastrophic threat is signaled, humans are quick to aggregate, defend and aggress. We only need to be led to believe that the threat is imminent. In recent years, at least 13 Red states have enacted laws forbidding foreign laws in America, in a reaction against the false belief that Muslims are moving to enact Sharia (Islamic law) in their states. To date, there have been no proposals for Sharia law in the U.S., however. This is an imagined enemy.

At the same time conservative states are enacting laws that they depict as defending religious freedom. These laws essentially attempt to protect Conservative Christians from having to serve gays, lesbians, and transgender individuals. Whatever our views on these laws, it should be clear that those enacting these laws feel under siege and losing ground. They believe that they are protecting their freedom, liberty and way of life. And when those sentiments are held, violence has never been far behind. It was not long ago that the same states were enacting laws against Blacks, and they fought violently to preserve their freedom then too. We are currently at our third Tea Party. The first was in Boston, the second was the rallying cry of the South as they fought the "Second War of Independence" (aka, the Civil War) against Northern Aggression, and the third is being forged by the Conservative Right.

We will look next at how the prism of bias alters our thinking so that we become convinced of our own truth. Everywhere we look, we see evidence of "our side," and we lose the ability to step back and see the cracks and fissures, let alone the gaping holes, in our arguments. Our tribal genetics insures that we aggregate with others who support our viewpoint and our brains adopt filters that stream a constant propaganda tape of our own making. Because the biological pressures on our thinking exist below the level of awareness, we never see them. We cannot detect when our primitive mid and deep brain are in control of our thinking, and our forebrain barely engaged.

The greater the environment signals threat and the loss of personal, social and material resources that we value, the greater the primitive engagement on the individual, family and tribal level. Indeed, because we are so threat-sensitive, our news, film, and conversations constantly reinforce threat, paradoxically to prepare us to defend against it. As the force of threat accelerates the perceived need for walls, figurative and literal ones, and weapons spirals and gains speed and momentum, leaving us more aghast at each news cycle, but at the same time unable to look away.

NOTE

1. The term "tribe" actually fell out of favor in anthropology in the latter part of the 20th century, in part because of its pejorative use in labeling by Western colonial nations and scholars referring to non-Western "primitive" peoples. I am favoring the term "tribes" precisely because of its biological basis, and not implying that it is inherent in any given culture. Americans, Armenians, communists, English soccer hooligans, and Hamas may all act like tribes. It is a deep part of us that is always expressed to a degree, but becomes prominent under threat. For anthropologists the term "bands" may be more appropriate, but because it is not generally known, it would obfuscate the points I will be making.

REFERENCES

1. Rice, O. K. (1982). *The Hatfields and the McCoys*. Louisville: University Press of Kentucky.
2. Novogrod, J., & Engel, R. (2015, August 25). ISIS terror: Yazidi woman recalls horrors of slave auction. *NBC News*. Retrieved February 26, 2017, from http://www.nbcnews.com/storyline/isis-uncovered/isis-terror-yazidi-woman-recalls-horrors-slave-auction-n305856
3. Wilson, E. O. (1978). *On human nature*. Cambridge, MA: Harvard University Press.
4. Buss, D. (2015). *Evolutionary psychology: The new science of the mind* (5th ed.). New York: Routledge.
5. Arie, S. (2003, September 20). Blood feuds trap Albania in the past. *The Guardian*. Retrieved February 26, 2017, from https://www.theguardian.com/world/2003/sep/21/sophiearie.theobserver
6. Maher, A. (2013, June 20). Many Jordan teenagers 'support honour killings'. *BBC News*. Retrieved September 5, 2017, from http://www.bbc.com/news/world-middle-east-22992365
7. BBC News. (2011, December 3). 'Honour' attack numbers reveals by UK police forces. *BBC News*. Retrieved December 18, 2017, from http://www.bbc.com/news/uk-16014368
8. Sullivan, K. (2016, July 23). The rise of black nationalist groups that captivated killers in Dallas, Baton Rouge. *The Washington Post*. Retrieved September 5, 2017, from https://www.washingtonpost.com/national/inside-the-black-nationalist-groups-that-captivated-killers-in-dallas-baton-rouge/2016/07/23/c53aef66-4f89-11e6-a422-83ab49ed5e6a_story.html?utm_term=.c47ec908ed68
9. Warren, D. (1996). *Radio priest: Charles Coughlin, the father of hate radio*. New York: Simon & Schuster.

10. Islamic State of Iraq and al-Shām (Director). (2014). *There is no life without Jihad* [Motion Picture].
11. Zelin, A. Y. (2014, June 19). Al-ḥayāt media center presents a new video message from the Islamic state of Iraq and al-shām: 'There is no life without Jihad'. *Jihadology*. Retrieved September 26, 2017, from http://jihadology.net/2014/06/19/al-%E1%B8%A5ayat-media-center-presents-a-new-video-message-from-the-islamic-state-of-iraq-and-al-sham-there-is-no-life-without-jihad/
12. Harwood, J. (1989, July 27). Newt Gingrich: GOP's Bare-Knuckles Battler. *St. Petersburg Times*, p. 1A.
13. Beers, D. (1989, September 1). Newt Gingrich: Master of disaster. *Mother Jones*. Retrieved September 5, 2017, from http://www.motherjones.com/politics/1989/09/master-disaster/
14. Gingrich, N. (1978, June 24). *Speech to College Republicans*. Atlanta: Atlanta Airport Holiday Inn. Retrieved September 5, 2017, from http://www.pbs.org/wgbh/pages/frontline/newt/newt78speech.html
15. Mogelson, L. (2017, April 20). The recent history of bombing the shit out of 'em. *The New Yorker*. Retrieved September 5, 2017, from http://www.newyorker.com/news/news-desk/the-recent-history-of-bombing-the-shit-out-of-em
16. Savage, C. (2017, January 25). Trump poised to lift ban on CIA 'black site' prisons. *The New York Times*. Retrieved September 5, 2017, from https://www.nytimes.com/2017/01/25/us/politics/cia-detainee-prisons.html?rref=collection%2Fsectioncollection%2Fus&action=click&contentCollection=us&region=stream&module=stream_unit&version=latest&contentPlacement=4&pgtype=sectionfront
17. Reilly, K. (2017, August 17). President Trump praises fake story about shooting Muslims with pig's blood-soaked bullets. *Time*. Retrieved September 5, 2017, from http://time.com/4905420/donald-trump-pershing-pigs-blood-muslim-tweet/
18. Schleifer, T. (2016, March 10). Donald Trump: 'I think Islam hates us'. *CNN Politics*. Retrieved September 5, 2017, from http://www.cnn.com/2016/03/09/politics/donald-trump-islam-hates-us/
19. Farley, R. (2016, March 16). *Trump's false Muslim claim*. FactCheck.Org. Retrieved September 5, 2017, from http://www.factcheck.org/2016/03/trumps-false-muslim-claim/
20. Trump, D. (2015, December 7). *Donald Trump statement on preventing Muslim immigration*. New York. Retrieved February 26, 2017, from http://ichef-1.bbci.co.uk/news/624/cpsprodpb/E11D/production/_87092675_000001atrump.jpg
21. Public Policy Polling. (2015, December 18). *Trump leads grows nationally; 41% of his voters want to bomb country from 'Aladdin'; Clinton maintains big lead*. Public Policy Polling. Retrieved September 7, 2017, from http://www.publicpolicypolling.com/pdf/2015/PPP_Release_National_121715.pdf

22. Trump, D. (2016, February 29). State of the Union. (J. Tapper, Interviewer).
23. Landers, E., & Masters, J. (2017, November 30). Trump retweets anti-Muslim videos. *CNN Politics*. Retrieved December 18, 2017, from http://www.cnn.com/2017/11/29/politics/donald-trump-retweet-jayda-fransen/index.html
24. Troy, D. (2012, November 9). *The real republican adversary? Population density*. Dave Troy: Fueled By Randomness. Retrieved February 26, 2017, from http://davetroy.com/posts/the-real-republican-adversary-population-density
25. Moore, A. (2014, May 14). Top 10 most racist states in America. *Atlanta Black Star*. Retrieved September 5, 2017, from http://atlantablackstar.com/2014/05/14/top-10-racist-states-america/
26. Chae, D. H., Clouston, S., Hatzenbuehler, M. L., Kramer, M. R., Cooper, H. L., Wilson, S. M., et al. (2015). Association between an internet-based measure of area racism and black mortality. *PloS One, 10*(4), e0122963.
27. Pew Research Center. (2014, September 10). *Growing concern about rise of Islamic Extremism at home and abroad*. Pew Research Center. Retrieved February 26, 2017, from http://www.people-press.org/2014/09/10/growing-concern-about-rise-of-islamic-extremism-at-home-and-abroad/
28. Blow, C. M. (2015, November 23). Anti-Muslim is anti-American. *The New York Times*. Opinion Pages. Retrieved February 26, 2017, from https://www.nytimes.com/2015/11/23/opinion/anti-muslim-is-anti-american.html?_r=0
29. Malcolm, N. (1996). *Bosnia: A short history*. New York: NYU Press.
30. Kalyvas, S. N., & Sambanis, N. (2005). Bosnia's Civil War: Origins and violence dynamics. In P. Collier, & N. Sambanis (Eds.), *Understanding Civil War: Evidence and analysis—Africa: V. 1* (pp. 191–229). Washington, DC: World Bank Publications.
31. McWhirter, C. (2011). *Red summer: The summer of 1919 and the awakening of Black America*. New York: Henry Holt and Company.
32. Essig, S. (2005). *Race riots*. Encyclopedia of Chicago. Retrieved February 26, 2017, from http://www.encyclopedia.chicagohistory.org/pages/1032.html
33. Chicago Public Library. (1996). *Deaths, disturbances, disasters and disorders in Chicago: A selective bibliography of materials in the municipal reference collection of the Chicago Public Library*. Chicago: Chicago Public Library.
34. Grossman, R. (2015, September 25). Chicago's Lager Beer Riot proved immigrants' power. *Chicago Tribune* Retrieved February 8, 2018, from http://www.chicagotribune.com/news/history/ct-know-nothing-party-lager-beer-riot-per-flashback-jm-20150925-story.html
35. Ural, S. J. (2006). *The harp and the eagle: Irish-American volunteers and the union army, 1861–1865*. New York: New York University Press.

36. Unknown. (1942). *Japs keep moving—This is a white man's neighborhood.* Retrieved September 20, 2014, from http://oberlinlibstaff.com/omeka_hist244/exhibits/show/japanese-internment/item/217

37. Weglyn, M. (2000). *Years of infamy: The untold story of America's concentration camps.* Seattle: University of Washington Press.

38. Niiva, B. (Ed.). (1993). *Japanese American history: An A-to-Z reference from 1868 to the present.* New York: Facts on File, Inc..

39. Reagan, R. (1990). *An American life: The autobiography.* New York: Simon & Schuster Adult Publishing Group.

40. Raju, M. (2016, May 20). Dems' new fear: Sanders revolt could upend Democratic convention. *CNN.* Retrieved February 26, 2017, from http://www.cnn.com/2016/05/17/politics/democrat-bernie-sanders-revolt/

41. Dunbar, R. (1998). The social brain hypothesis. *Evolutionary Anthropology: Issues, News, and Reviews, 6*(5), 562–572. https://doi.org/10.1002/evan.v26.1.

42. Flinn, M. V., Geary, D. C., & Ward, C. V. (2005). Ecological dominance, social competition, and coalitionary arms races: Why humans evolved extraordinary intelligence. *Evolution and Human Behavior, 26*(1), 10–46.

43. Hill, R., & Dunbar, R. (2003). Social network size in humans. *Human Nature, 14*(1), 53–72.

CHAPTER 3

We Believe What Protects Us and Our Tribe

There are two ways to be fooled. One is to believe what isn't true;
the other is to refuse to believe what is true. *(Søren Kierkegaard,*
twentieth-century Danish philosopher [1])
Truth is the greatest enemy of the state. *(Dr. Joseph Goebbels, Reich*
Minister of Propaganda and Chancellor of Nazi Germany (for one
day) [2])

It would appear obvious that people seek the truth and that we would scan
our environment, including the political environment, for truth. After all,
in truth lie "the answers." We wish to see ourselves as rational beings, not
blind to our emotions and prejudices. It is in the nature of conscious
thought that we are not aware of underlying biases, motivations, and ways
of seeing the world. Who would want to get up at a meeting at work or in
a discussion with one's partner at home and begin with the phrase, "Based
on my distorted view of the world and this situation, and the fact that I
feel threatened, I think   ?" Instead, we imagine that we have the facts
with crystal clarity. We see ourselves as having clear and even brilliant
insights into ourselves, politics, the economy, raising our children, han-
dling our love lives, and determining how our favorite sports teams ought
to be managed. That our "brilliance" only increases with liquor should
have been a warning, but our biases are deeply camouflaged in our need
to see ourselves as correct and justified.

© The Author(s) 2018
S. E. Hobfoll, *Tribalism*,
https://doi.org/10.1007/978-3-319-78405-2_3

On one important level humans are quite rational. We have a good grasp of our surrounding reality and process that which we see with our own eyes with good accuracy. Indeed, our survival depends on it. If we did not accurately detect and dodge when something was coming at us, it would hit us. If we did not know that an attacker was dangerous, we would be killed or badly injured. We even develop a generally accurate sense of social danger, and know who at work are our supporters and who are our detractors. We can conclude that for the most part, as long as the environment is that which is known to us directly, we have fairly accurate appraisal systems. This also makes evolutionary sense in that humans' only knowledge was based on what they experienced or what their immediate social group said was knowledge.

It is with more ambiguous information that the prism through which we see the world is often highly distorted. We know this when we refer to others, but we stubbornly believe that our own vision and insights are rather faultless. We can see the biases in others but are blind to our own.

Let me begin with some examples from everyday life before we venture into the darker world of threat, fear, and politics. Unfortunately, our brains only have a superficial need to look for truth beyond our immediate vision, hearing, touch, and smell. Rather, we are primed to search for self-confirming information and to denigrate, disregard, and deny information that is counter to our already decided upon ways of being in the world. We seek information that will protect us, our family, and our tribe. This is true of our religious beliefs, our marriages, and our politics. Indeed, there is no better tie between our self-esteem and our biology than the search for self-affirming information.

Some simple examples are illustrative. When was the last time you changed your spouse's mind about some belief that they held strongly? I don't mean got them to grudgingly go along with you on something, but changed their mind? And by the way, when was the last time your spouse or partner changed your mind? When was the last time you convinced anyone who was committed to a political position that they were wrong and you were right? Over time, some strongly held views can migrate, and many Americans have changed their views on same-sex marriage, as illustrated by polling numbers over the past 10 years. Except, of course, those who hold extreme positions on either side, where there is little change. When views become intertwined with people's identity—be it their identity as pro-Israel, Islamic fundamentalist, conservative, liberal, or pro-life—factual or logical argument will seldom alter their views.

3.1   WE ARE INDIVIDUALS-NESTED IN FAMILIES-NESTED IN TRIBES

On May 3, presidential candidate Donald Trump accused candidate Ted Cruz's father of being tied to the assassination of President Kennedy in 1963. Taking the story from the *National Enquirer*, an infamous tabloid that makes up the most insane and vitriolic rumors and reports them as news, the soon-to-be presumptive Republican candidate for president of the most powerful nation on earth said,

> *"His father was with Lee Harvey Oswald prior to Oswald's being—you know, shot. I mean, the whole thing is ridiculous," Trump said during a Fox News phone interview. "What is this, right prior to his being shot, and nobody even brings it up. They don't even talk about that. That was reported, and nobody talks about it. I mean, what was he doing? What was he doing with Lee Harvey Oswald shortly before the death, before the shooting? It's horrible."* [3]

Raising the specter of such a wild conspiracy is the pinnacle of inflammatory politics. It is irresponsible, reprehensible, and speaks of either fundamentally flawed judgment or fundamentally flawed ethics by Trump. For Trump's supporters it did not make one iota of difference and they went to the primary polls and gave him a landslide victory over Cruz in Indiana the next day. How can thoughtful, mostly rational people, who know the president must have excellent ethics and judgment, screen out information to such an extreme extent? We must admit that they do screen out such information and disregard it, or themselves believe it.

This all becomes quite clear when we understand that there is one thing that we must defend. I call it the **self-nested in family-nested in tribe**. I wish there was an easier term for this, but in the 30 years of research on stress and threat, I have not found a simpler term for this fundamental three-part connection. It appears to be biologically fixed and defines who we are as humans. Although complex, we can at least deconstruct this complex concept in simple terms. Once understood, we will have insight into how we can process information and how little truth matters in belief, and matters even less when we are threatened.

3.2   PROTECTING THE SELF, THE FAMILY, AND THE TRIBE

The self is both physical and psychological. It is a natural and a biological requirement that we protect the biological self. If someone strikes us or attacks us they could injure or kill us. But if we think about it, we often describe the self by saying, "This is who I am." And so, exactly as we state this, to attack the psychological self is also to attack our essence, who we are. Psychology often called this the ego or one's identity. We guard this sense of our self almost as strongly as we guard our physical self. Information that supports the view of the self is accepted and information that is inconsistent or a threat to the self is defended against.

Next is the family. I often apply a simple test to show how much we are attached to family. Would you stand in the way of a bullet to protect your child? If they became deathly sick would you have asked God to rather have made you sick? If you answered yes, then what this means is that family is more part of you, or more highly prized, than your self is. You would forfeit yourself for your family.

The family is the cardinal biological social unit. Children are the biological future, but the family would also be at great risk and deeply threatened by the loss of the mother or father. Grandparents and other kin were also required to sustain the family unit. Cultures developed different rituals for preserving the family, and this refers back to the leash concept of our behavioral genetics that evolved with our evolution. The attachment to family is on a rather short leash, meaning family will be represented across cultures. But how that family is manifested is on a longer leash, meaning it will vary significantly. Families may be matriarchal or patriarchal. Families may have gay partners or practice polyandry. Married couples most typically entered the man's family's home, but not always. English law transferred title and land to the firstborn son, so as not to dilute and divide the land, but other countries evolved other forms of family legacy. Humans have been existing in families before they were humans and in our pre-human evolutionary form. This means we have biological push to form families in some form.

The tribe, as I have already discussed, is the principal biological grouping beyond the family and it is set by several million years of development. The tribe was necessary for sustenance, daily food, and protection. Families could not survive without the tribe as they were too vulnerable to attack and did not have the numbers to provide food, protection, and knowledge of survival. Our tribal psycho-biology explains so much about how we practice our politics, why terrorism emerges, and why wars are fought. But little is written about our tribal self and it is the least well understood part of the *self-nested in family-nested in tribe*.

The preeminent anthropologist Owen Lovejoy explains in his work several attributes of early human and hominids that are critical in understanding our tribal behavioral genetics. Humans, Lovejoy argues, do not descend from apes and have a separate unique evolutionary history. Our clade (evolutionary tree) and that of the ape differed from our clade's earliest beginnings. Unlike apes, human fathers are protective of their young, male apes are disinterested. Humans also became bipedal and upright very early in our evolutionary history. This had a profound impact on our tribal origins. Being upright humans could travel great distances for hunting and foraging. Apes, not being upright, are much more limited in their territory. Being bipedal also affords the use of tools, as the hands become free. Mothers, however, do not become free to roam as they are tied to protection of the young and old. And so the tribe begins, with family structures of bread winner-hunter, and nurturer-protector. Make no mistake about it, women in our tribal origins also evolved as vicious, committed, strong protectors. They were often left alone at the hearth with the young and the old and had to fight off attack from wild beasts and invading tribes [4].

But something else changes according to Lovejoy with human's evolutionary advancement. Males and females within the tribe had to cooperate to survive. Evidence suggests typical tribal or band size of 100–150 people. Of course, there would be jealousy, aggression, and coveting of resources, but everyone needs everyone else to survive given the social complexity that occurs with band size of these numbers. Everyone needs to maximize children's survival for a next generation. The group has to sustain a certain number of hunters, fertile women, children, and protectors to sustain itself. Nor can men or women be merely promiscuous to ensure survival of their genes. Getting pregnant or impregnating someone is the easy part. In fact, humans became less efficient at reproduction with its lowered importance. Protecting the offspring to adulthood, in contrast, takes tremendous cooperation. And, it is the outsider, those threats that come from outside the tribe that become the threats that the tribe must aggressively protect against. Weather, wild beasts, vermin, and neighboring tribes become the threat.

This profoundly changes how we see humans and our behavior in groups. Humans' behavioral genetics, passed from one generation to the next in our DNA, had to become strongly cooperative within the tribe and strongly defensive against the outsider. It seems simple, but when we lost our sectorial canine complex (those scary teeth that monkey's bite with), we could no longer dominate by mere aggression. We had to dominate through joining and cooperation. "Smart and together" replaced "vicious and ascendant" and no one human could rule without others. This occurred 4–6 million years ago, long before *Homo sapiens*, which is what we are, evolved a mere 200,000 years ago.

This means that these insider-outsider demarcations and strong tribal ties run to our deepest behavioral genetics [5]. Critically important here is also evidence that this need to rely on cooperation, competition and collation among humans exerted the strongest pressure on brain development and is what propelled brain size and intelligence to so markedly advance compared to other species. So the advancement of our brains and our inherent genetics for cooperation, competition and coalition building are largely interwoven [6]. Said another way, humans became smart because cooperation requires enormous brain capacity and complexity.

This evolutionary history is what makes us *individuals, nested in family, nested in tribe*. We can act alone, but we depend on the family for reproduction, parenting, and companionship, and we depend on the tribe for sharing resources within and protection from without. Beliefs about the self, family and tribe are vital and information from the outside is highly suspect. We will believe the most insane things and reject the most rational arguments if it supports the self-nested in family-nested in tribe. Once we have committed to the tribe we are able to cheer as we watch our enemies blown to bloody defeat and support our leaders for bombing them into the stone age. We might see Secretary Hillary Clinton as politically manipulative and weak for staying with Bill during his philandering, but we just don't hold it against her once we have chosen her to be our leader. Those who "Burn for Bernie," supporting Senator Bernie Sanders for president, hardly process that his plans make little economic sense, and they are the most intelligent young segment of the electorate. They are burning for Bernie and truth does not dissipate their passion. It is not processed. True, this becomes harder when candidate Donald Trump lies about 70 percent of the time [7], and continues this into his presidency, but the process is no different. As he famously stated, *"I could stand in the middle of 5th Avenue and shoot somebody and I wouldn't lose any voters."* [8]

3.3   You Must Tell the Tribe What They Want to Hear

When Barack Obama succeeded in killing Osama bin Laden, the architect of the September 11 attack on the World Trade Center and Pentagon, surveyors asked citizens of Ohio who they thought was responsible for killing bin Laden. At the time Mitt Romney was running against Barack Obama for president, so they were asked "Was Obama or Romney responsible for killing Bin Laden?" Sixty-two percent said either Romney was responsible for killing bin Laden, or stated they didn't know [10]. Romney, at the time, held no political position and the news had been filled with scenes from the White House Situation Room as President Obama, Secretary Hillary Clinton, Defense Secretary Gates, and Chairman of the Joint Chiefs Admiral Mullen watched on during the tense operation. Defense Secretary Robert Gates, a Republican, had stated, "I've worked for a lot of these guys and this is one of the most courageous calls—decision—that I think I've ever seen a president make." [11] But that is just not how Ohio Republicans saw it. The prism through which they screen the world blinded them to accurate information (Image 3.1).

Image 3.1   *Situation Room* by Pete Souza [9]

We have a limited ability to detect our own prisms of perception, but can see them with better clarity when we view them in others. The extreme nature of ISIS's views offer an opportunity of understanding how truth can be distorted, and such understanding is essential if we wish to defeat ISIS. Inaccuracy in our understanding of an enemy is dangerous.

ISIS at this date is in territorial retreat, but remains powerful in its ability to inspire terrorism and anti-Western hatred. Their central thinking on key pivotal points, that are at their core, are bizarre and far outside the realm of rational thought, and yet they are quite rational in most other ways.

The key to understanding ISIS is seeing that ISIS is an apocalyptic sect, as are many fundamentalist Christians and some sects of Chasidic Jewry. Like fundamentalist Christians and Chasidic Jews, they believe that certain events must transpire to bring us to the end of days prophesized in their bible. Where they differ from fundamentalist Christians and Chasidic Jews is to the ends to which they believe they must go to bring on the days of prophesy.

We must understand how cults screen in and broadcast out information through a distorted prism that is consistent with their lynchpin tribal beliefs. We have seen several cults in recent decades, but we are used to thinking of cults numbering in the dozens or perhaps hundreds. The *Branch Davidians* amassed an armory of weapons and their leader, David Koresh, believed that the end of the world was near and that he was married to all women. The siege of their Waco, Texas, compound ended in a bloody federal raid and the death of 77 members. *Heaven's Gate* made headlines in 1997 when 39 members of the cult committed mass suicide. They prophesized that a spaceship would take them away to a Garden of Eden. They were found clad in black attire and gym shoes with arm patches that read "Heaven's Gate Away Team." The 900 members of the *Peoples Temple*, led by Jim Jones, committed mass suicide, drinking poison mixed with Flavor Aid after moving their cult from the U.S. to Guyana in South America. Estimates on the number of ISIS fighters varies, but it is believed that there are perhaps 30,000 people who have travelled from other countries to join ISIS [12]. The Syrian Observatory for Human Rights estimates there are 80,000–100,000 ISIS fighters [13]. Whatever the true numbers, their adherents are numerous.

The ISIS prophesy is an extremist version of the stages of world's end found in the Old Testament (Torah), New Testament, and Koran. ISIS believe that they must cause a war of East and West. They believe that such a war will bring about the prophesy that Jesus, who they consider the second-greatest prophet after Mohammed, will lead them to defeat their enemies. ISIS also counters widespread Muslim opposition to their cause by simply believing that those who do not pledge allegiance to them are apostate, and therefore conveniently non-Muslims and consequently deserving of death. ISIS are strict adherents to their inaccurate interpretation of an imagined seventh-century Islamic state that they believe will bring about the apocalypse. They await the defeat of the army of Rome at Dabiq in Syria, and that this will initiate the next cascade of apocalyptic prophesies [14]. Their interpretation of the Koran is clearly out of step with most Muslims, but it is deeply Islamic. When such beliefs are so deeply held, they are immune to outside persuasion. As in other cults, they are not only willing to die for their cause, they feel obligated to do so.

A rational viewpoint would then argue that ISIS adherents are irrational and even insane to hold such beliefs. But if you listen to their videos you will hear rational, calm, decisive argument. ISIS uses complex military strategies that require high level thought about integration of forces and weaponry. Their recruitment videos are better than any I have ever seen for the U.S. military. They have advanced knowledge of use of the internet on a technical level. Their interpretations of the Koran are not in themselves extreme, and they follow Koranic text with careful logic. What defies rational thought is they make a leap to a foregone conclusion, and it is in the distance of that leap that they leave reality and enter a world of dangerous fantasy. Argument, logic, and thought must support the tribe. Ergo, the Koran must support their extreme conclusions. It is a dangerous leap, but its structure is no different than the denial of climate change by Republicans. One has to discount an overwhelming amount of informed expert opinion to come to these conclusions.

3.4   THE THREAT OF LOSS AND THE END OF TRUTH

The question arises as to whether the departure from truth politics to fear politics is predictable, and it clearly is. Perhaps the answer is obvious when we accept that those who are most susceptible to fear messaging are those who feel threatened or who have experienced loss. A rape victim will naturally be overly alert to any hint of threats in the environment that had anything in common with the original trauma. In fact, it is adaptive that she overinterpret threats until reality is again safe. Caution is largely functional as long as it is not paralyzing.

But we can also create perceived realities through repeated messaging from trusted sources, especially when we already have some level of agreement or belief in the message. Hence, if you constantly warn a child to the extreme about the dangers of strangers, or Blacks, or Jews, they will believe that every stranger, Black, or Jew is a threat. Repeated fear messaging produces fear, and if it comes repeatedly from believed sources, be they parents or talk radio, they become reality. This was the Nazi's chief propagandist Joseph Goebbels' brilliant insight. By constantly telling the German public of the evil of Jews in newspaper, books, radio and film, he created a reality that allowed every "good, thinking" German to be proud to hate Jews. It is the only way to get several hundred thousand otherwise civilized citizens to participate in the murder of 6 million Jews. The tribe must adjust its reality to protect itself from existential threat. The Jew must be seen as posing an existential threat.

Examining the social and economic climates in the U.S. allows great insight about the threat of loss and already occurring losses that the middle class have experienced. Without this sense of profound loss, the presidential campaigns of two figures so different, Donald Trump and Senator Bernie Sanders, and Trump's election, could never have occurred. Median family income fell since when George W. Bush took office in 2000–2014 by about 7–8 percent from about $58,000 to $53,700 in 2014 dollars. The jobless rate has steadily improved, but not for those without high school degrees. For them the jobless rate is almost three times higher than for college grads. The footprint of white men in the job market is shrinking markedly. White men's representation in the job market has fallen from about 90 percent in the 1950s to about 72 percent in 2016, or about a 20 percent drop [15] (Fig. 3.1).

Fig. 3.1   U.S. Male Labor Force Participation Rates. (Adapted from U.S. Bureau of Labor Statistics [16])

Our brains are wired not to react to loss, but to overreact to loss or even the whiff of threat of loss because it is adaptive to do so. It causes us to be alert and diligent and motivated. It pushes us to rise to the occasion, to be vigilant against attack, and to protect hearth and home. But chronic loss also takes a toll on our emotions and our bodies. Those with a bachelor's degree have markedly lower rates of death due to drug addiction and suicide in 2013 than they did in 1999. In contrast, those with a high school education or less, that segment of the population that has experienced these marked losses of status and position and who are threatened by further loss and threat, have experienced a catastrophic rise in death rates from 1999 to 2013. No other Western nation has experienced this reversal in loss of life due to drug and alcohol addiction and suicide. Despite getting more obese as a nation, diabetes deaths have held constant and lung cancer deaths are down, but deaths by despair—suicides, deaths by poisoning, and deaths from chronic liver diseases—are all on the rise [17] (Fig. 3.2).

It makes sense that an even more direct indicator of being under attack, and therefore needing to hear certain truths and not others, would be arming yourself. So, it is instructive to examine who buys guns, especially military style weapons. White non-Hispanics own twice as many guns as

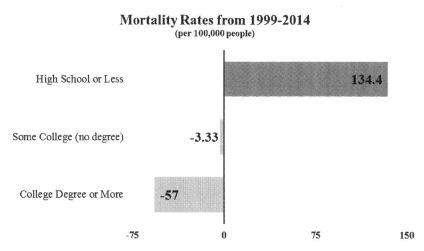

Mortality Rates from 1999-2014
(per 100,000 people)

Fig. 3.2   U.S. mortality rates by education level. (Adapted from Case and Deaton [17])

do Blacks and Hispanics. Republicans are about 2.2 times more likely than Democrats to own a weapon. Conservatives are nearly two times more likely to own a gun than those who identify themselves as liberal. Men are 9 times more likely to own a gun than a woman. Some of these differences represent differences in lifestyle and a fondness for hunting, but that is only a small part of the differences [18].

Data on assault-style rifles are harder to ascertain. It is estimated that there may be as many as 2.5–3.3 million AR-15 assault-style rifles in the U.S., and this is only one of the popular models available of the most military weapon allowed by law [19]. This was the weapon that Adam Lanza used at Sandy Hook to kill 20 children and 6 educators. Consistent with this logic, it is middle-aged White men, again that group who have experienced loss of jobs, income, and status, who are overwhelmingly buying these weapons. The late historian Richard Hofstadter wrote in his book *The Age of Reform* that White men in the U.S. are "losing in status and respect," and feel "bypassed and humiliated" by their loss in economic and social standing, and lash out at those who have usurped them and fight to regain power and status [20]. The "Man Card" is depicted in a recent advertisement for assault-type rifles. The assault-like weapon is the man card, reestablishing men's power and reversing their sense of humiliation (Image 3.2).

Nor is this reemergence of right-wing, militaristic White males isolated to the U.S. Western Europe has experienced a similar rise in White men who see themselves as victims and threatened by loss. Since the 1990s, Sweden has been a European center for rising anti-immigrant and anti-Semitic political organizing and grassroots efforts, often using popular music as a vehicle to attract young adherents. Led by the Swedish Resistance Movement and other neo-Nazi group, they have managed sizable representation in the Swedish parliament by popularizing their message to a general public fear of the infusion of Syrian refugees. In 2014, the Sweden Democrats, whose roots are in the country's neo-Nazi movement, became the country's third leading party. It should be no surprise that the supporters of the Sweden Democrats are largely unemployed urban and rural men [22]. As in the U.S. its supporters are those who have been left behind by the changing nature of the Western economy.

Image 3.2   Bushmaster "Man Card" Advertisement [21]

3.5   THE NEED TO SILENCE TRUTH

In each of these instances, we see that the threatened self, family, or tribe adopt a defensive posture and that a major aspect of this posture is to be open to certain truths and closed to others. However, this opening then needs to be exploited. In both the U.S. and Europe television has played some part of this. The politically motivated station does so by making an important shift. They declare mainstream media as biased in favor of the left and declare themselves as purveyor of the truth. Fact checking would quickly debunk much if not most of what they say, but we have already seen that facts have little to do with deeply believed truths. Indeed, as the Nazi propagandist Goebbels so astutely understood, the principal enemies of the fear-based narrative are intellectuals and the university.

There was no point in seeking to convert the intellectuals. For intellectuals would never be converted and would anyway always yield to the stronger, and this will always be "the man in the street." Arguments must therefore be crude, clear and forcible, and appeal to emotions and instincts, not the intellect. Truth was unimportant and entirely subordinate to tactics and psychology. [23]

The Nazis moved early and quickly to take over the university, knowing that professors would be an impediment to propaganda, perversion of science, and the Nazi need to be the sole voice to the young. Peter Drucker, an Austrian economist and professor, wrote as follows:

What made me decide to leave right away, several weeks after Hitler had come to power, was the first Nazi-led faculty meeting at the university. Frankfurt was the first university the Nazis tackled, precisely because it was the most self-confidently liberal of major German universities, with a faculty that prided itself on its allegiance to scholarship, freedom of conscience and democracy. The Nazis therefore knew that control of Frankfurt University would mean control of German academia. And so did everyone at the university. [24]

Likewise, the Soviet Union could not afford for scientific findings to dispute ideology. In the mid-1930s Stalin moved to support scientists and scientific methods that argued against genetics as a science. Mendelian genetics (supporting Darwin) was seen as a danger to communist ideology for its support of survival of the fittest. Likewise, principles of reinforcement theory and B.F. Skinner's findings on behaviorism were seen as dangers to communist thinking. They could not allow that people were motivated by being directly rewarded for their work. This disallowed Soviet scientists from participating in the global scientific community and Soviet psychology and physiology was retarded in the process.

Led by Trofim Lysenko, a pseudoscience was created within the Soviet Union's scientific establishment. The ideas of Lysenko were based on the proposition that if you created a trait in humans in one generation (actually any living form plant or animal) that it would be inheritable in future generations. In a simple example, if you trained a citizen to be more willing to work for the state, her progeny would inherit this tendency. So, communism's shaping of human behavior and demanding people act for the good of all was pitted against what the Soviets saw as a capitalistic "survival of the fittest" and people motivated by just rewards for work well done. Lysenkoism instead argued that his data showed that once trained by society, these new traits would be inherited by future generations.

This pseudoscience devastated Russia's ability to benefit from much of science, and it was only reversed when in 1962 leading Soviet physicists Yakov Borisovich Zel'dovich, Vitaly Ginzburg, and Pyotr Kapitsa presented a case against Lysenko. This began to unravel support in Russia of pseudoscience, but it took some decades to rebuild the scientific community [25, 26].

When ideological movements of the far left or far right take over, they begin by claiming that the outsider of their tribe is an enemy and that that enemy has control of the apparatus of media, banks, universities and government. This means that any information that has or will come from these sources is tainted and indeed designed as part of the conspiracy against the new movement or order. At step two, they engage in creating new sources of "truth" that continue to poison the legitimate sources of knowledge, government and science. This has been a design of the right in the U.S. and Europe for two decades, and the creation of tribal politics and the demonization of their opponents has been relentless. As President Trump tweeted on February 17, 2017

> The FAKE NEWS media (failing @nytimes, @NBCNews, @ABC, @CBS, @CNN) is not my enemy, it is the enemy of the American People! [27]

The echo chamber of this is seen in the support of this viewpoint, with an overwhelming 60 percent of Trump supporters seeing the press as the "enemy of the people." And, the more actually truthful the media is objectively, the less they see it as truthful [28, 29].

The silencing of free speech has also been a double-standard by the far liberal left, at the same time as they criticize the right for their tendencies. Beware the speaker who heads to college campuses to speak in favor of conservative issues, a pro-Israel stance, challenging radical feminism, or for some semblance of logic on issues of genderized bathrooms. A stance against the liberal left in academia is often met not with debate, but with an attempt at silencing. The difference between such acts and most of what this chapter has covered is that universities have mainly stood up to such attempts to gag speakers and silence more conservative faculty, and the extreme left in the U.S. has virtually no political power above the level of a few local governments. In Great Britain, the university has nearly ceased to be a place where fair discussion of Israel can occur, and where the logic that supports terrorism is rampant.

My thesis is that were the extreme left to gain political power as in several communist and far-left-leaning countries, they would respond as do the extreme Right in the U.S. and Europe. Truth and science are threats to the extremes on both sides of the political spectrum. It is not surprising that Venezuela's responses to criticism of their human rights record was to expel Human Rights Watch, and in so doing to attempt to silence any opposition criticism [30]. Beware the extremes on both sides of the political spectrum, as they protect tribal politics with extreme actions.

3.6   The Need to Invalidate Science

The vilification of science itself is perhaps the most egregious and dangerous aspect of the denial of truth, for if science is seen as mere opinion, then the very anchor of modern medical, technological and energy advancement is disemboweled. The stripping of science from its basis in empirical confirmation has been a hallmark of extremist political movements, but has moved even to centrist Republican positions more recently.

The following are quotes from media and politicians that illustrate the rejection of science and the scientific method and its replacement by scripture or whatever is politically convenient.

Cholesterol has nothing to do with heart disease. Nothing wrong with saturated fats. (Rush Limbaugh, March 8, 2011 [31])

Do you know we have more acreage of forest land in the United States today than we did at the time the Constitution was written. (Rush Limbaugh, February 18, 1994 [32])

Obama is a clown. You don't have to be a scientist to know that the President doesn't know what he's talking about when he says fossil fuels are the energy of the past. We have more oil than we need. We'll never run out of it. It's all we've got. (Rush Limbaugh, March 8, 2011 [31])

Carbon dioxide is not a harmful gas; it is a harmless gas ... And yet we're being told that we have to reduce this natural substance and reduce the American standard of living to create an arbitrary reduction in something that is naturally occurring in the Earth. (Michele Bachmann, House floor speech, April 22, 2009 [33])

I think there are a substantial number of scientists who have manipulated data so that they will have dollars rolling in to their projects. I think we're seeing it almost weekly or even daily, scientists who are coming forward and questioning the original idea that man-made global warming is what is causing the climate to change. (Rick Perry, Candidate for President, Aug. 17, 2011 [34])

Perry is just fabricating false information. Actually over 97 percent of publishing scientists agree that humans are responsible for climate change. Indeed, the small segment of scientists who doubt climate change being of human origins are not experts in climate science [35].

...the idea that man, through the production of CO_2 ...is somehow responsible for climate change is, I think, just patently absurd ... To me, this is an opportunity for the left to create—it's really a beautifully concocted scheme. (Rick Santorum, Candidate for President June 8, 2011 [36])

All that stuff I was taught about evolution and embryology and the Big Bang Theory, all this is lies straight from Hell. And it's lies to try to keep me and all the folks who were taught that from understanding that they need the Savior. (Paul Broun, Member U.S. Congress and Tea Party Caucus, 2007–2015 [37])

3.7   THE INVALIDATION OF THE UNIVERSITY

The invalidation and even vilification of the university has been a cornerstone of the "very conservative" right. Indeed, the Republican Party is the only denier of the legitimacy of climate science among conservative political parties in the Western world [38]. Margaret Thatcher moved the

British Conservative party stance to adopt climate change as a high priority in 1988. The German government called for an aggressive program to reduce CO_2 emissions in 1988, and the current German conservative party has climate change as a major plank of its party's platform [39].

There is a simple reason why universities are liberal bastions. Education leads to liberalism, and it sticks long after people leave their college campuses. Among adults with postgraduate degrees, Democrats lead Republications by a huge margin of 57 percent to 35 percent. Among those with college degrees and some postgraduate education the difference is narrower, but still substantially favors Democrats (49–42%) [40]. As professors nearly all have advanced postgraduate degrees they are going to fall into the group of liberals, and not conservatives. Indeed, the Republican assault against academia is really an assault against those with more education. Knowledge is not a danger to fiscal conservatism, but it is a threat to any political body or entity that is in the business of distorting knowledge, left or right. The university is also a haven for tolerance, or at least has been historically, as from its outset, universities were places where new ideas were entertained. Indeed, owing in part to its tolerance, women are increasingly represented in academia. This will be devastating for Republicans as women with postgraduate education tilt Democratic over Republican 64 percent to 29 percent, a 35 point spread [41]. Indeed, the Right should be scared of universities and education.

Given that access to education is part of the American dream, one wonders to which constituency this assault on the fountainhead of knowledge—the university—is geared toward. White evangelicals tend to accurately see the university as secular, its science in opposition to strict biblical interpretation of how the world was created, and a place of openness to lifestyle choices that threaten their view of the traditional family. Evangelicals are of course overwhelmingly Republican (68–22%). Less-educated White men are also largely Republican leaning (54–33%), and so again we have those who have lost jobs to the more educated elements of society as a natural enemy of those who stole their jobs, status, and middle-class position.

By attacking the university, Republicans are not only delegitimizing knowledge they are preaching to exactly what their choir wants to hear. If the university is not a source of knowledge and unbiased science, then the world was created in 6 days about 5800 years ago and men walked the earth with dinosaurs and did not descend from earlier life forms. The fossil record and scientific techniques such as advanced physics of thermoluminescence, potassium argon dating, paleomagnetism are fallacious or even conspiratorial concocted as part of the war on Christianity. If the university is worthless, then White men, whom we as a society have failed to educate and train for the highly skilled demands of today's economy, can blame "liberal intellectuals," instead of the politicians who let them down.

3.8   WOMEN, THE TRIBE, AND LOSS'S IMPACT: BREAD AND ROSES

According to our work on stress, and what we have called Conservation of Resources (COR) theory, the loss of resources and ongoing threat of further loss will equally impact women as it does men. Women, however, manifest loss's impact in very different ways than men. Nearly all the literature has focused in psychology and sociology on the level of the self and women's greater tendency to experience depression than men, at about a 2–1 level [42]. In contrast we know little about how women react to the ongoing economic losses and threats from terrorism that we face daily in the news, and even less about how these threats impact women socially and politically.

Although we all recognize that women are different than men, how they are different politically is typically treated superficially. Politicians seek women's votes by addressing issues directly relevant to women, such as equal pay, abortion rights, childcare, and family leave. These issues are of course especially relevant to women, but it implies that women are not interested in broader issues in the political discourse. Instead, I believe a sounder argument can be made for women as the most reasoned and thoughtful voting group. They are less politically emotional and volatile than men, and are less easily led by demagogues and political fads [43]. While men may "stick to their guns," women stick to their principles. This suggests that women may be less impacted by biased prisms and tribal defensiveness and remain better analyzers and processors of threat, loss and responding to it.

The 1912 Lawrence Textile Strike is a sterling exemplar of the maturity, depth, and breadth of women's political awareness and perspective. Called the *Bread and Roses movement*, women went on strike for better pay, but also for better quality of life for workers. "Hearts starve as well as bodies; give us bread, but give us roses" was a philosophy that created a paradigm shift in workers' rights [44]. The woolen mills in Lawrence, Massachusetts, were mainly worked by women immigrants, divided by language and not integrated into the labor movement. The workers were overwhelmingly young women, girls really, ages 14–18 who worked a backbreaking 56-hour week. Male-dominated unions in the U.S. have still not caught up with the forward nature of their insights about workers' rights. They altered the labor struggle by demanding both higher wages and less hours, along with improved conditions for workers. Their cause was called "bread and roses," as the bread stood for better wages, but their plea was that quality of workers' and families' lives was equally essential, and this was poetically represented by "the roses."

The tactic of bread and roses advanced by these labor women was also entirely novel. They could not stand to watch their children starve as the strike stretched on. In a strategic move, they sent hundreds of their hungry children to be cared for in the homes of sympathetic families in New York and Vermont [45]. This astute move not only protected their children and allowed strikers to continue without fear for their families, it rallied a broader and more politically powerful allegiance across New England. With this move, Congress was forced to hold hearings after public opinion swelled in strikers' favor after the overzealous factory owners had police block the further exodus of children to families who could feed and care for them.

If women are less emotional and more rational in their politics than men, and less likely to overreact because they feel their honor insulted, then we would expect women to have less hawkish views, place more emphasis on education, and be less prone to react to fear politics. Among Republican women, who we would expect to be more conservative, only 37 percent support the further right-leaning Tea Party. What is key here is what issues Tea Party supporters, mostly male, strongly believe in. Although fiscally conservative, their strongest views are anti-science and racist. Tea Party supporters were found by Abramowitz in a survey of them to disregard science as indicated by their opposition to clean energy (81%) and opposing stem cell research (71%). Tea Party supporters oppose health care reform (88%), which may be just a reaction against government overreach, but they also believe Blacks' problems are that "they just don't try hard enough" (65%), and believe that Blacks should not receive the favors they are getting by such programs as affirmative action (82%) [46].

Conservative women just do not seem to buy in to this more blind-to-the-facts and more racist view of America's problems.

3.9   WOMEN SEEM HARDER TO PUSH INTO HATE-BASED
AND FEAR-BASED AGENDAS

Today, women across cultures continue to support bread and roses. A recent survey from the Greenberg Quinian Rosner Research Center (2016) found women more likely than men to favor lowering taxes to business in order to help middle-class families, a conservative viewpoint. But they at the same time markedly favored roses issues compared to men. They were much more likely than men to favor paid sick leave (75–67%), tax credits for childcare for working parents (66–56%), and requiring employers to give workers predictable work schedules (66–56%). Quality public education is likewise a top priority for women compared to men [47].

Women are also consistently socially more tolerant than men. Women are more likely than men to favor government sponsored health care, guaranteeing good jobs for people, and providing aid for poor children. They are more likely than men to believe that treating people more equally would solve many of the problems we have in this country. Women are less likely than men to directly and indirectly hold attitudes that support class, ethnic, and sexual intolerance. Across cultures and different political contexts, men are more likely to support hierarchy enhancing policies, survival of the fittest, whereas women are more likely to favor policies that offer support and give people a helping hand [48].

Of course, women's "nurture and build" strategy could be partially an outgrowth of their tribally-based behavioral genetics, but it does not seem to rise and fall based on fear and threat if it is. Certainly, women could be—and in many ways must be—enacting in some part what they are genetically endowed to do, and this could be tribal as well, as women could be behaving tribally as protectors of the hearth and home. But their thinking seems more influenced than men's by a rational and less emotional, and more stable set of attitudes and a steadier reaction against threat. Men move toward fight and flight, what Harvard's Jim Sidanius and his colleagues in their important and thorough work call *social dominance orientation*, whereas women favor "support and protect" strategies [48]. As in sports, women are often fans, but they seldom move from fan to fanatic.

Looking across this data, it appears that although the pull to tribal protectionism and reactivity must exist in both men and women's genetic underpinnings, it seems less easily evoked among women. Women live under more threat and experience more loss than men due to their being more likely to be single parents, poorer economically, and more vulnerable to violence due to rape. Women have repeatedly been found to be more fearful of crime, and more recent work shows them to be more fearful than men of terrorism and more likely to make personal choices such as seeking information about terrorism or avoiding places that might prove dangerous, both reasonable if perhaps exaggerated strategies considering the true low risk of being caught up in the U.S. in a terrorist attack [49]. But they do not appear to translate this personal set of fears to tribal, fear based react and attack strategies.

How we should react to terrorism and our enemies as a tribe finds women consistently less likely to favor war, and they were markedly less in favor of going to war with Iraq in November 2001 (68% vs. 80%), and notably strongly more in favor of attempting further negations compared to men (59–34%). Women were also much more in favor of going into Iraq if the U.S. could build a coalition through the United Nations compared to men. Men were more likely than women to want to invade Iraq whether or not the U.N. voted to authorize a coalition invasion. Women did come around to favoring the war, but they took much more convincing on what we have unfortunately learned were false "facts" regarding Iraq's position of weapons of mass destruction [49].

3.10   ENGINEERING TRUTH THROUGH FEAR

External threat clearly makes us fearful and this moves us to more conservative positions. We become more protective of the self, the family, and the tribe, and truth suffers in the process. But fear can and is also given to manipulation and the extreme right and extreme left use this tool to motivate political action and support in their favor. It appears that this is especially true for men and that women are more reasoned in their political action. Education is also a defense against the twisting of truth and the manipulation of fear politics of the aggressive tribe. The right in the U.S. claims a war against Christianity, a takeover of media by liberal conspirators, a war on White America, Mexican rapists invading from the south, and Syrian terrorists invading from the East. It is not enough that we must fight terrorists for them, we must place all Muslims as suspect.

The war metaphor is powerful, as we of course consider ourselves on the right and morale side of these wars. The danger is in the slippage that has occurred from war on an issue as a metaphor, to use of the war metaphor to actually arm ourselves and attack our opponents. The use of the war and threat metaphors are marketing strategies. Johnson asserted his war on poverty as an attempt to rally support for fighting poverty and discrimination and promoting equal rights. You might be for or against such a liberal sets of policies, but the policy is not intended to attack those who disagree, the war is on poverty. We have migrated from the use of the war metaphor to the use of the actuality of war and the eliciting of fear politics and tribal responding. In this war it has been instrumental and advantageous for extremists to destroy faith in traditional sources of truth, science, and open media, and to replace them with propagandized, distorted versions of truth. To do so they must twist facts to meet their ideology, rather than face facts to shape their ideology.

REFERENCES

1. Kierkegaard, S. (1962). *Works of love.* New York: Harper Perennial.
2. Holocaust Education & Archive Research Team. (2007). *Joseph Goebbels.* Holocaust Education & Archive Research Team. Retrieved February 8, 2018, from http://www.holocaustresearchproject.org/holoprelude/goebbels.html
3. Cameron, J. (2016, May 3). Ted Cruz's dad Rafael played role in John F. Kennedy assassination, Trump claims. *New York Daily News.* Retrieved September 20, 2017, from http://www.nydailynews.com/news/election/ted-cruz-dad-involved-john-f-kennedy-assassination-trump-article-1.2623025
4. Lovejoy, C. O. (2009). Reexamining human origins in light of Ardipithecus ramidus. *Science, 326*(5949), 74e1–74e8. https://doi.org/10.1126/science.1175834.
5. Dunbar, R. (1993). Coevolution of neocortical size, group size and language in humans. *Behavioral and Brain Sciences, 16*(4), 681–694. https://doi.org/10.1017/s0140525x00032325.
6. Alexander, R. D. (1979). *Darwinism and human affairs.* Seattle: University of Washington Press.
7. Konnikova, M. (2017, January/February). Trump's lies vs. your brain. *Politico Magazine.* Retrieved September 5, 2017, from http://www.politico.com/magazine/story/2017/01/donald-trump-lies-liar-effect-brain-214658
8. Leonhardt, D., & Thompson, S. A. (2017, December 14). Trump's lies. *New York Times.* Retrieved December 20, 2017, from https://www.nytimes.com/interactive/2017/06/23/opinion/trumps-lies.html?_r=0
9. Souza, P. (2011). *Situation room.* Executive Office of the President of the United States. Retrieved from https://www.flickr.com/photos/35591378@N03/5680724572
10. Baumann, N. (2012, September 10). 15 percent of Ohio GOPers say Romney deserves credit for bin Laden raid. *Mother Jones.* Retrieved March 7, 2017,

from   http://www.motherjones.com/mojo/2012/09/ohio-republicans-poll-romney-bin-laden

11. CNN. (2011, May 16). Gates praises Obama's call on bin Laden raid. *CNN*. Retrieved March 7, 2017, from http://www.cnn.com/2011/US/05/15/gates.cbs.interview/

12. Kirk, A. (2016, March 24). Iraq and Syria: How many foreign fighters are fighting for Isil? *The Telegraph*. Retrieved March 7, 2017, from http://www.telegraph.co.uk/news/2016/03/29/iraq-and-syria-how-many-foreign-fighters-are-fighting-for-isil/

13. Aljazeera. (2014, August 19). *Islamic State 'has 50,000 fighters in Syria'*. Aljazeera. Retrieved September 5, 2017, from http://www.aljazeera.com/news/middleeast/2014/08/islamic-state-50000-fighters-syria-2014819184258421392.html

14. Wood, G. (2015, March). What ISIS really wants. *The Atlantic*. Retrieved March 7, 2017, from https://www.theatlantic.com/magazine/archive/2015/03/what-isis-really-wants/384980/

15. Glaeser, E. L. (2017, July). The war on work—And how to end it. *City Journal*. Retrieved September 4, 2017, from https://www.city-journal.org/html/war-work-and-how-end-it-15250.html

16. U.S. Bureau of Labor Statistics. (n.d.). *Civilian labor force participation rate: Men*. Federal Reserve Bank of St. Louis. Retrieved September 5, 2017, from https://fred.stlouisfed.org/series/LNS11300001

17. Case, A., & Deaton, A. (2015). Rising morbidity and mortality in midlife among white non-Hispanic Americans in the 21st century. *Proceedings of the National Academy of Sciences, 112*(49), 15078–15083. https://doi.org/10.1073/pnas.1518393112.

18. Morin, R. (2014, July 15). *The demographics and politics of gun-owning households*. Pew Research Center. Retrieved March 7, 2017, from http://www.pewresearch.org/fact-tank/2014/07/15/the-demographics-and-politics-of-gun-owning-households/

19. Boyle, J. (2014, December 3). *Military-style AR-15 rifles: 'The market is saturated'*. *USA TODAY*. Retrieved March 5, 2017, from http://www.usatoday.com/story/news/nation/2014/12/03/military-style-ar-rifles-market-saturated/19836755/

20. Hofstadter, R. (1955). *The age of reform*. New York: Vintage Books.

21. Gray, E. (2012, December 17). Bushmaster rifle ad reminds us to ask more about masculinity and gun violence. *Huffington Post*. Retrieved September 5, 2017, from https://www.huffingtonpost.com/emma-gray/bushmaster-rifle-ad-masculinity-gun-violence-newtown-adam-lanza_b_2317924.html

22. Groll, E. (2016, September 16). How a former neo-Nazi party became Sweden's third-largest. *Foreign Policy*. Retrieved March 9, 2017, from http://

foreignpolicy.com/2014/09/16/how-a-former-neo-nazi-party-became-swedens-third-largest/

23. Trevor-Roper, H. (Ed.). (1978). *Final entries of 1945: The diaries of Joseph Goebbels.* London: Putnam.

24. Drucker, P. (1994). *Adventures of a bystander.* Piscataway: Transaction Publishers.

25. Gordin, M. D. (2012). How Lysenkoism became pseudoscience: Dobzhansky to Velikovsky. *Journal of the History of Biology, 43*(3), 443–468. https://doi.org/10.1007/s10739-011-9287-3.

26. Joravsky, D. (1996). *The Lysenko affair.* Chicago: University of Chicago Press.

27. Anapol, A. (2017, December 4). Poll: Majority of Trump supporters say media is 'enemy of American people'. *The Hill: 26.* Retrieved December 20, 2017, from http://thehill.com/blogs/blog-briefing-room/363098-poll-majority-of-trump-backers-say-media-is-enemy-of-american-people

28. Greenwood, M. (2017, February 17). Trump tweets: The media is the 'enemy of the American people'. *The Hill.* Retrieved December 20, 2017, from http://thehill.com/homenews/administration/320168-trump-the-media-is-the-enemy-of-the-american-people

29. Durkheimer, M. (2017, July 27). *'Fake news' leads to no news for the Trump base.* Forbes. Retrieved December 20, 2017, from https://www.forbes.com/sites/michaeldurkheimer/2017/07/27/fake-news-leads-to-no-news-for-the-trump-base/#501a38d52bb3

30. Reuters. (2008, September 19). Venezuela expels U.S. rights group for criticism. *Reuters.* Retrieved March 7, 2017, from http://www.reuters.com/article/us-venezuela-rights-idUSN1948835520080919

31. Foster, S. (2013, August 21). *50 of the worst things Rush Limbaugh has ever said.* Addicting Info. Retrieved February 8, 2018, from http://addictinginfo.com/2013/08/21/50-of-the-worst-things-rush-limbaugh-has-ever-said/

32. Wilson, J. (2011). *The most dangerous man in America: Rush Limbaugh's assault on reason.* New York: St. Martin's Press.

33. Johnson, B. (2009, April 24). *Stumped by science: Michele Bachmann calls CO2 'harmless,' 'negligible,' 'necessary,' 'natural'.* ThinkProgress. Retrieved February 8, 2018, from https://thinkprogress.org/stumped-by-science-michele-bachmann-calls-co2-harmless-negligible-necessary-natural-ba603ff8ef05/

34. Johnson, B. (2011, August 17). *Rick Perry: 'Substantial number' of climate scientists have 'manipulated data' for money.* ThinkProgress. Retrieved February 8, 2018, from https://thinkprogress.org/rick-perry-substantial-number-of-climate-scientists-have-manipulated-data-for-money-8e139fce3719/

35. Cook, J., Nuccitelli, D., Green, S. A., Richardson, M., Winkler, B., Painting, R., et al. (2013). Quantifying the consensus on anthropogenic global warming in the scientific literature. *Environmental Research Letter*, 8(2), 024024.
36. Samuelsohn, D. (2011, June 9). Santorum: Climate change is 'junk'. *Politico*. Retrieved February 8, 2018, from https://www.politico.com/story/2011/06/santorum-climate-change-is-junk-056599
37. Horowitz, A. (2012, October 6). Paul Broun: Evolution, big bang 'lies straight from the pit of hell'. *The Huffington Post*. Retrieved February 8, 2018, from https://www.huffingtonpost.com/2012/10/06/paul-broun-evolution-big-bang_n_1944808.html
38. Båtstrand, S. (2015). More than markets: A comparative study of nine conservative parties on climate change. *Politics & Policy*, 43(4), 538–561. https://doi.org/10.1111/polp.12122.
39. Pettenger, M. E. (2007). *The social construction of climate change: Power, knowledge, norms, discourses*. Burlington: Ashgate Publishing.
40. Pew Research Center. (2015, April 7). *A deep dive into party affiliation: Sharp differences by race, gender, generation, education*. Pew Research Center. Retrieved March 7, 2017, from http://www.people-press.org/2015/04/07/a-deep-dive-into-party-affiliation/
41. Martin, L. A., Neighbors, H., & Griffith, D. (2013). The experience of symptoms of depression in men vs women. *JAMA Psychiatry*, 70(10), 1100–1106. https://doi.org/10.1001/jamapsychiatry.2013.1985.
42. Kaufmann, K. M., Petrocik, J. R., & Shaw, D. R. (2008). *Unconventional wisdom: Facts and myths about American voters*. Oxford: Oxford University Press.
43. Weir, R. E. (2013). *Workers in America: A historical encyclopedia*. Santa Barbara: ABC-CLIO Interactive.
44. Eisenstein, S. (1983). *Give us bread but give us roses: Working women's consciousness in the United States, 1890 to the first world war*. London: Routledge.
45. Abramowitz, A. (2011). *Partisan polarization and the rise of the Tea Party movement*. American Political Science Association Annual Meeting Paper. Retrieved March 9, 2017, from http://faculty.washington.edu/jwilker/353/AbramowitzTea.pdf
46. American Women. (2016, September 19). Women and the 2016 elections. *American Women*. Retrieved May 13, 2017, from http://www.americanwomen.org/research
47. Sidanius, J., Levin, S., Liu, J., & Pratto, F. (2000). Social dominance orientation, anti-egalitarianism and the political psychology of gender: An extension and cross-cultural replication. *European Journal of Social Psychology*, 30(1), 41–67.

48. Nellis, A. M. (2009). Gender differences in fear of terrorism. *Journal of Contemporary Criminal Justice*, *25*(3), 322–340. https://doi.org/10.1177/1043986209335012.
49. Moore, D. (2002, November 19). *Gender gap varies on support for war.* Gallup. Retrieved May 13, 2017, from http://www.gallup.com/poll/7243/gender-gap-varies-support-war.aspx

CHAPTER 4

Historical Threat and the Priming of Tribal Violence

> We shall fight on the beaches, we shall fight on the landing grounds, we shall fight in the fields and in the streets, we shall fight in the hills; we shall never surrender, and if, which I do not for a moment believe, this island or a large part of it were subjugated and starving, then our Empire beyond the seas, armed and guarded by the British Fleet, would carry on the struggle… *(Winston Churchill in a speech to the House of Commons on the 4th of June 1940 [1])*

Throughout history we are called on to respond to existential threat to the tribe. For much of the world the Nazi and Japanese imperial attacks in Europe and the Pacific created a unifying tribal response comprised of both solidarity and counter-violence. On September 11, 2001, four passenger airliners were hijacked by 19 members of al-Qaeda who had been hiding in plain sight in the U.S. American Airlines Flight 11 and United Airlines Flight 175 crashed into the north and south towers of the World Trade Center (WTC), respectively. A half hour later, American Airline Flight 77 was crashed into the Pentagon, the very symbol of U.S. military might, killing 125 military personnel and civilian defense workers. Not two hours later, both 110-story towers collapsed, killing 2996 individuals, constituting the worst attack on U.S. soil since Pearl Harbor and the worst loss of civilian life since the Civil War. In response, the U.S. raged for retribution and entered a war against Iraq highly questioned today, and certainly against a country that had little or nothing to do with the September

© The Author(s) 2018
S. E. Hobfoll, *Tribalism*,
https://doi.org/10.1007/978-3-319-78405-2_4

11 WTC attacks. The next 11 years resulted in the death of between 151,000 and 1 million Iraqis, in addition to the 4500 U.S. service members who lost their lives.

I will neither attempt here to criticize nor justify this war of retribution. Hindsight is 20/20. Rather, it is clear that the attacks and the loss of American lives resulted in a primitive response, a search for someone to blame and then someone to punish. None of the hijackers were from Iraq and Iraq was known to have no ties to the attack. Of the 19 hijackers, 15 were Saudi Arabian, 2 were from the United Arab Emirates, 1 was from Egypt, and 1 from Lebanon. Lashing out in anger and pain, 72 percent of Americans supported the war at the time, with most Americans giving strong support [2]. That is an overwhelming percentage of members of the American tribe.

I am not the kind of person who places an American flag by their door. I have never thought I had to prove my patriotism in that way. As a civilian and military officer, I have prided myself on being strategic and not being captured in emotions. The day after the WTC attack I found seven American flags in my garage that must have been left over from some parade my kids were in. I planted all seven defiantly in my front yard. Let freedom wave, and damn if Muslim terrorists were going to attack my country and think they would get away with it. I was quite emotionally ready to carpet bomb and would not have stopped at mere water boarding, or cared about the results. Such was my emotional state in those first days.

I recall a colleague sobbing in her office after the attack. We assumed she was mourning the loss of life, but when her crying subsided her remarks give insight into my thesis here. What she said was, "I am shaking with anger because I want to kill them and I don't know who "them" even is. I'm a pacifist against war and killing. I'm not supposed to feel like this?" Her aggressive, visceral reaction was experienced by millions of Americans. Her deep tribal biology was evoked from a million-year-old imprinting that overrode, at least for a time, what she thought was her liberal core beliefs about humanity.

We react to the killing of members of our tribe, and nations are very much tribes, with a deeply felt emotionality. The national anthem of the U.S. is about the glory of a flag, flags being tribal symbols since ancient times. It is notable that it ends in a question that stirs the American soul. After the night's bombardment by British forces in the War of 1812, the poet Francis Scott Key asks, "Does that star-spangled banner yet wave o'er the land of the free and the home of the brave?" [3] The flag and group identity become inseparable and inspirational. During the U.S. revolutionary war, the American flag also depicted a coiled rattlesnake with the motto "Don't tread on me," a rallying cry for American's sense of defiant independence that has ever since been part of the American identity. Military units historically protect their battle flag at all costs, holding it more sacred than human life sacrificed in its defense. During the Napoleonic Wars, the taking of a French Eagle, their battle symbol, by British troops was the most devastating defeat, and the British soldiers who captured one were rewarded with military honors as if they had overcome a battalion and not its symbol.

4.1   BUILDING TRAUMA NARRATIVES TO PROTECT THE TRIBE

We mourn each loss of life, and the death of nearly 3000 individuals is tragic. But nations wear tragedy on their chests. Like tattoos, they are stories deeply engraved in the national character. If we feel as we do over the death of 3000 members of our nation, what is felt by nations for whom such loss is not a drop of blood in the bucket of their dead, and for whom loss is seen as generational and ongoing?

Our research clearly establishes that as individuals we are much more deeply affected by loss than by gain. Our emotions, cognitions, and neurophysiology are loss-centered, and nearly oblivious to gain [4]. As I have developed in prior chapters of this book, when the individual or family is threatened, we reorient to protect and defend the self or the family. When the tribe in the form of a military unit, organization, nation, religious group, or even sports team is threatened, we respond to defend and protect from our evolutionary wiring on the tribal or band level. But, as we are each wired as individuals, the question arises as to how we create a tribal priming of the "defend and protect" response? In other words, what is the mechanism that connects our biological self and its psyche with the joined psyche of the "band of brothers?"

On the individual and family level, the experience of trauma produces memories that are nearly indelible and very different from other kinds of memories. The memories associated with PTSD are reexperienced as if they are reoccurring afresh with much of the original intensity and sense of reality. They even produce a physiological reaction that mimics the original trauma response. These memories serve a vital evolutionary purpose in our survival. The brain changes with PTSD in a way that serves to mimic the "alert, defend, and aggress" biological system for ready fight or flight. Indeed, when PTSD is chronic the very structures of the brain change. Neuroendocrine, neurochemical, and neuroanatomical alterations occur, in a sense sacrificing the individual for the sake of building an indelible alert and defend system [5].

As a tribe, however, we are a collection of people, each with their own brain. Over time, those who have been traumatized, who served as sentinels against repeated traumas, will recover or eventually die off. This would leave the tribe vulnerable again, as the hyper-alert system against trauma will have disappeared. The defense against this dangerous possibility in many lower animals is a genetic encoding of danger. For example, animals that are vulnerable to hawks will have a built-in warning system that alerts them when the shape of that hawk appears [6]. It does not need to be learned. Humans appear to have this built in system for heights, but the threats to humans, other than the general fear of the stranger, is too complex for one-to-one genetic encoding.

How do humans overcome this potentially disastrous genetic deficiency? They do so by having in their behavioral genetics a genetic push toward storytelling. Storytelling creates a narrative that is repeated and exaggerated, just as PTSD exaggerates the story of the trauma for the individual. Jews, Armenians, Russians, Palestinians, African Americans, ISEL, al-Qaeda, and Cuban refugees, all develop narratives that become powerful truths in their constant retelling. Indeed, it is believed that our brains enlarged markedly for the very purpose of communication and social interaction [7]. We are genetically pushed to share stories not just to talk, but because listening is embedded in our DNA as key to survival of the individual, family, and tribe.

The immediate experiences of individuals teach them "knowing how" and "knowing that," but through storytelling we learn to know what the trauma was like, we learn it as a shared experience. Our tribal genetic programming is not so hard-wired as to dictate the stories, but instead shapes us so that we will develop a narrative of danger and feel push both to hear it and repeat it. Our genetics endow us with an affinity toward such messaging.

The Jewish Passover Haggadah does not just retell the Exodus from Egypt 3500 years ago to a people's long dead ancestors. It joins Jews in the Exodus from slavery in Egypt, and how they are expected to respond to it. It also makes a connection from the Exodus from slavery to the history of persecution of Jews across the centuries. In this way, the tribal narrative goes beyond the retelling of one trauma, it weaves together repeated traumas and repeated responses, making "narrative connections" that are as convincing as an experienced attorney making her summation before the jury, connecting the dots and weaving the strands of fabric into the narrative's tapestry [8].

The tribal trauma narrative then takes another essential step. It demands that we recite the narrative as if it is occurring to us, the participant. It is not about a long dead people, but rather the Haggadah reads...

> *And if your son asks you in the future, saying, What are the testimonies, and the statutes, and the judgments, that the Lord our G-d commanded you? You will say to your son, **We** were slaves to Pharaoh in Egypt; and the Lord brought **us** out of Egypt with a mighty hand. The Lord gave signs and wonders, great and harmful, against Egypt, against Pharaoh, and against all his household, before **our eyes:** And he brought **us** out of there to bring **us** in, to give **us** the land that he promised **our** fathers.* (Deuteronomy 6:20–23)

The dictum of making it something that happened to us and not just them is explicit in the Haggadah:

> *In every generation, each person must regard **himself or herself as if he or she had come out of Egypt.***

Nor is the expectation to adopt the narrative left to choice without severe consequences. Those who do not accept the narrative as their own are rejected, and historically exile meant likely death, and certainly isolation. The Passover Haggadah warns that the son that denies the exodus's relevance to himself is banished.

> *What does the wicked son say? "What does this drudgery mean to you!" To you and not to him. Since he excludes himself from the community, he has denied a basic principle of Judaism. You should blunt his teeth by saying to him: "It is for the sake of this that the Lord did for me when I left Egypt. For me and not for him." If he was there he would not have been redeemed.*

And what of the people who do not inherit the narrative as an obligation? Psalm 137 is clear and vivid.

By the rivers of Babylon we sat and wept when we remembered Zion.
If I forget you, O Jerusalem, may my right hand forget its cunning.
May my tongue cling to the roof of my mouth if I do not remember you, if I
do not consider Jerusalem my highest joy.

And what of those who have threatened us in this way? What do we owe those who threaten our tribe? Psalm 137 continues…

Daughter of Babylon, doomed to destruction, happy is he who repays you for
what you have done to us—he who seizes your infants and dashes them against
the rocks.

Individual trauma experience alters the brain and our trauma response system. The personalized tribal narrative imprints the trauma experience for the group. Told from childhood and linked to emotional storytelling and often emotional current experience, such as a terrorist attack in modern Jerusalem, the trauma narrative defines the parameters of how a people will respond. So, (1) the threat from outside is named, (2) multiple traumas are interwoven, (3) the individual is seen as belonging to a tribe that is both current and historical, and (4) severe consequences for not adopting the narrative as one's own are enumerated. And most certainly, these four parts are told as truth, with the expectation that members of the tribe will live and abide by them. The tribe does not turn its other cheek, but is expected to aggressively respond. The tribe's narrative imprints this indelibly.

4.2   The Creation of Loss and Resilience Narratives for Great Tribal Loss

For Russia, World War II (WWII) shaped a generation. Some 9 million soldiers died fighting. Between 7.5 and 9.5 million civilians died due to military violence and acts of genocide, and perhaps another 8.6 million died due to disease and famine. Total losses due to the war are estimated at a staggering 27 million lives lost. This represents a loss of nearly 14 percent of the total population of the Soviet Union, and perhaps 13 percent of Russia proper. In comparison, the total losses for the U.S. totaled an estimated 419,000, and for the UK 450,000, which represented one-third of 1 percent of the population of the U.S., and less than 1 percent of the population for the UK. Stated another way, Russia lost over 43 times more lives than did the U.S. during WWII.

4.3   THE SIEGE OF LENINGRAD IS PERHAPS AN ULTIMATE TRIBAL NARRATIVE

For Nazi Germany to win WWII they had to defeat the Goliath Russia to their north. It was both tactically and ideologically necessary for Germany to defeat communism and what they saw as an inferior people. The siege of Leningrad began in September 1941 and lasted 872 days, or nearly two and a half years. It was one of the longest sieges in history and one of the most devastating and heroic for a nation to endure. Leningrad, formerly St. Petersburg, was the main base of the Soviet Baltic Fleet, housed great industry, and was the symbolic capital of the Russian Revolution. German Army Group North led by Field Marshall Wilhelm Ritter von Leeb aimed to capture the city and turn it over to their Finnish allies. The Nazis were confident that a siege would starve the city in a matter of weeks. Their military successes from all directions only increased their optimism, as they rolled over defending armies in a matter of weeks. Leningrad was, however, not to be compliant with the Nazi plan.

Famine raged in the city, and bombardments from the air and artillery were ceaseless. The Russians created a narrow corridor over nearby Lake Lagoda to bring in food, medical supplies, and reinforcements and to evacuate the wounded and vulnerable. They called the road alternatively the *Road of Life* and the *Road of Death* as it meant life but saw profound losses.

It is estimated that 1,500,000 Russians died between shelling, bullets, disease, and famine—famine being the largest cause of death. To feed the public, the minimal bread was fortified with saw dust to give it substance [9–11]. One mass grave at the railway town of Voldgda, filled with refugees who failed in their flight, contains the remains of about 20,000 people [12]. Imagine Chicago, Melbourne, Los Angeles, Buenos Aires, or Yokohama, cities of similar size, losing half the lives of their inhabitants.

The simple diary of 6-year-old Tanya Savicheva, who, although evacuated, later died of tuberculosis, tells the story in words that few poets could emulate. The child's diary, printed in her broad block letter handwriting on a handful of sheets, read:

Page 1: Zhenya died on Dec. 28th at 12:00 P.M. 1941
Page 2: Grandma died on Jan. 25th 3:00 P.M. 1942
Page 3: Leka died on March 17th at 5:00 A.M. 1942
Page 4: Uncle Vasya died on Apr. 13th at 2:00 after midnight 1942

Page 5: Uncle Lesha on May 10th at 4:00 P.M. 1942
Page 6: Mother on May 13th at 7:30 A.M. 1942
Page 7: Savichevs died.
Page 8: Everyone died.
Page 9: Only Tanya is left. [13]

It would be a gross misjudgment to think that such loss is responded to with a sense of defeat, as the opposite is true. The narrative for Russians of Leningrad is not in any way one of failure. Instead the tribal response to such loss is one of resilience against the "other," the enemy who eternally lurks from the outside to destroy Mother Russia. Men were already serving in Russian forces elsewhere and so women greatly outnumbered men in the city. Women worked tirelessly in factories, starving as they worked. They dug graves for the masses of dead, fought in fire brigades, built defenses, and joined the few older men left to defend the city with weapons. The men being older and often in too poor health to join the Soviet Army succumbed quickly to starvation and disease. The women came to realize that the fate of their families and the city rested on them, if not the fate of Russia itself. Women became mother, wife, daughter, worker and fighter, with the roles merging into a new sense of womanhood [14]. One of the most dangerous tasks was serving in rooftop fire brigades against incendiary bombs. The rooftop fire brigades were the most vulnerable to these bombings, as others sought shelter, they fought to extinguish fires on rooftops that would have slaughtered their families below, with other women manning anti-aircraft guns.

The narrative of Russia becomes twofold. *They are against us* and *we will unite to prevail against all odds.* Even 60 years after the siege of Leningrad, NATO is seen as an aggressive threat through Russia's eyes, rather than a defensive response to Russian aggression as perceived by the West. The U.S. and Europe are seen as the constant aggressor against Russia, and Putin is only defending Russia from this assault. In this dual narrative, the enemy is seen in every act, and can be easily cast to be so when Russia holds central control over media and information. Russia, in turn, is seen by Russians as powerful, resourceful, and requiring sacrifice. "Of course," they say, "our battles have always taken a heavy toll," but sacrifice is accepted with a sense of pride and purpose. Sacrifice evokes the sense of heroism of Leningrad. Russia has experienced major economic setbacks due to Western sanctions over her invasion of the Ukraine and the drop in oil prices from $100 to $40 dollars per barrel. But Putin does not need to use internal military power to support his regime. Portrayed as the hero fighting for Russia against Western aggression, his approval rating has soared, and sits at about 80 percent or above [15].

4.4   ISRAEL, AND NEVER AGAIN

National loss narratives are seldom perceived as recent, they emerge from a long history of repeated ongoing loss. Modern Israel does not begin its history with the founding of the State of Israel in 1948. As told in the Passover Haggadah over hundreds of years...

> *In each and every generation they rise up against us to destroy us. And the Holy One, blessed is He, rescues us from their hands.*

No people have been so persecuted in the history of the world. Egyptian enslavement, early nations attacking and persecuting Jewish practice, murder of Jews in Muslim capitals from the time of Mohammed, Christian persecution and pogroms led by Church leaders and becoming a central tenet and obligation for Christians against Jews occurred for centuries. Jews were expelled from Spain, England, France, Hungary, Austria, and Portugal. Each of these expulsions were catastrophic, and hundreds of thousands perished and were sent away without home or hope. Jewish women were raped for centuries without recourse. Jews in Yemen married their children at age 2, to protect them from rape by virtue of their being married women. Ulysses S. Grant even managed to expel Jews from Tennessee. And then of course the Holocaust occurred, with the murder of 6 million Jews.

The Nazi Holocaust of Jewish Europe was unleashed beginning in 1933 with the formation of concentration camps and the formation of ghettos for the Jewish populace. As the Nazis quickly conquered new territory in Western and Eastern Europe when the war began, specialized paramilitary units called Einsatzgruppen murdered Jews, mainly in mass executions. Finding the pace and resources required for such murder too slow and the number of soldiers involved too costly, the Nazis established the "final solution" involving transport to extermination camps and systematic murder by more efficient methods in gas chambers. In total it is estimated that about 6 million Jews, including 1.5 million children, were murdered. In the end virtually two-thirds of the 9 million Jews of pre-war Europe were murdered. This is a story that many of my generation grew up with as we count over 150 members of my family, most of them children, murdered, mainly at Treblinka in Poland.

From this burning platter Israel is served up and through historical happenstance and the will of a people a new state was created. Since before its statehood Israel has been attacked from all quarters and known little peace. Prior to Israel as a state, there were constant battles with Palestinians. At the moment of its birth, Israel was attacked by its Arab neighbors from all directions. Since 1948, Israel fought the War of Independence, ongoing infiltrations of fighters from Syria, Egypt, and Jordan during the 1950s, the 1956 Suez Crisis, the 1967 Six-Day War, The 1973 Yom Kippur War, Palestinian insurgency against Northern Israel from Lebanon throughout the 1970s, The 1982 Lebanon War, 20 more years of conflict on the Lebanon border, The First Intifada (Arab Uprising) (1987–1993), the 2006 Lebanon War, the 2008 Gaza War, Operation Pillar of Defense against Gaza in 2012, and Operation Protective Edge in 2014.

Whatever political arguments might be made to the contrary, and the Palestinians have their own loss narrative, for Israelis it is a war of existence. Until 1967 the Palestinians possessed all the land they claim to only now fight to get back. Israelis know that Hezbollah and Hamas, the militant Palestinians who stand against them, have as their central tenet the complete taking back of all the lands of Israel. For Israel it is often said, "We must win every war. They only need to win one."

The Israeli National Anthem speaks of the essence of the Jewish view, pairing a 3500-year history of loss and longing with the *raison d'être* of the State. Called "Hatikvah" ("The Hope"), it reads:

> *As long as in the heart, within,*
> *A Jewish soul still yearns,*
> *And onward, towards the ends of the East*
> *An eye still gazes toward Zion:*
> *Our hope is not yet lost.*
> *The hope two thousand years old.*
> *To be a free nation in our land*
> *The land of Zion and Jerusalem*

Israel is further isolated within a territorial siege and what they see as the European left's anti-Semitism. The only exit from Israel, a country the size of New Jersey, is through air travel or by sea, the latter being impractical for all but short vacation voyages. British and French intellectuals have been at the forefront of anti-Israeli actions, claiming Israeli war crimes and Apartheid, and silent on Palestinian attacks against Israel. This leaves the U.S. as the single stable ally, and oddly Germany in Europe as a stable anchor within Western Europe.

I lived at Israel's narrowest point, just north of Tel Aviv. From my rooftop near the Mediterranean Sea, the West Bank was only about 9 miles. A modern tank assault traverses 9 miles in less than half an hour. I recall pointing out the nearby lights of the West Bank town of Qalqilya to a rather anti-Israeli European colleague from my patio rooftop. His response was illuminating: "Stevan, are we safe now? Maybe we should go downstairs," as if "downstairs" would bring safety from a rocket attack or sniper who had infiltrated. He could not sustain his anxiety for a few minutes in a place where most of Israel's population live their lives. Israelis in the south, near Gaza, have faced over 10,000 rocket attacks from Gaza and have some 60 seconds to find shelter from the moment of launch. The Israeli Defense Forces website, which, however accurate, depicts Israel's view on the threat it faces, is displayed in Fig. 4.1, showing relentless threat and attack [16].

As rational thinkers, distant from attack, with our children and families safe, we easily can talk about the need for Israeli restraint in responding to the Palestinians. But as tribal members, no nation can or has or will allow this to occur. No government would survive the next election. We have

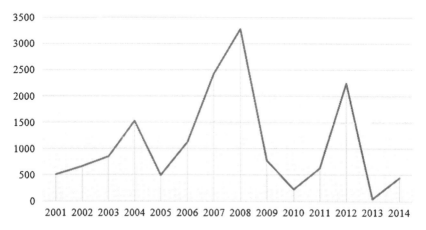

Fig. 4.1   Rocket attacks on Israel from the Gaza Strip between 2001 and 2014. (Adapted from Israel Defense Forces [16])

seen fear politics in the U.S. within a fraction of the threat and loss of life. When attacked by terrorists in Paris in November 2015, French President François Hollande vowed a "merciless" response to the Paris attacks:

> *"The exceptional and unprecedented threat posed by this group to the entire international community requires a strong, united and unambiguous response from the security council,"* French ambassador, François Delattre, <u>said</u> on Thursday: *"This is the goal of our draft resolution, which calls on all member states to take all necessary measures to fight Daesh" [also referred to as ISIS].* [17]

No matter that already before the Paris attacks that French, U.S., and Russian bombers launched air strikes across civilian areas of ISIS held Syria, because ISIS fighters were embedded within civilian populations [18]. Thousands of civilians have been killed, the very acts that France, Russia and Britain have charged against Israel and with a tiny portion of justification compared to what Israel faces.

Again, it is not my purpose here to justify Israel, but only to point to how we react when it is our tribe that is threatened. Reason and proportionality are sacrificed without hesitation. The built-in protection of the tribe and retribution against those that threaten the tribe lead to primitive responding. We can drop fire bombs on Dresden in Germany and atomic bombs on Hiroshima in Japan and kill hundreds of thousands to protect our tribe, without disturbing our appetite for lunch. Literally.

Like Russia, Israelis have transformed their loss narrative into a resiliency narrative. Israel will stand up to any and all attacks to defend its population. It adopts a common Russian and indeed Middle Eastern philosophy of fighting fire with ten times the fire, believing that brute force is the only policy that the enemy will listen to. The Israeli Defense Forces are considered among the best military in the world. As is well known, women are conscripted into the military along with men. The drill sergeants who trained me were almost all women. They radiated strength and expected me to respond to their strength in training.

At the same time, Israel proves its resilience, no less to itself, as it invests in industry, technology, and science and prides itself as a world leader in each of these areas. This is all part of the narrative that "we will neither be deterred nor diminished." Outsiders may claim Israel as an Apartheid State, but Arab students fill Israeli universities. Currently, 14.4 percent of bachelor's degrees, 10.5 percent of master's degrees, and 5.9 percent of PhDs were awarded to Arabs within Israel. Among Arab students 67.2

percent were women. More than half (55.4%) of Arab PhD candidates were women [19]. Palestinian students not only fill Israeli universities, one of the most liberal, educated Arab cultures in the world is blossoming in Israel [*The New York Times*, 1-3-16; opened 5-18-16]. A recent poll showed that while Arabs living in Israel favor some sort of combined state solution, 85 percent were satisfied with life in Israel and 60 percent of the Arabs polled were satisfied with their economic situation, both figures only slightly below those for Jewish Israelis, and much better than felt by Arabs in Europe [20].

My argument is that Israel invests in science, education, technology, medicine, and its Arab population because it sees such acts as illustrating their resilience and exceptional tribal character, where others would turn to Apartheid or ethnic cleansing. The narrative of loss means that threat is answered with iron force, but that the country also sees itself as generous, advanced, modern, exceptional, and progressive. Indeed, Israel's first prime minister, David Ben Gurion, emphasized that Israel should be a moral and social beacon to the world [21], fulfilling words of the Prophet Isaiah, "*Yea, He saith, 'It is too light a thing for you to be My servant, to establish the tribes of Jacob, and to restore the scions of Israel, and I shall submit you as a **light unto the nations**, to be My salvation until the end of the earth'*" (Isaiah 49:6). There is hardly a more resilient and lofty aspirational template for a nation that this.

4.5   PALESTINIANS: A TRAGEDY WITH POLITICAL PERPETUATION

It is only fitting that we next examine Palestinian's sense of loss and the tragedy and resilience they have face and created. Beyond their clear loss and justified struggle, I use them as an example of how the tribal response experienced through national loss of small states and peoples can be manipulated by larger forces and other nation's agendas. As a tribe, Palestinians have been among the most manipulated people in modern history, and their tribal struggle and sense of loss has been intentionally perpetuated by the former Soviet Union and other Arab and Muslim states for strategic purposes.

Palestinians call the 1948 exodus of Arabs from the territory claimed as the original borders of Israel as the "Nakba," the "catastrophe." A multitude of disputed factors went into the exodus of Palestinians into neighboring regions in 1948, and the occupation of territories that Israel took control of following the 1967 Six-Day War, further increased that plight. One attributed cause of the flight in 1948 was the right-wing Zionists' massacre of Palestinians at Deir Yassin, causing a panic. Others fled Israel at the behest of invading Arab countries' broadcast of evacuation orders to clear the way for invading Arab armies, expecting the civilians to quickly return on their victorious army's heels. Many of the wealthier classes evacuated for greener pastures. Still others refused to live under Jewish control.

The massacre at Deir Yassim's exact details are disputed with Israelis and Palestinians telling different stories, but the narrative that matters for Palestinians is their own, and the Jewish narrative simply has no relevance for them. On April 9, 1948, Israeli independence was being fought desperately. The main fighting group for Jews was the Haganah. Two extremist splinter Zionist groups were the Irgun and Lehi, and it was they who entered the village of Deir Yassim, killing 107 inhabitants, including women and children [22]. News of the terror sparked fear among Palestinians, and many fled upon hearing the news. Indeed, the Irgun bragged of 240 killed, a story which was picked up by international news services [23]. British Assistant Inspector-General Richard Catling of the British Palestinian Police Force, with Britain still in charge of Palestine, investigated the massacre. He wrote of rapes of Arab women, which have been disputed as Catling was an enemy of Jewish aspirations. Again, pro-Israelis may reject his account of the atrocities, but the Palestinian narrative will take his recorded testimony as that of an external objective force that serves to validate "their truth." You cannot pick another nation's narrative sources.

I interviewed many of the women folk in order to glean some information on any atrocities committed in Deir Yassin but the majority of those women are very shy and reluctant to relate their experiences especially in matters concerning sexual assault and they need great coaxing before they will divulge any information. The recording of statements is hampered also by the hysterical state of the women who often break down many times whilst the statement is being recorded. There is, however, no doubt that many sexual atrocities were committed by the attacking Jews. Many young schoolgirls were raped and later slaughtered. Old women were also molested. One story is current concerning a case in which a young girl was literally torn in two. Many infants were also butchered and killed. [24]

For Palestinians, the exodus of Arabs was forced by European Jews, whose claim to the land they deny as antiquated and obsolete. They date Zionism's beginning as a radical movement of the late nineteenth century. Their narrative denies Israel's right to defend itself, as they either grant those rights as a political reality they are forced to accept, or see them as rights taken by violence and therefore illegitimate. While accepting that terrible things may have happened to Jews in Europe, they often claim that Jews lived peacefully with full rights in Arab countries, which is a point that Jewish Israelis of course refute. So, Israel is seen as occupying a land with force, confiscating property not theirs and killing Arabs at will. For them, the occupation of the holy sites in Jerusalem are a further insult, as Jerusalem is a site of the Prophet Mohammed, and from where he ascended to heaven.

Israeli occupation of the West Bank and Gaza results in a constant shaming for Palestinians. This especially occurs at border crossings, as Palestinians enter Israel for work, family visits and medical attention. The border crossings are tense on the Israeli side for fear of suicide bombers or other terrorists crossing into Israel. The border patrols themselves are at great risk and are often attacked. Finding a suicide bomber might result in suicide detonation and killing of the soldiers and all those around. The fear factor for border patrols and their general antipathy for Palestinians breeds an aggressive stance and interaction with those crossing. Sadly, this is one of the main points of interactions between Israelis and Palestinians. For Palestinians it is a reminder of their being a conquered people, a people who have lost their homeland, and a people who must respond with meekness if they are to pass into Israel for work and family.

Imagine the sense of outrage and anger when Israel strikes with tanks and bombers into Gaza. There is no doubt that Hamas manipulates Israel through rocket attacks to get this Israeli response. Indeed, this has occurred precisely when Hamas sees its coffers lacking funds [25]. Hamas also clearly places its military and its arsenal, rooted within the community and even using hospitals and schools, as testified by international observer groups that are overwhelmingly sympathetic to their cause [26]. But what the Gazans see is the destruction that is wrought. Hamas is acutely aware of how to manipulate tribal fervor.

Following months of rocket attacks from Hamas-held Gaza, Israel entered Gaza in July 2014. From the Israeli point of view, this was a protective response, and again likely manipulated by Hamas to get Israel to react in a way that creates the kind of international film coverage that no

Web-based propaganda can ever hope to achieve. Earlier in June, three Israeli teenagers were kidnapped and murdered by Hamas members. The Israeli response was devastating. According to the UN office for the Coordination of Humanitarian Affairs, over 270,000 Palestinians were displaced, 872 homes were destroyed or severely damaged, 373,000 children required psychosocial support (which can be read as making them fervent devotees to the tribe against Israel), and nearly half a million Palestinians required emergency food assistance [27]. The Palestinian Authority claimed that 73 mosques were destroyed completely.

The cost in human life was horrific. The invasion resulted in the death of between 296 and 315 children and 2200 Palestinians overall [28]. Another 10,000 Palestinians, including over 3000 children, were wounded. Israeli official accounts were somewhat lower, but mainly differed as to the percentage of militant fighters versus innocent civilians who were killed.

Rational thinking has little to do with how those who experience such an attack respond. People's cognitions in such instances are generated by emotional and biological parts of the brain-mind connection, leading to hatred and resolve. The invasion of Gaza may have been necessary from Israel's viewpoint, but it must also be understood as creating incendiary fuel for the Palestinian struggle and their tribal identity to stand up against Israeli brutality. It does not matter that Hamas was cited for using human shields, hiding within schools and hospitals, and launching attacks from amidst populated urban areas. Indeed, they do this to create the tribal loss narrative and to etch it indelibly in the Palestinian psyche [29].

Each day of Israeli intransigence and violent action, as seen by Palestinians, is a further wounding that must be resisted until the Zionist state is defeated. Every Jewish settlement in the West Bank, occupied by Israel since the 1967 Six-Day War is a testimony to Israeli disregard for international rights. Daily border crossing of Palestinians into and out of Israel occur under high security and often with disrespect for those crossing, and each incident is a burning insult. I am sure pro-Israeli readers are countering these accounts with what they see as the "facts," but the point is that Palestinians and anti-Israelis were countering the earlier accounts of Jewish history, especially Israeli history, with equal resolve as to the ownership of facts. Whichever side you as reader took, is the very heart of the prisms and biases that we hold and for which we seldom have self-insight.

4.6   WHEN SHAME AND LOSS MIX: THE CREATION
OF SALAFI JIHAD

Jihadists hold the devout belief that they are staging a holy war against the West who are attacking them. Importantly, this includes what they see as the Westernization of the Middle East, or at least a brand of Islam that is more liberal and open. Al-Qaeda and now ISIS see a Western, Christian world that is attacking and killing Muslims across the Middle East and Africa. They also see a Middle East that is sliding toward Western culture and openness. They point to attacks on Muslims in Chechnya, Somalia, Palestine, Syria, Iraq, and by non-Muslim Indians in Kashmir. But given that much of this violence against Islam occurred after the September 11 attacks and is perpetrated by Muslims on Muslims, other reasoning has to be given for their *Casus belli*.

As much as their motivation to protect, their tribal angst is multiplied by the powerful source of shame and the incursion of Western liberalism into their own societies. The incursion of Western ideas itself is deeply shaming as it reflects cultural dominance. One of the greatest insults that bin Laden felt was that Christian troops from U.S. and allied forces were invited to Saudi Arabia, home of the most holy city of Mecca. A further shame within this shame was that female coalition forces were brought to protect the holy city Mecca from the invasion forces of Iraq as part of the Kuwait war, or first Persian Gulf War. The keen insights of Jessica Stern, research professor at Boston University's School of Global Studies and co-author of *ISIS: The State of Terror*, wrote,

> A principal source of the threat to the West is that the Islamic State and its Salafi jihadi ideology have metastasized into the banlieues of Europe. It appeals, in Islamic State's words, to the people *"drowning in oceans of disgrace, being nursed on the milk of humiliation, and being ruled by the vilest of all people."* To those oppressed, the Islamic State promises the chance *"to remove the garments of dishonor, and shake off the dust of humiliation and disgrace, for the era of lamenting and moaning has gone and the dawn of honor has emerged anew. The sun of jihad has risen."* [30]

We see here how the Jihadists' sense of shame is multiplied by the second-class status of Muslims in Europe. In France, Muslims are poor, discriminated against in work and education, and harassed by police. In Germany, Muslim guest workers may not obtain German citizenship, generations after they are invited into the country to work. Their education and employment levels make them a constant underclass, with limited rights [31].

Further light is thrown on their sense of shame and humiliation by a recent U.N. report on the failure of the Arab world to produce meaningful contributions to humanity. Jihadists may point to the great age of enlightenment, the Islamic Golden Age, but this age of enlightened caliphates ended some 800 years ago. The Arab Human Development Report is an independent set of reports by the U.N. Development Programme. It was researched and written entirely by leading Arab scholars—it is an all-Arab report. The reports decries the lack of human rights within Arab countries, pointing to its dampening effect the acquisition, diffusion, and production of knowledge in Arab societies. The report cites widespread illiteracy in the Arab world and even greater limits to education of girls and women [32].

The report is damning of the pervasive human insecurity in the Arab world caused by Arabs and their governments. They find the Arab investment in education to be intolerably low. With all the wealth of Saudi Arabia and the Gulf States, there are no Nobel Prizes in medicine, none in chemistry, and none in economics. There are two Nobel Prize winners in literature from the Middle East, one from Egypt and one from Turkey. Orhan Pamuk of Turkey, one of the two winners of the Nobel Prize in Literature, lives in fear for his life in Turkey from Muslim extremists who have threatened him for heresy. In 2005 his books were burned in a nationalist rally.

Of course, the Nobel committee's Westernized judgment of literature may be biased. But in terms of sheer numbers of publications the Arab world is singularly behind virtually all others— West, East, and Middle East. A U.N. survey found that Americans read an average of 11 books a year, Britons read 8 books, while the average Arab reads 4 pages [33]. The survey further found that one book title is published per 12,000 population in the Arab world, one book per 500 people is published in Britain, and one book is published in Israel for every 125–150 people, second in the world to the People's Republic of China. This means that 80 times more books are published in Israel per capita than in the Arab world. Nor is this a matter of being Muslim, as Iran and Turkey are world centers of literature. We can see how this report has reverberated in the Arab world.

Fahed al-Fanek, writing in the Jordanian newspaper *Al-Ra'I*, *wrote the following:*

[Arab] oil wealth is matched by social backwardness, and the only other region of the world with an income level lower than ours is sub-Saharan Africa. Productivity is decreasing, scientific research is virtually nonexistent, the region is suffering a brain drain, and illiteracy afflicts half of Arab women. The report was only diplomatic concerning implicit criticisms of extremist Islamist movements as a cause of the culture of backwardness and absence of fertile ground for democracy. Interestingly, the report found that the total number of books translated into Arabic yearly is no more than 330, or one-fifth of those translated in a small country like Greece.

Indeed, the total number of books translated into Arabic during the 1,000 years since the age of Caliph Al-Ma'moun [a ninth-century Arab ruler who was a patron of cultural interaction between Arab, Persian, and Greek scholars— WPR] to this day is less than those translated in Spain in one year. [34]

For Jihadists, the tribal solution is simple. They must reject the U.N. report on Arab Human Development or admit to shame and responsibility. As the report rails against al-Qaeda's and ISEL's version of attacks on human rights, and particularly their oppression of women, they must reject the report and its liberal basis. This does not mean that they do not feel the shame of their lack of accomplishment and the pride they would feel in the long lost Arab Renaissance of the Arab Golden Age, but their only recourse is through the violent recapturing of honor.

4.7   SHAME, AGGRESSION AND TRIBAL NARCISSISM

Psychological research sheds other important light on the relationship between loss, shame and aggression. Specifically, men who have experienced traumatic circumstances, which often has occurred in the Arab world, are likely to react to shame with aggression. On the level of the individual, the interaction of loss, shame, and trauma often translate to family violence [35]. On a nationalist level, such aggression is pointed outward toward the "other" and enemy, but in either case shame is like gasoline on a fire, it is incendiary.

Tribal narcissism appears to be a cardinal attribute of both fascist and communist tribal ideology. The combination of raging anger and aggression is often seen in narcissists, who exhibit explosive rage and hostility when they are shamed. The narcissist is in love with himself and can only see his own self view. In al-Qaeda and ISEL's response we see all of the vanity, self-absorption and sense of entitlement that we see in clinical narcissism on an individual level. The narcissist must reject others' interpretation of reality as these are highly threatening and undermine the narcissist's worldview in which they are central.

When attacked from the outside, the answer for the narcissist individual is aggressive rage, and for the shamed Jihadist, their interpretation is likewise the only interpretation. No authority from Islam or outside of Islam can override theirs. First formulated by Freud, but well researched in modern psychology, "narcissistic rage was first extensively described by the psychoanalyst Heinz Kohut (1972)," [36] and his insights clearly translate to tribal narcissism, helping us to understand its deeply emotional, irrational basis.

> [T]he need for revenge, for righting a wrong, for undoing a hurt by whatever means, and a deeply anchored, unrelenting compulsion in the pursuit of all these aims ... are the characteristic features of narcissistic rage in all its forms. [37]

4.8   THE HINGE OF RESILIENT RESPONDING

Nations and peoples who have experienced great loss are especially prone to a tribal response to protect, defend and aggress. The successful emergence from such profound loss—the hinge of transformation to tribal resilience—occurs when their history becomes incorporated into a loss narrative that is accompanied by a phoenix-like rebirth. In this way their narrative is transformed and becomes a story of empowerment mixed with sacrifice. These narratives are deeply felt, and no doubt often justified. However, as we have seen in this chapter, they are also given to manipulation through the political process. Many leaders, of small groups, popular uprisings and insurgencies, and nations have exploited our evolutionary push for attachment and devotion to the tribe for their own power and aggrandizement. Like a tidal wave, tribal fervor becomes a powerful force that once set in motion is difficult to reverse and its biology overcomes rationality, replacing the lens of rational judgment with a set dogma that must be fully narcissistically supported.

But this chapter has also shown that shame and humiliation are emotional co-travelers that accompany loss. Those nations and people who have experienced great loss often respond with a profound and deeply embedded sense of shame, humiliation and rage. In the case of Russia, Israel, and Iran this shame is mitigated by a great sense of pride and accomplishment which is based on their contributions as societies to their own citizens and to the world. For the Arab world, there is little basis for this sense of pride, other than the pride of extremist dedication itself. They must not only violently reject the West, they must reject the Arab Middle East and Gulf States. The Golden Age of Islam that they yearn for was one of enlightenment, but it is neither approached in the Gulf States' materialism and conservative practice of Islam, nor in the violent rage of ISIS, al-Qaeda, or Boko Haram.

As we will examine next, shame, aggression, and tribal narcissism are group responses that long for, and attach easily to authoritarian, narcissistic leadership. The flock longs for its shepherd in the form of someone who will acknowledge their pain, and turn with them against their enemies. That such leadership fits with a more primitive kind of society, translates to even modern and advanced cultures, such as where cultured pre-WWII Germany quickly devolved into an ugly pattern of hatred and persecution. It is such a powerful force that we would be smart to beware of it in our own times and our own nations, as its seeds exist and gain strength as the real and perceived threats to us and our ways of life become more salient.

References

1. International Churchill Society. (n.d.). *We Shall Fight on the Beaches.* International Churchill Society. Retrieved February 8, 2018, from https://www.winstonchurchill.org/resources/speeches/1940-the-finest-hour/we-shall-fight-on-the-beaches/

2. Newport, F. (2003, March 24). Seventy-two percent of Americans support war against Iraq. *Gallup News.* Retrieved September 10, 2017, from http://www.gallup.com/poll/8038/seventytwo-percent-americans-support-war-against-iraq.aspx

3. Key, F. S. (1779–1843). *The Star Spangled Banner.* Garden City: Doubleday, Doran, & Co. 1942.

4. Hobfoll, S. (1998). *Stress, culture, and community.* New York: Springer.

5. Sherin, J. E., & Nemeroff, C. B. (2011). Post-traumatic stress disorder: The neurobiological impact of psychological trauma. *Dialogues in Clinical Neuroscience, 13*(3), 263–278.

6. Mitchell, M. D., Chivers, D. P., Cormick, M. I., & Ferrari, M. C. (2015). Learning to distinguish between predators and non-predators: Understanding the critical role of diet cues and predator odours in generalisation. *Scientific Reports, 5,* 13918.

7. Dunbar, R. I., & Shultz, S. (2007). Evolution in the social brain. *Science*, *317*(5843), 1344–1347.
8. Carroll, N. (2001). On the narrative connection. In W. V. Peer & S. B. Chatman (Eds.), *New perspectives on narrative perspective* (pp. 21–42). New York: State University of New York Press.
9. Glantz, D. M. (2001). *The siege of Leningrad, 1941–1944: 900 days of terror.* Minneapolis: Zenith Press.
10. Goure, L. (1962). *The *siege of Leningrad.* Redwood City: Stanford University Press.
11. Kirschenbaum, L. A. (2006). *The legacy of the siege of Leningrad, 1941–1995: Myths, memories, and monuments.* Cambridge: Cambridge University Press.
12. Reid, A. (2011, September 15). Myth and tragedy at the siege of Leningrad – Gallery. *The Guardian.* Retrieved May 18, 2017, from https://www.theguardian.com/books/gallery/2011/sep/15/siege-leningrad-history-anna-reid
13. Mikhaylenko, N. (2013, January 20). Leningrad siege: The captive's diary. *Russia Beyond The Headlines.* Retrieved March 25, 2017, from https://rbth.com/multimedia/2013/01/30/the_girl_who_survived_the_siege_of_leningrad_22349?crid=325369
14. Simmons, C., & Perlina, N. (2005). *Writing the siege of Leningrad: Women's diaries, memoirs, and documentary prose.* Pittsburgh: University of Pittsburgh Press.
15. Birnbaum, M. (2016, March 6). How to understand Putin's jaw-droppingly high approval ratings. *The Washington Post: 13.* Retrieved January 5, 2018, from https://www.washingtonpost.com/world/europe/how-to-understand-putins-jaw-droppingly-high-approval-ratings/2016/03/05/17f5d8f2-d5ba-11e5-a65b-587e721fb231_story.html?utm_term=.bf6d796b2d18
16. Israel Defense Forces. (n.d.). Rocket attacks on Israel from Gaza. *Israel Defense Forces.* Retrieved April 8, 2017, from https://www.idfblog.com/facts-figures/rocket-attacks-toward-israel/
17. Prupis, N. (2015, November 21). UN council approves French resolution for 'all necessary measures' against ISIS. *Common Dreams.* Retrieved May 6, 2017, from http://www.commondreams.org/news/2015/11/21/un-council-approves-french-resolution-all-necessary-measures-against-isis
18. Cooper, H., Gordon, M. R., & MacFarquhar, N. (2015, September 30). Russians strike targets in Syria, but not ISIS areas. *The New York Times.* Retrieved September 10, 2017, from https://www.nytimes.com/2015/10/01/world/europe/russia-airstrikes-syria.html
19. Skop, Y. (2015, October 15). More Arab students in Israel attending university in new academic year. *Haaretz.* Retrieved May 18, 2017, from http://www.haaretz.com/israel-news/.premium-1.680454
20. Cherry, R., & Lerman, R. (2014, October 1). Slow but certain integration in Israel. *US News and World Report.* Retrieved May 26, 2017, from https://www.usnews.com/opinion/articles/2014/10/01/arabs-are-slowly-but-surely-integrating-into-israel

21. Jewish Telegraphic Agency. (1958, June 13). *U.S. Jewry will not survive without link with Israel, Ben Guion says*. Jewish Telegraphic Agency. Retrieved June 11, 2017, from http://www.jta.org/1958/06/13/archive/u-s-jewry-will-not-survive-without-link-with-israel-ben-guion-says
22. Kananah, S., & Zaytuni, N. (1988). *Deir Yassin: Destroyed Palestinian villages*. Birzeit: Birzeit University Press.
23. Morris, B. (2004). *The birth of the Palestinian refugee problem revisited*. Cambridge: Cambridge University Press.
24. Collins, L., & Lapierre, D. (2007). *O Jerusalem!* New York: Simon & Schuster.
25. United Nations Office for the Coordination of Humanitarian Affairs. (2014, August 3). *Occupied Palestinian territory: Gaza emergency situation report (as of 3 August 2014, 1500 hrs)*. United Nations Office for the Coordination of Humanitarian Affairs. Retrieved May 5, 2017, from https://www.ochaopt.org/sites/default/files/ocha_opt_sitrep_04_08_2014.pdf
26. Chandler, A. (2014, September 12). Hamas quietly admits it fired rockets from civilian areas. *The Atlantic*. Retrieved September 10, 2017, from https://www.theatlantic.com/international/archive/2014/09/hamas-quietly-admits-it-fired-rockets-from-civilian-areas/380149/
27. United Nations Office for the Coordination of Humanitarian Affairs. (2014, August 2017). *Humanitarian bulletin: Monthly report June-August 2014*. United Nations Office for the Coordination of Humanitarian Affairs. Retrieved September 10, from http://fschuppisser.ch/gaza/ochaall.pdf
28. Israel Ministry of Foreign Affairs. (2015). *Palestinian fatality figures in the 2014 Gaza conflict*. Israel Ministry of Foreign Affairs. Retrieved June 14, 2017, from http://mfa.gov.il/ProtectiveEdge/Documents/PalestinianFatalities.pdf
29. Christian, P. J. (2011). *A combat advisor's guide to tribal engagement: History, law and war as operational elements*. Irvine: Universal Publishers.
30. Stern, J. (2015, November 18). Why the Islamic State hates France. *PBS NewsHour*. Retrieved June 10, 2017, from http://www.pbs.org/newshour/updates/why-islamic-state-jihadis-are-enraged-by-france/
31. Wilpert, C. (2013). Identity issues in the history of the postwar migration from Turkey to Germany. *German Politics and Society, 31*(107), 108–131. https://doi.org/10.3167/gps.2013.310209.
32. United Nations Development Programme. (n.d.). *Arab Human Development Reports (AHDR)*. United Nations Development Programme. Retrieved June 10, 2016, from http://www.arab-hdr.org/
33. Fleisher, M. (2008, August 12). UN survey: Arabs read approximately 4 pages per year. *Arutz Sheva*. Retrieved September 10, 2017, from http://www.israelnationalnews.com/News/News.aspx/128752
34. al-Fanek, F. (2002). Rhima Khalaf drops a bomb. *World Press Review, 49*(9). Retrieved June 10, 2017, from http://worldpress.org/Mideast/663.cfm

35. Schoenleber, M., Sippel, L. M., Jakupcak, M., & Tull, M. T. (2015). Role of trait shame in the association between posttraumatic stress and aggression among men with a history of interpersonal trauma. *Psychological Trauma: Theory, Research, Practice, and Policy, 7*(1), 43–49. https://doi.org/10.1037/a0037434.

36. Krizan, Z., & Johar, O. (2015). Narcissistic rage revisited. *Journal of Personality and Social Psychology, 108*(5), 784–801. https://doi.org/10.1037/pspp0000013.

37. Kohut, H. (1972). Thoughts on narcissism and narcissistic rage. *The Psychoanalytic Study of the Child, 27*, 360–400.

CHAPTER 5

The Primal Emergence of the Authoritarian Father-Leader

Nationalist movements, extremist cults, and extremist political groups of the left and right all represent manifestations of tribal emergence of the primitive self that emerges on the level of the collective. In the overwhelming number of cases accompanying these collective movements an authoritarian father-leader emerges. This tribal authoritarian leader combines a kind of father-like authoritarian form of compassion and ruthlessness, spreading the message of great danger from external and internal threats, for which only he has the solution. The authoritarian father-leader emerges in cults such as the Fundamentalist Church of Jesus Christ of Latter-Day Saints and the violent cult of Charles Manson's Manson Family. It is also witnessed in political extremism of the right and left, with an endless list of leaders from Robespierre, to Mussolini, to Hitler, to Juan Perón, to modern-day Kim Jong-un and Vladimir Putin. Although we had imagined the U.S. would be immune to this after the experience of McCarthyism, first candidate and now President Donald Trump borrows dangerously from the authoritarian father-leader playbook.

Extremist groups of the left and right share a common psychological trait known as dogmatism. Dogmatism was first researched by the famous psychologist Milton Rokeach [1]. Returning home from the devastation and death brought about by World War II (WWII), which followed the emergence of Nazism, Japanese imperialism, and Italian fascism, psychologists and psychiatrists felt compelled to make sense of how hundreds of millions of people could support such extremist worldviews. How did

© The Author(s) 2018
S. E. Hobfoll, *Tribalism*,
https://doi.org/10.1007/978-3-319-78405-2_5

101

ordinary citizens operate death camps, enforce slave labor, and machine gun hundreds of thousands of civilians next to mass graves and commit the endless list of atrocities that WWII engendered? Rokeach had the keen insight that authoritarianism was not only a trait of the far right, but also a trait of the far left. To understand the emergence of the authoritarian father-leader and his attractiveness, we must first understand his powerful appeal. Why would certain groups or types of groups be so drawn to these ruthless leaders who are often caricatures and viewed as highly offensive, and even ridiculous by others who have not drunk the Kool-Aid of the political extremes, the cult, or the extremist movement?

Dogmatism was viewed by Rokeach as a personality trait that includes rigidity in thinking, closed mindedness, and strong inflexible opinions. People high on dogmatism strongly agree with statements such as "The things I believe in are so completely true, I could never doubt them," "I am so sure I am right about the important things in life, there is no evidence that could convince me otherwise," "I am absolutely certain that my ideas about the fundamental issues in life are correct," and "People who disagree with me are just plain wrong and often evil as well" [2]. Such endorsements reflect their rigid, inflexible thinking, and need for being entirely correct and convinced of their position. They are more likely to hold extreme views of the right or left, more likely to endorse fundamentalist religious doctrine, or "religiously" believe in their philosophy. They go beyond patriotism, and tend to endorse nationalist philosophies that are buoyed by prejudice and a claim to the only acceptable path for love of country.

People high on dogmatism hold members of their own group in high favor, and are xenophobic and disdainful of outsiders. Globalism and internationalism is anathema to them, unless one means their takeover of the world! The dogmatic personality style is also associated with seeing the world as dangerous and those high on the dogmatism personality trait are more likely than those low in dogmatism to believe we must arm ourselves or isolate ourselves from others. At the extremes, those highest on dogmatism of the left and right see themselves as superhuman and near to God and their enemies as subhuman and demonic, as we see in philosophies of racial superiority, racial purity, and beliefs in being God's direct messengers.

Some attributes that are co-travelers of dogmatism are far from intuitive, but profoundly shape how they see the world and the political and social ends they endeavor to impose as movements. Those high on dogmatism are often nostalgic for the past, meaning the traditional world they fantasize was the past, and so would want to "make America great again," which for them means going back to the "good old days." For them, the good old days included racial segregation, women "knowing their place" and being homemakers, Hispanics being back in Mexico behind a wall "where they belong," and White men who are unskilled having high-paying jobs, or at least jobs that paid higher than those held by Blacks or Hispanics. Today their message involves sending Mexicans back across the border or keeping Muslims out. In 1926 it was about keeping Jews and Italians out, and certainly keeping Blacks "in their place." For the dogmatism of the right in particular, the "good old days" is a euphemism for turning the process of increased social justice and equality backwards [2].

Dr. Carl Bingham, a psychologist and professor of no less a place than Princeton, was in the forefront of the anti-immigrant movement following World War I. This wave of anti-immigrant sentiment coincided with the push to send African Americans back to the South and out of Northern cities where they had migrated during World War I in response to the nation's labor needs. In a twisted use of psychological science to promote racism and ethnocentrism, he provided falsely interpreted psychological studies to support the dogmatism of the right and the populist sentiment that was looking to close the borders to preserve American superiority and to prevent the immigration of the "other" as tainted, inferior, and to be feared. Quoting Brigham,

>...mental tests had proven beyond any scientific doubt that, like the American Negroes, the Italians and the Jews were genetically ineducable. It would be a waste of good money even to attempt to try to give these born morons and imbeciles a good Anglo-Saxon education, let alone admit them into our fine medical, law, and engineering graduate schools. [3]

Although Bingham was later to entirely recant his findings as unfounded, the damage was done and American tribalism and fear of the "other"— Jews and Italians being at the forefront of what were seen as depraved and inferior peoples—essentially closed her borders to immigration in 1926, lasting until after WWII.

Insight about the closed-minded nature of dogmatism is illuminated when we consider the surprising list of things that Nazis were against. We are all aware of their morbid hatred of Jews and gypsies. Less well known is their vehement rejection of modern architecture and art, which they saw as degenerate. They idolized women being in the home and in the kitchen. They abhorred modern styles of dress. Abstract art and music were proscribed and punished. Under the Weimar government of the 1920s that proceeded Nazism, modern art and jazz flourished. Germany was a leading center of the avant-garde. It was the birthplace of abstract musical expression, Expressionism in painting, and Expressionistic filmmaking. The Nazis saw such art and music as miscreant and contributing to a breakdown of proper German society. By 1937 such art and music were seized or purged as subversive. The works of artists, including Heckel, Max Beckmann, Henri Matisse, Pablo Picasso, and Vincent van Gogh, were presented to the public in what they called a "Degenerate Art Exhibition" that was meant to evoke revulsion in the German viewer [4].

The soaring modern architecture of Mies van der Rohe was rejected, and van der Rohe eventually fled to the U.S. Instead the Nazi's esteemed the overdone Hansel and Gretel architecture of traditional Germany [5]. Dogmatism is a closing of much more than the political mind. The closed mindedness of dogmatism results in individuals being attracted to black and white solutions, stark insider-outsider divisions, fear of the new and unknown, and a search for affiliation that will support these views. The gray, the abstract, the new, and unknown are all deeply anxiety provoking for those high in dogmatism.

5.1   FREEDOM AND THE FEAR OF ITS UNKNOWN

People high on dogmatism are much more susceptible to the politics of the tribe in their affiliation. The system and worldview they create is a self-fulfilling prophesy and as they aggregate in groups they gain further devotion to their worldview, replete with its fear of others, its envisioning of a dangerous world and the need for simple, straightforward solutions. They cling on one hand to complex conspiratorial theories, but must have a clear enemy. They can tolerate little questioning of their viewpoint and those who do question are immediately cast as outsiders, a fifth column. Human response to threat, as I have outlined, exists largely in older evolutionary brain structures and not in our rational forebrain, which came late in human development and those high in dogmatism are largely driven by anxiety and fear.

People high on dogmatism want "THE" answers as individuals and, as they form groups, believe they have THE answers. Having a clear, distinct, and inflexible set of answers provides comfort from the existential anxiety of freedom that Sartre discussed in great depth [6]. This is an odd paradox as right-wing groups often decry the imposition of government and the consequent lack of freedom as individuals. They call themselves freedom fighters, Tea Partyists, individualists, but then replace freedom with an endless list of dos and don'ts of acceptable behavior.

The brilliant psychoanalyst and philosopher Erich Fromm saw authoritarianism as an expression of the fear of freedom. The new system they create, with its rules and covenants, is what Fromm called "negative freedom" or freedom *from* doing things, but it does not include freedom *to do* things. This is classically displayed in fundamentalist movements that promote religious freedom and then dictate their codes and mores on the rest of society denying their religious freedom. So, as the Protestant movement of Martin Luther departed from all the rules of Catholicism, they imposed new rules equally restrictive if not more so [7]. As discussed in an earlier chapter, those Americans who endorse the Tea Party, a conservative economic movement, also endorse restrictive social laws, rejection of many principles of civil rights, and antipathy to changes in marriage rights for gays and lesbians that on their surface are irrelevant to their economic reform philosophy [8]. With their claimed prioritization of greater freedom, most of their views are aimed to restrict freedom multiplicatively. They wish to use authoritarian tactics to impose their will against those taxes, laws, and practices that have been chosen through a free society and its representation of the people, by the people and for the people. They are displeased with what democracy has brought. About 60 percent of those who identify with the Tea Party rejected the will of the people electing President Obama as President, and largely believe that he was not born in the U.S., or at least doubted he was—making him an illegitimate president [9].

Not only those who have a dogmatic personality type are at risk of thinking or behaving in a dogmatic fashion in high threat or major loss circumstances. Specifically, when threatened and fearful, we humans become more rigid and defensive, more dogmatic. "Terror management theory" (referring to terror of fear, not fear of political terrorism) has found that when people feel threatened they cling to more dogmatic viewpoints, clearer sets of rules, and deeper in-group versus out-group divisions [10]. In our own research, those who are threatened by warfare and actual terrorism tend to move to the right politically and become more militant and dogmatic in their beliefs [11]. As fits our evolutionary genetics, we become more rigid and move to defend and aggress when our tribe is threatened.

Herein lies the window of opportunity for the entre of the totalitarian dogmatic authoritarian father-leader. Dogmatism and its accompanying fear of freedom and need for clear rules, creates an affinity to deep-set tribal affiliation and a need for a tribal leader who will provide clarity, as well as aggress against all who threaten us. Just as dogmatism cannot tolerate abstract art and expressionism, it cannot tolerate abstract ideals. It demands firm, restrictive laws, tight borders, and inflexible rules. The need for absolutes means an absolutist leader is needed. When real world circumstances signal clear danger, as during war, when we are threatened by terrorism or when we frame political arguments as wars on enemies rather than differences between patriots, larger groups of people move toward dogmatic thinking and the desperate need for the authoritarian father-leader who will lead his sheep to safety.

5.2   The Authoritarian Father-Leader and the Role of Dominance

As tribalism emerges, we still believe we are being rational, but our emotions increasingly take center stage on our brain and behavior. Convinced of their cause by the distorted cognitive prism created by threat circumstances, the behavioral genetic push of tribalism seeks the simple, but powerful answers of the authoritarian father-leader. When mixed with dogmatism and its own push toward rigid interpretation of events and solutions, a leader who speaks in clear, simple, and usually simplistic terms about solutions and about protecting the tribe gains affinity. As complexity is anathema to rigid tribal thinking, there is little need for content within the message, only the headlines. Indeed, as the content gets filled in, as eventually it must, its incoherence and internal contradictions hardly matter. In a kind of reverse emotional thinking, the incoherencies and contradictions become truths because they are rigidly tied to the headline messages. For the radical jihadist, killing non-believers, or for that matter their children, pleases God.

Although they come in several shapes and sizes, there are several core elements that must be present in such leaders [12]. They must tell a simple, straightforward story in bold-faced headlines. They must appear attached to and of the people. In fact, the narcissistic tribal leader often does not come from the people, but their populist image must create a mythology of a transformation that makes them part of those they represent. They must be transformed like the biblical Moses, who was an Egyptian prince whose mother found him among the reeds, floating in a basket made by his Hebrew mother. In truth, they are often an outsider. Hitler was an Austrian. Napoleon was a Corsican. Stalin was a Georgian. Mao was the son of a wealthy landed family. Trump is the son of a wealthy real estate developer who showed disdain for his workers, and has been charged with cheating them of their hard-earned wage [13].

The archetypal leaders of extremist movements must be harsh and a fighting force toward the threatening outsider, but are often loving and compassionate to their loyal followers. They must appear powerful and willing to act ruthlessly to protect the tribe. They are usually traditionalists, but at the same time their own story may become cult-like in its retelling. Although often not religious in a strict sense, they create a new movement which becomes a kind of religion.

Democracy is obviously a late arrival to our evolutionary history and therefore hardly encoded in our genetics. Although human tribes might not have had one single leader, authoritarianism and male domination and ascendency is a clear pattern in band culture and in our primate clade (our evolutionary branch), and therefore deeply embedded in our tribal behavioral genetics. Dominance hierarchies are clear in nonhuman primates that preceded human evolution, but that determined much of our genetic patterns.

Male dominance often includes sexual dominance patterning, which after all was the evolutionary purpose of dominance. In male mandrills, those who move up in the hierarchy have a consequent increase in testicular volume and an increase in circulating testosterone, and increased reddening of their sexual skins. This in turn prepares them for their sexual dominance over other males lower in the hierarchy [14]. If this seems irrelevant to humans, think not only of current polygamy, but that King Solomon had 700 wives and 300 concubines. Indeed polygamy was only banned for all Jews after creation of the State of Israel in 1948. For Christians, monogamy was more a contribution of Roman tradition than the New Testament, but in any case, Christianity began long after our evolutionary blueprint was encoded [15].

Understanding the tribal pattern of asserting sexual dominance of the ascendant male, it is no surprise how often political power figures are exposed for their sexual dominance. The tie in with male dominance and sexual dominance was made painfully obvious in the explosive revelations of the #MeToo movement, accusing politicians, business tycoons, and media stars of a litany of sins from use of power to gain sexual advantage to outright rape [16]. That the U.S. elected a leader against whom no fewer than 15 women came forward with accusations of his sexual misconduct, with multiple marriages and divorces of the most beautiful women, and who was heard on tape bragging about sexually molesting women, epitomizes not just the aspect of sexual dominance, but also the willingness of the tribe to be led by such a figure [17].

5.3   Narcissism and the Mystique of Dominance: The Dark Triad

The powerful authoritarian father-leader is an ideal that is longed for by the extremes of the political left and right, the cult, and the extremist group. That it is sought by both right and left is further evidence of its genetic, tribal basis in our species. The authoritarian father leader amplifies the need for affinity and belongingness of members of the group, and asks for sacrifice to the higher calling of the dream they provide. That dream may range from political domination, to spiritual salvation, to psychotic meanderings, and they lay claim to the playbook of that ideal. They are often feared, but they are as often loved as well.

The tribe, fueled by fear and dogmatic in their approach to solutions, has as its complement a leader characterized by what personality research has labeled the "dark triad" [18]. The dark triad consists of narcissism, Machiavellianism and psychopathy. The narcissistic aspect of this triad includes grandiosity, sense of entitlement, dominance, and an unflinching sense of superiority. The narcissist is self-absorbed and frames the world through their own eyes, frequently lacking empathy. They crave loyalty and allegiance and must be the constant focus of attention. Machiavellianism is the attribute of a keen sense of how people and systems can be manipulated, mixed with a cold, emotionless approach where any means justify the ends. Appropriately, it was a concept based on the work of *Niccolò* Machiavelli, entitled *The Prince*, on how to manipulate in politics in the sixteenth century [19] and translated to a psychological concept by Christie and Geis in the 1960s [20].

It is the psychopathic aspect of the dark triad that moves us from what might otherwise be a self-centered and perhaps successful leader to the often toxic and dangerous style of leadership. Psychopathy is best known when we frame it with the word "killer," as in "psychopathic killer," but the concept relates to a more general personality type. The psychopath is self-centered and manipulative, as would be the narcissist, but lacks a sense of anxiety, compassion, or guilt when his acts harm others. Some authoritarian father-leaders, such as Idi Amin of Uganda, Pol Pot of Cambodia, and Hitler, have been guilty of genocide, but their psychopathy is toward a greater end, and not the need to kill found in the individual psychopathic killer. Of course, given their need for political dominance, they may and have murdered millions. Their psychopathy allows them to do this with relaxed "reasoned" justification (see Fig. 5.1).

Mind you, a bit of any of these traits can be a good thing and may even be required to lead. The healthy personality should have a high view of themselves to a degree and often appear narcissistic. They must be Machiavellian enough to know intimately how to "work the system." Without a touch of psychopathy one cannot be a leader because some people will nearly always be harmed by decisions that may benefit the many. An executive may need to close one factory, putting one hundred out of work, to save the company and the jobs of, say, 5000. A touch of psychopathy allows the executive to sleep at night. Certainly, a head of state may need to send young men, and now women, to war, for some greater good. But, the Dark Triad speaks to a leader who is highly narcissistic, highly Machiavellian, and at times dangerously high on psychopathy. Such leaders when in business may be destructive to their colleagues and may even be toxic. But, the dark triadic political or cult leader (as noted in the figure here) is dangerous to the extreme and the authoritarian need for dominance adds a violent dimension that portends death and destruction to any foe from the outside or from within.

The psychopathic and narcissistic aspects nearly always portend troubled waters in the authoritarian father-leader's relationships with their extremist or cult followers. They can be deeply loyal to those who are loyal

Fig. 5.1 The characteristics of a "dark triadic" leader. (Adapted from Paulhus and Williams [10])

to them, even if out of sheer Machiavellianism, but are hypersensitive and are often paranoid to any hint of disloyalty or criticism. This includes their adamant disallowal of the ascendency of any follower who threatens them by themselves creating a position of strength within their movement. The authoritarian father-leader must stand alone on the pedestal, singularly receiving the glow of adulation and adoration. This means that there is often a love of them mixed with a fear of them. Once fully in power, they may only need the fear aspect to retain their secure, dominant stance.

5.4   POWER AND THE CULT OF PERSONALITY: THE GOOD, THE BAD, AND THE UGLY

The authoritarian father-leader is a power figure that answers the tribal needs of the group, nation or cult. We must remember and certainly must appreciate that they are nearly always inspirational and visionary, and that their goals are in many instances laudatory. Undoubtedly, the authoritarian father-leader has repeatedly altered society and many authoritarian father-leaders have answered their tribes' needs for liberation, freedom, and casting off the yoke of oppression, just as many authoritarian father-leaders have been evil oppressors.

Certainly, one of the most inspirational, history-altering, and liberating authoritarian father-leaders of modern times was Mao Zedong. Like most authoritarian father-leaders, his reputation and footprint on history depends on who is writing that history, but even accepting his destructiveness and ruthlessness, no historian can deny many positive and far-reaching aspects of his leadership and imprint on bringing China from a feudalist state, repeatedly vulnerable to outside attack, to a modern world power.

Born to a wealthy farming family, Mao was deeply influenced by the Chinese nationalist movement and evolving Marxism in Russia. In his early years, China was ruled by an imperial dynasty, which was toppled in the several iterations of what was collectively called the Revolution of 1911, giving birth to a fledgling Chinese Republic. This did not, however, mark the end of tribalism in China, but more so the beginning, as the imperial dynasties had lost a series of stinging defeats to the West in the Opium Wars and to Japan in the first Sino-Japanese war. At the same time, the agrarian society was failing to modernize and meet the challenges of the modern industrial world, not least of which the ability to create an effective modern military to protect herself from the West and her aggressive ally to the East, Japan.

Mao emerged as a brilliant military strategist during the Chinese Civil War, during which he defeated the nationalists, creating the People's Republic of China in 1949. Mao was the embodiment of the authoritarian father-leader. He was as loved by his devotees as he was destructive to his enemies. With a vision for agrarian China to rapidly transform into a world power, he launched the Great Leap Forward campaign in one of the most comprehensive feats of social engineering the world has ever known. It was the seemingly impossible vision of the Great Leap Forward to create a modern industrial power out of a backward, landowner-based feudal agrarian system, with the intent of making this transformation in a little more than a decade. The campaign succeeded in industrializing China and creating a powerful modern military force, but at the cost of between 18 and 45 million lives lost.

In 1966, Mao went on to introduce the Great Proletarian Cultural Revolution, removing what he called "counter-revolutionary" elements, a violent attack on persons, institutions and cultural artifacts that remained tied to old China. Throughout these periods of turmoil, destruction, and some would say genocide, he raised the status of women, introduced greatly improved health care, created sweeping educational reform, and increased life expectancy. Critically, he created a China that could no longer be threatened by the West or Japan.

Mao had an enormous cult of personality. He was loved and revered. Mao's image was displayed everywhere and his *Little Red Book*, officially known as *Quotations from Chairman Mao Tse-tung*, was carried throughout the nation. His quotes were displayed in homes and offices in adorned frames, as would be the words of Jesus or Mohammed in Christian and Muslim homes. To achieve his goals, it is believed that his programs were collectively responsible for the genocide of between 40 and 70 million people through forced labor, executions, and starvation. The brilliant general, poet, philosopher, and leader fulfilled the dark triad and won his people's hearts through his vision of their advancement, merciless to any who challenged that vision. He brought to action as he believed. His name and his movement became synonymous [21–23]. Always articulate, Mao wrote:

Revolution is not a dinner party, nor an essay, nor a painting, nor a piece of embroidery, it cannot be so refined, so leisurely and gentle, so temperate, kind, courteous, restrained and magnanimous. A revolution is an insurrection, an act of violence by which one class overthrows another. [24]

5.5   THE AUTHORITARIAN FATHER-LEADER: IF I SAY IT, IT BECOMES TRUE

Few authoritarian father-leaders in modern times display the political cunning of Vladimir Vladimirovich Putin, who rose to the rank of Lieutenant Colonel in the notorious Russian KGB. He is known as a skilled politician and Machiavellian in the extreme. He shows a keen understanding of the Russian people and their need for a muscle-flexing, authoritarian father-leader and capitalizes on the Russian attraction to one clear voice from above that was honed under communism, and perhaps prior to that, under feudalist Czarist Russia. He is willing to steamroll any opposition, but prefers the use of circumscribed modern warfare, skilled political maneuvering, quiet assassination, and waving the flag of Russian preeminence.

Most illustrative of Putin's leadership for an understanding of primitive politics and the role of fear politics is his engineering of the internal media that he controls to shape a story that perfectly complements the fears, aspirations, and leadership expectations of the Russian people. He is a sterling example, like Mao, of the need for an argument that is logical only to his audience, caring little about its logic to those without the prism of his own country's history of loss and resiliency narrative. He relies on the authoritarian father-leader as the holder of truth, and the then backwards logic that any interpretation he provides must be true. Mao looked for eternal truths and philosophies that were timeless. Putin manages this game despite having reversed the advances of Russian democracy, risked Russia in wars of little gain and major economic and global loss, and nearly destroyed the strength of the ruble. He has created a Russia that can barely pay its bills and is relying on its deep financial reserves to stay afloat. And his popularity among the Russian people appears to have never been better, having an approval rating within Russia of 89 percent in 2015 because he has reasserted the Russian tribe as a superpower once again [25].

Putin carefully orchestrates his image as the ultimate alpha male. He is photographed and filmed in race cars, descending in a deep water submersible, firefighting from the air, flying military jets, and participating in martial arts. He is shirtless on horseback, shirtless hunting big game with high-powered rifle, and shirtless fishing. He is photographed as a judo master. His image is broadcast looking distinguished at balls surrounded by beautiful women. His imagery is that of a superhero, who should be envied by men and adored by women. It is a caricature straight out of Marvel Comic Books or a James Bond movie and it is orchestrated and designed as would be those films. It is cardboard thin, with no depth, and completely scripted. And it works.

In thinking of Russia and the manipulation of the press, one might immediately think that the ceiling-shattering approval ratings of Putin are fake. What is fake is the image he creates and his control of news and views, but the approval this brings is apparently quite valid. Putin is revered and he is commonly referred to as *batyushka*, the holy father. When Putin is the likely shadow behind the killing of a political opponent such as Boris Nemstov, public opinion is more likely to hold the attribution of Putin's guilt as a manipulation by the West to destabilize Russia.

Iana Bakunina for the *New Statesman*, Britain's longstanding political magazine, interviewed everyday Russians to hear what they had to say. They see Putin as asserting Russian pride and international ascendency. He is seen as having built a middle class, which they see the West, not Putin, as undermining. He is seen as restoring social welfare, especially popular among the many Russians who have not made the transition to the post-Communist market economy. But, what interviews revealed was most important was Putin's tribal leadership, restoring power and pride in Russia, building their military capacity, and reasserting Russia's position as a superpower [26]. By fulfilling the role of authoritarian father-leader, Putin is able to ignore logic and rational political interpretation of his actions. He powerfully fulfills the emotional needs of Russian's tribalism. He is not speaking to the cognitive forebrain, but to the survival-based, emotional, "protect and defend" regions of older brain structures that we all hold and that play a more prominent role given Russia's history of loss and threat and their particular resiliency narrative. His actions and their consequences do not need to answer to logic, they need to answer to genetically based, threat and loss evoked, aspects of our tribal brain.

5.6   THE AUTHORITARIAN FATHER-LEADER IN 140 MAXIMUM CHARACTERS

Donald Trump has created a movement without a philosophy whose only attribute as a movement is Trump's style and bravado. His willingness to take on authority is the essence of his appeal, and he does so using many of the bully tactics of the archetypal authoritarian father-leader mixed with a school yard level of discourse. Against candidates of his own party his attacks were personal and juvenile—"lyin' Ted" for Ted Cruz, "little

Marco" for Marco Rubio. In other cases he used unsubstantiated, baseless, poison pen tactics—"Jeb Bush is an embarrassment to his family." On Senator John McCain, who spent five and a half years in North Vietnam's notorious "Hanoi Hilton" prison where he was repeatedly tortured, "He's not a war hero...He is a war hero because he was captured. I like people who weren't captured." This from the mouth of someone who used five deferments to not serve is the height of hypocrisy.

Trump clearly inherited an electorate that sees itself as let down by political process and the rational arguments that either political party present. He is a leader without an agenda, without policy, without content, and without consistency. Listen to the debates of Nixon and Kennedy. They are complex, erudite, foundational, philosophically rich, and expressed in postgraduate language. Agree or disagree with conservative philosophy, it is a rich, complex philosophy. Agree or disagree with pro-life and pro-choice positions, they are based on complex thought, spiritually informed and rationally presented, even while being deeply emotional. Arguments about the degree and role of military presence of America in the world is a highly complex topic for which both parties have waxed and waned, usually (if not always) with complex thought-out arguments. The complexity of the use of military presence, military force, and the art of diplomacy are ever-evolving because world circumstances are ever-evolving.

Trump has replaced the use of rational argument with the language of the authoritarian father-leader, absent of content. "We are the best." "They are the worst." "I am a unifier." "I'm very much a unifier." "I will be a great unifier." "You're disgusting." "I am, like, a really smart person." "I believe strongly in being smart." "I think the political press is among the most dishonest people that I've ever met." "You could see that there was blood coming out of her eyes." "Blood coming out of her whatever" [attacking Fox News Meghan Kelly]. He mocks a disabled reporter mimicing the disability. "Some of the media is honest. But most of the media... is scum. Absolutely dishonest."

His proposals are baseless and collapse under any scrutiny. "I will build a great wall—and nobody builds walls better than me, believe me—and I'll build them very inexpensively. I will build a great, great wall on our southern border, and I will make Mexico pay for that wall. Mark my words." "When Mexico sends its people, they're not sending the best. They're not sending you, they're sending people that have lots of problems and they're bringing those problems with us. They're bringing drugs. They're bring crime. They're rapists... And some, I assume, are good people." "An 'extremely credible source' has called my office and told me that Barack Obama's birth certificate is a fraud."

Trump weakens his opponents through vitriol and innuendo. Borrowing from the tactics of the *National Enquirer*, a cheap scandal-mongering tabloid, Trump makes dangerous accusations that are baseless and without substance. These accusations are the complement of many of the dogmatic right-wing followers' conspiracy viewpoints that typically mark the extremist dogmatic who sees enemies lying behind every bush and always feels in dangerous waters. It hardly matters how absurd the conspiracies. So, he accused Republican presidential opponent Ted Cruz's father of conspiring to assassinate President John F. Kennedy. Following the deadly massacre of 50 individuals in an Orlando nightclub in June of 2016, Trump implied that President Obama was somehow involved with the terrorists in a conspiracy. Looking at the text, there is not even a coherent line of thought, only several vaguely connected fragments of thought.

> *We're led by a man who is very—look, we're led by a man that either is not tough, not smart, or he's got something else in mind. And the something else in mind, you know, people can't believe it...People cannot believe, they cannot believe that President Obama is acting the way he acts and he can't even mention the words 'radical Islamic terrorism.' There's something going on. It's inconceivable. There's something going on.* [27]

The threat of terrorism evokes our evolutionary-based tribal behavioral genetic motivation to circle the wagons and prepare for attack. Trump exploits this by railing against Muslims, claiming he would carpet bomb them, and advocating for surveillance of American Muslims on the basis of their faith. And of course, his audience, high on dogmatism and pushed further to the right with their fear, applaud without any thought to the fact that this is constitutionally forbidden and that we are no longer the America we stand for were we to enact such policy.

Trump is banking on the formula that his raising the fear of people who already have great fears of Muslims will lead to a longing and need for the authoritarian father-leader. His strategy regarding framing his opponent is classic, framing "crooked Hillary" as an ineffective, fragile woman versus his powerful father image. He bet, and won, that the dominant alpha male will be the preferred choice, and the higher the fear, the more he is hoping this tribal formula will be effective. What he is entirely lacking, compared to other effective authoritarian father-leaders, is the content beneath the headlines that those who have succeeded at this dangerous game have mastered. His strategy depends on a populace too fearful and too absorbed in their own conspiracy frameworks to look beyond his 140-character tweets for coherent content.

5.7   FROM RADICAL ISLAM TO MESSIANIC JIHAD

Although most Arabs no longer live in strictly organized tribes, even traditional Arab nations and movements are generally tribal in their social structure as well as their ascendant leaders. Saudi Arabia is both ruled and mainly owned by the 200 or so senior members of the Saudi family. Trickle-down power to others is also through tribes and their Sheiks. The authoritarian father-leader is also modeled on tribal political structure across the Arab world, even if the form of government is varied. Many Arab leaders, such as Gamal Abdel Nasser of Egypt, King Hussein of Jordan, and Mohammed VI of Morocco, are characterized by their political astuteness and ability to play the complex power politics of the Middle East. Others like Muammar Gaddafi of Libya, Bashar al-Assad of Syria, Saddam Hussein of Iraq, and Hosni Mubarak of Egypt were more threatening and forceful to the point of ruthless and very much personified the dark triad of Machiavellianism, narcissism, and psychopathy. But, the migration toward radical Islam and now messianic radical Islam in the form of ISIS markedly changes the calculus of the make-up of the authoritarian father-leader and the tribal politics of the Arab world. As Hitler created a philosophy that justified his psychopathic policies, these radical Islamic leaders have directed a form of Islam that justifies genocide, encourages attacks on civilian targets, and enforces officially sanctioned degradation and even enslavement of girls and women.

Since June 2014, Abu Bakr al-Baghdadi has led ISIS as the self-proclaimed Second Emir of the Islamic State of Iraq. Although much of his image is a propaganda-created mythology, he is believed to hold a PhD in Islamic Studies and to have lived as a simple cleric. He was detained and held by U.S. forces in Iraq as a civilian internee at Camp Bucca, but released as a "low level prisoner." He masterminded several large-scale bombings and suicide attacks as leader of what was called al-Qaeda in Iraq or alternatively the Islamic State of Iraq.

By his personal decree, al-Baghdadi appointed himself the leader of the Islamic State of Iraq and the Levant (ISIL), or alternatively the Islamic State in Iraq and Syria (ISIS). By this Machiavellian move he dispelled ties with al-Qaeda and expanded his target of domination beyond the borders of Iraq. In a narcissistic chess move of the grandest proportions, he quickly declared himself the Caliph of a worldwide caliphate.

Al-Baghdadi's ascendant message is to march on "Rome," meaning the combined forces of the West, to establish a caliphate extending from the Middle East across Europe. One of his greatest talents is to capitalize on existing tribal groups who he loosely knits together in temporary coalitions to fight their common enemies. This allows him to enter any nation where the undercurrents of disputes are already well-brewed and exploit them in apparent harmony as if they, ISIS, were a single unit. In fact, they are disjointed, only temporarily organized and disperse as easily as they form depending on the political winds and the way that region's battles are trending. The West mistakes this as a grand movement, but the movement, while large, is not integrated or having a common core. It is reminiscent of wars of the Western Middle Ages, where regional "kings" organized forces comprised of unaffiliated "lords" and knights who could muster some fighting force, often changing sides and dispersing as quickly as they formed.

A pivotal point missed by the West, and hardly touched upon by the Western press outside of a few prescient articles marked by exceptional investigative journalism, is that ISIL is a messianic movement [28]. Unlike the Palestinian movement or al-Qaeda, it is not in this for the long game, or at least the long game as part of the world as we know it. It cannot succeed by actually establishing a lasting caliphate, because without the messianic end of days occurring, al-Baghdadi knows that he would be destroyed by both Western military superiority and indeed Arab military might. As in the case of most cults, the logic of its path ends at a rather near point that is not really carefully considered.

In the case of ISIL, they understand and believe that their only path of success is through bringing on the end-of-days battle, with Jesus (who they believe is their prophet as Islam supersedes Christianity and Judaism, and adopts their prophets) leading the warriors of Islam against "Rome" meaning the West. And yes, you just read that correctly, they believe the resurrected Jesus will lead the triumphant Islamic forces. Every call for Jihadists to attack Westerners and non-believing Muslims, is at the behest of this messianic mission. Such is the dream of the narcissist, Machiavellian, psychopath, unless he is indeed inspired by God in his mission, and then he is only Machiavellian. Al-Baghdadi must lead a temporary caliphate in order to obtain a post-apocalyptic lasting caliphate. As anyone who does not accept their brand of Islam is *takfiri* (an apostate) and being *takfiri* is punishable by death, their path follows a narrow Quranic corridor in a high stakes game of their knowing God's true will and heart.

The current ISIS has a limited life span. But it will morph and transform as the seeds of dogmatic discontent will repeatedly result in reemergence of continuously transforming movements. Whether one sees them as a Medusa or phoenix depends on which side of this struggle one is on, but in either case they will reproduce and have to be fought in each iteration. We can defend ourselves and attack them at every opportunity, and by so doing limit the death and destruction each version will offer, but their tribal energy and structure has lasting power and authoritarian father-leaders will readily spring up to inherit the mantle of messianic leadership.

5.8   Tribal Hatred for Fun and Profit: The Puppet Masters

The human level of protection of the tribe and one's people is heartfelt, often necessary and even rational, and engraved with the strength of our evolutionary biology. However, at the same time, an understanding of behavioral genetics and our evolutionary tribal capacities to defend, protect and if necessary sacrifice for the tribe, are easily manipulated.

Charismatic, and sometimes violent leaders, often exploit the evolutionary behavioral response and use their control of media and the foundations of power politics to meet their own goals as alpha males, which is itself a genetically based archetype. Certainly, in some cases they themselves feel the same patriotic or religious fervor as their supporters, but there is often much psychopathy mixed in with whatever they feel in their hearts or is driven by their evolutionary-developed brains. Indeed, the psychopath is mainly driven by narcissism and lacks social conscience, and so is driven by self-aggrandizement and not the needs of the tribe.

There is great profit in leading tribal or nationalist fervor that does not occur in more democratic forms of government. Vladimir Putin is estimated to be worth \$40–\$70 billion. King Adulyadej of Thailand, whom it was illegal to criticize, was worth over \$30 billion before his recent death. Kim Jong-un, the leader of North Korea, with an average citizen income of about \$1800, is estimated to be worth \$4–\$5 billion. Bashar al-Assad, president of Syria, has an estimated worth between \$500 million and \$1.5

billion [29]. *Forbes* magazine estimated that at his death Libyan dictator Muammar Gaddafi was worth an astounding $200 billion [30].

Terrorism is also big business and many terrorist leaders live as playboys, enjoying great wealth. Much of their money is used to support the expenses of terrorism, but their leaders often enjoy the perks of power to support a lifestyle of comfort. ISIS is estimated to run a $2-billion-a-year franchise. Hamas is a $1-billion organization. In Gaza, Hamas siphons money meant for the population's welfare not only to wage war against Israel, but for their own luxury. Like a mafia organization, those that do not adhere to their leaders find that their businesses and banks suffer "misfortunes." Their leaders live in luxury villas and pocket great sums for their and their families' luxury lifestyle. Hezbollah is a $500-million-a-year business. In addition to financial support from nations such as Iran, they produce and traffic in drugs. They also win over the public by providing relief, education, loans, and welfare, often filling the gap that their violence has created in the destruction of government organizations and a poverty created by their ongoing violence. The Taliban are estimated to have a yearly income of $400 million in a region of the world where the average yearly income is about $500 [31].

Yasser Arafat, the father of the Palestinian people, and the leader of Fatah, Hamas's competitor in the Palestinian cause, was estimated to be worth as much as $3 billion. At the time of his assuming the role of leader of the Palestinian Authority he was estimated to be worth a small fraction of this amount [32]. As he lived a frugal lifestyle, much of this money paid for luxuries enjoyed by his family and many of his leaders, who were not so austere.

Ali Hassan Salameh was known as the "Red Prince." He was also the chief of operations for Black September, the militant Palestinian organization that masterminded the 1972 Munich Olympics massacre of Israeli athletes. He led a life of luxury and wealth and was married to Georgina Rizk, the former Miss Universe. Al-Qaeda leaders Ramzi Yousef and Khalid Shaikh Muhammed were the architects of the 1993 and 2001 World Trade Center attacks, respectively. They traveled the world mixing violent acts with lavish spending [33].

Mullah Mohammed Omar gave birth to the Taliban movement. He founded the Islamic Emirate of Afghanistan, creating the hopes of a new Islamic state based on strict Quranic principles. The Taliban recognized him as their supreme leader and "commander of the faithful." He preached to his impoverished followers a message of simplicity. As "commander of the faithful" he argued for a fundamentalist interpretation of the Koran, with ever spiraling dictums of new rules. Women were discouraged from leaving their homes and their education was forbidden. The very charge of adultery, homosexuality or even immodesty led to severe punishment and often death. Mullah Omar ascended with popular support in large part for the war he took against corrupt local war lords who exploited the post-Soviet chaos to gain power. He was sickened by the warlords' practice of kidnapping children and raping them. Taliban means "students of Islam," and with quickly increasing support of the faithful, Mullah Omar gained control over a wide region of Kandahar Province [34].

Mullah Omar gained the devotion of his followers by protecting them against both outside infidels and local war lords who defied the holiness of Islam. As I have covered earlier, people's response to sexual exploitation by an enemy is one of the most powerful and primal motivations that our evolutionary biology is shaped to respond to. Mullah Omar's enforcement of the beliefs of the faithful was brutal, but by all accounts he was believed to live as a simple, quiet, thoughtful man. He was respectful of those who came to them and known as a teacher. Yet, even this devoted leader appears to have succumbed to a lifestyle that was quite opposite of his preaching. Before fleeing from the allied invasion of Afghanistan, the man who gave birth to the Taliban lived in a "lavish palace of gaudy pink bathrooms, courtyards, garages larger than most Afghan homes…a kitchen, including a Whirlpool dishwasher, was in one corner of the sprawling two-level house," part of a 10-acre compound [35].

"This was the blood money of the Taliban. Mullah Omar collected this money after he became the leader," says Abdul Shakkar, a Karzai supporter who was going through the ruins. "Before that, he had nothing. In the beginning, he declared to the whole nation of Afghanistan that 'I have come as a mullah, and I believe in the Holy Quran.' After that he changed. He became a lover of money, and he sold the blood of the mujahedeen who fought for 22 years."

5.9   THROWING RED MEAT TO THE BELIEVER

In the end, authoritarian father-leaders can only exist with a following who supports them with all the evolutionary tribal strength built into our genetics. They are the complement of a longing to be led in a certain direction. They and their movements typically only sustain momentum with a leader in place. The grassroots movements may meander and generate support and action, but their strength and vision are translated into major force only when an authoritarian father-leader enjoins his vision and influence.

This does not mean that underlying the Taliban is not a conservative version of Islam that denies rights to women and will fiercely defend any power that attempts to change their way of life. Likewise, the Tea Party will continue to be uncompromising, even though it means that they will not obtain what Ronald Reagan always thought was the great value of a gain of some portion of the conservative philosophy. The dogmatic all-or-none mind is inflexible and blind to the options that a flexible approach might gain. And they await the authoritarian father-leader, even if the content that that leader brings actually has little to do with their philosophy, as is the case with the movement behind President Donald Trump.

The leader's authoritarian approach becomes more important than the fulfillment of their actual dreams. For such irrational thinking to be so determinant can only occur with enormous genetic push. The longing for the authoritarian father-leader is built into all of our genetics, but tempered by rational thought as long as threat and fear of loss do not become dominant vectors in people's minds. Under conditions of high threat and loss, however, our tribal genetics flourish and dominate our "thinking" and actions, creating political movements of great moment and sometimes grave danger to the world for which the authoritarian father-leader is key.

With radical Islam and now Messianic Islam raging war East and West, it is imperative that we understand the tribal, evolutionary nature of their outcry and actions. We have continued to attempt to understand and frame these movements from a rational viewpoint, rather than from its evolutionary-based, genetically driven emotional origins. We will examine this next, as we look to the biological need to protect, defend, and aggress when loss is experienced massively as it has been experienced for fundamentalist Muslims, often as a byproduct of their own lack of leadership and their own version of truth.

REFERENCES

1. Rokeach, M. (1966). *The open and closed mind*. New York: Basic Books.
2. Crowson, H. M. (2009). Does the DOG scale measure dogmatism? Another look at construct validity. *The Journal of Social Psychology, 149*(3), 265–283. https://doi.org/10.3200/socp.
3. Brigham, C. (1923). *A study of American intelligence*. Princeton: Princeton University Press.

4. Adam, P. (1992). *Art of the third Reich*. New York: H.N. Abrams.
5. Dyckhoff, T. (2002, November 29). Mies and the Nazis. *The Guardian*. Retrieved June 10, 2017, from https://www.theguardian.com/artanddesign/2002/nov/30/architecture.artsfeatures
6. Sartre, J.-P. (1956). *Being and nothingness*. New York: Philosophical Library.
7. Fromm, E. (1941). *Escape from freedom*. New York: Farrar & Rinehart.
8. Montopoli, B. (2012, December 14). Tea Party supporters: Who they are and what they believe. *CBS News*. Retrieved March 6, 2017, from http://www.cbsnews.com/news/tea-party-supporters-who-they-are-and-what-they-believe/
9. Condon, S. (2010, April 14). Poll: 'Birther' myth persists among Tea Partiers, all Americans. *CBS News*. Retrieved June 23, 2017, from http://www.cbsnews.com/news/poll-birther-myth-persists-among-tea-partiers-all-americans/
10. Greenberg, J., Pyszczynski, T., & Solomon, S. (1986). The causes and consequences of a need for self-esteem: A terror management theory. In R. F. Baumeister (Ed.), *Public self and private self* (pp. 189–212). New York: Springer.
11. Hobfoll, S., Canetti-Nisim, D., & Johnson, R. J. (2006). Exposure to terrorism, stress-related mental health symptoms, and defensive coping among Jews and Arabs in Israel. *Journal of Consulting and Clinical Psychology, 74*(2), 207–218. https://doi.org/10.1037/0022-006x.74.2.207.
12. Post, J. M. (2004). *Leaders and their followers in a dangerous world*. Ithaca: Cornell University Press.
13. Graham, D. A. (2017, January 23). The many scandals of Donald Trump: A cheat sheet. *The Atlantic*. Retrieved December 20, 2017, from https://www.theatlantic.com/politics/archive/2017/01/donald-trump-scandals/474726/
14. Ray, W. J. (2012). *Evolutionary psychology: Neuroscience perspectives concerning human behavior and experience*. Thousand Oaks: Sage.
15. Joyce, G. H. (1933). *Christian marriage: An historical and doctrinal study*. New York: Sheed and Ward.
16. Time Magazine. (2017, December 18). TIME's 2017 person of the year: The silence breakers. *Time Magazine, 190*(25).
17. Merica, D. (2017, December 12). Women detail sexual allegations against Trump. *CNN*. Retrieved January 12, 2017, from http://www.cnn.com/2017/12/11/politics/donald-trump-women-allegations/index.html
18. Paulhus, D. L., & Williams, K. M. (2002). The dark triad of personality: Narcissism, Machiavellianism, and psychopathy. *Journal of Research in Personality, 36*(6), 556–563.
19. Machiavelli, N. (1961). *The prince*. New York: Penguin Group.

20. Christie, R., & Geis, F. L. (1970). *Studies in Machiavellianism.* Cambridge: Academic.
21. Terrill, R. (2000). *Mao: A biography: Revised and expanded edition.* Red Wood City: Stanford University Press.
22. Lynch, M. J. (2004). *Mao.* London: Routledge.
23. Dikötter, F. (2010). *Mao's great famine: The history of China's most devastating catastrophe, 1958–62.* New York: Walker Publishing.
24. Columbia University. (2009). *Mao Zedong on war and revolution.* Asia for Educators. Retrieved November 12, 2017, from http://afe.easia.columbia. edu/special/china_1900_mao_war.htm
25. Nardelli, A., Rankin, J., & Arnett, G. (2015, July 23). Vladimir Putin's approval rating at record levels. *The Guardian.* Retrieved June 15, 2017, from https://www.theguardian.com/world/datablog/2015/jul/23/vladimir-putins-approval-rating-at-record-levels
26. Bakunina, J. (2015, March 4). Why do Russians still support Vladimir Putin? *New Statesman.* Retrieved June 10, 2017, from http://www.newstatesman. com/politics/2015/03/why-do-russians-support-still-support-vladimir-putin
27. CNN Wire. (2016, June 13). Trump attacks President Obama: 'There's something else going on'. *CNN Wire.* Retrieved September 10, 2017, from http:// q13fox.com/2016/06/13/trump-attacks-president-obama-theres-something-else-going-on/
28. Wood, G. (2015, March). What ISIS really wants. *The Atlantic.* Retrieved March 7, 2017, from https://www.theatlantic.com/magazine/archive/2015/03/what-isis-really-wants/384980/
29. The World Post. (2013, December 2). The richest world leaders are even richer than you thought. *The World Post.* Retrieved May 21, 2017, from http:// www.huffingtonpost.com/2013/11/29/richest-world-leaders_n_4178514. html
30. Durgy, E. (2011, October 25). Did Moammar Gadhafi die the richest man in the world? *Forbes.* Retrieved May 31, 2017, from https://www.forbes.com/ sites/edwindurgy/2011/10/25/did-moammar-gadhafi-die-the-richest-man-in-the-world/#1e728be276cf
31. Zehorai, I. (2014, December 12). The world's 10 richest terrorist organizations. *Forbes.* Retrieved May 31, 2017, from https://www.forbes.com/sites/ forbesinternational/2014/12/12/the-worlds-10-richest-terrorist-organizati ons/#4632315e4f8a
32. Rees, M. (2004, November 14). Where's Arafat's money? *TIME.* Retrieved May 31, 2017, from http://content.time.com/time/magazine/arti cle/0,9171,782141,00.html

33. The Washington Times. (2010, October 15). Editorial: The playboy terrorist. *The Washington Times*. Retrieved May 31, 2017, from http://www.washingtontimes.com/news/2010/oct/15/the-playboy-terrorist/

34. Rashid, A. (2010). *Taliban: Militant Islam, oil and fundamentalism in Central Asia*. New Haven: Yale University Press.

35. Gargan, E. (2001, December 15). A lavish lifestyle – For an Afghan. *The Baltimore Sun*. Retrieved June 2, 2017, from http://articles.baltimoresun.com/2001-12-15/news/0112150216_1_mullah-mohammed-omar-taliban-leader-mullah-lifestyle

CHAPTER 6

Radical Jihad and Paranoid Supremacists

"We call upon every *Muslim* in every place to perform hijrah [to migrate] to the Islamic State or fight in his land wherever that may be... This is because the battle is one between the allies of the Merciful and the allies of Satan, and so Allah ...will support His soldiers, grant His slaves authority, and preserve His religion, even if the days alternate between victory and *loss*, even if war is competition, and even if wounds afflict both parties.... *We call upon you so that you leave the life of humiliation, disgrace, degradation, subordination, loss, emptiness, and poverty, to a life of honor, respect, leadership, richness"* [bold added]. *(Abu Bakr al-Baghdadi, the leader of ISIS, May 14, 2015 [1])*

In these words, Abu Bakr al-Baghdadi, the leader of ISIS, underscores and epitomizes the key components that drive our genetic predisposition toward tribalism with a calling to the believers to defend, aggress, and sacrifice for the tribe. As I have highlighted in outlining the climate that elicits tribal behavior and how our tribal genetics direct our behavior, al-Baghdadi divides the world in black and white, between holy and Satanic, adopting the tribal tendency to fear outsiders and to view them as an existential threat. He demands dedication to the tribe, even at risk of one's own life and acknowledging that others must die. In this way, the tribe takes precedence over the family or individual self. He emphasizes the profound losses and threats that he believes have occurred to "true"

© The Author(s) 2018
S. E. Hobfoll, *Tribalism*,
https://doi.org/10.1007/978-3-319-78405-2_6

125

Muslims, listing humiliation, disgrace, degradation, subordination, loss, emptiness, and poverty. As we have seen in previous chapters, loss, and particularly loss that is infused with a deep sense of humiliation, is a primary driver of tribal genetics and the reactions of the tribe to defend and aggress. This sense of humiliation and offering of tribal pride and restoration of ascendency has been a clarion call for every extremist group from the Ku Klux Klan, the Nazis, imperial Japan, and White anti-government militia groups in the U.S. It is a powerful undertone in the 2016 British Brexit vote and the Trump candidacy for the White House, which he has continued during his presidency.

As an anecdote to loss and humiliation, al-Baghdadi offers rebirth, retribution, and honor with the acceptance of tribal affiliation. If you become committed to the tribe, even at risk of your life, you are offered transformation, but this is only offered for those who answer the call. Those who join ISIL will gain honor, respect, leadership, richness, and closeness with God. As we reviewed earlier, such leaders must rely on a dogmatic, inflexible legion of followers. As the powerful authoritarian leader, al-Baghdadi provides the authoritarian, narcissistic, Machiavellian, psychopathic leadership that such followings thrive upon and require. He has named himself Caliph of the world's true believing Muslims in a caliphate that includes much of the Middle East and conceptually includes the world. All others are apostate and must be put to death. No matter that the Muslim tradition of the Caliph is by acclamation of others, he believes himself anointed by God and able to declare this self-proclamation. Although contrary to Sharia law, anointment by force has a tradition in the Muslim world, and no doubt those who claimed to be Caliph by force before him likewise believed themselves the true messengers of God and His will. Al-Baghdadi in this way not only fulfills the tribal press for a strong authoritarian leader, he finds precedence in Muslim tradition. This tradition is not without controversy, but it is a controversy that exists from the first decades of Islam [2–4].

Nowhere is the rise of tribalism and all the markings of our primitive, genetically driven tribal selves more evident than in the movements that are known today as radical Islam and what I have called Messianic Islam. Once humans respond at the tribal level, brain, emotions, and behavior become dictated by the abhorrence of the "other," the impenetrable need to protect the self and the tribe, and a cognitive inflexibility to respond otherwise. Mid-brain and deep brain dominate mental functioning and emotional responding. That our tribal selves are deeply imprinted in our genetic code once again does not mean that we are slaves to our DNA. But rather that our genetics push us in certain directions that are elicited more powerfully when our biological and psychological needs signal a need for survival. Education, life circumstances, and the world around us all play a part in creating the environmental conditions that press us toward more tribal and primitive responding. If the environment signals loss, threat, humiliation, and harm to us or those things we love and value, we are more likely to respond along these built-in adaptive pathways.

We must be cautious with the term *primitive*. I do not refer to this as meaning a less well-evolved people or a lesser people. Much of the Middle East and Islam is erudite, educated, cultured, and advanced. Nor do I by any means suggest that Muslims are somehow genetically inferior. They are not and there is no evidence for racial or ethnic differences on such dimensions. Rather, by primitive, I continue to refer to that aspect of humans' built-in behavioral genetics that is more tribal in nature or more hard-wired on the individual or family levels, and part of **all our "primitive" evolutionary DNA**. Further, our tribal behavioral genetics also includes our drive to protect and nurture, as well as that aspect of our genetics that gives us empathy for other members of our group, and even the great human race. Indeed, although we often think of our sexuality as primitive, which it is, so is our search for God and meaning. Although sexual behavior and, say, search for food are on what we call a genetic "short leash," meaning the behavior is more clearly patterned and set, our search for God and meaning is on a longer leash, meaning it occurs across the species, but its genetics allows much greater variation.

6.1   RADICAL AND MESSIANIC ISLAM'S DEEP SENSE OF LOSS AND THREAT

Radical Islam is a tribal reaction against the threats of pluralism, the assault of global media that invades the Islamic world, just as it does our own living rooms, the undermining of their strict gender roles, and the perceived "war on Islam." It is disingenuous to argue that the West does not feel a need to control the Middle East and the oil that the entire modern world and world economy depend upon. The West clearly chooses allies and acts militarily and through clandestine (CIA) efforts and proxies to protect those interests and that need. We also certainly often choose to impose on their culture.

We must remind ourselves first and foremost that the Arab states were for the most part created by France and Great Britain after World War I and the defeat of the Ottoman Empire. The borders of much of the Middle East were the creation in 1916 of a single French and single British aristocrat, François Georges-Picot and Mark Sykes. These two men, chosen by the victorious allied governments, literally drew a map of the soon to be conquered territories and lettered them A and B, with A going to France and B belonging under the sphere of influence of Great Britain, like some children's board game. Their assignments had little to do with tribal or ethnic populations and were negotiated in secret without knowledge of the Arab world. As we know, the governments that emerged in these regions were either oppressive or unacceptable to most of the Arabs in the region or had to piece together coalitions from nonaligned constituent and sometimes rival groups [5, 6] (Image 6.1).

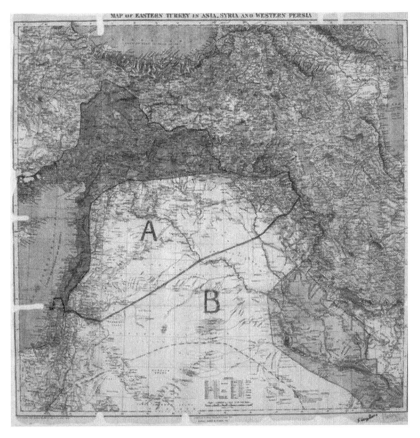

Image 6.1   Map of the Sykes–Picot agreement, 1916 [6]

We also wish to impose our moral will and cultural values on the region and have clearly acted on the basis of our moral code and worldview. We are incensed by radical Islam's treatment of women and girls, as illustrated by one of many news reports below, their barbarous acts, and their treatment of antiquities that we see as a world heritage. I am not saying that we should not feel this way, and I believe we must act upon it, but we cannot deny that we have done so in the past and continue to do so. And, impinging our will has consequences.

> *Attackers on a motorbike threw acid in the faces of three teenage girls on their way to school in Afghanistan's western Herat province on Saturday, an official told CNN. The girls, age 16 to 18, are students at one of the biggest girls' schools in Herat city, the provincial capital, said Aziz-ul-Rahman Sarwary, head of the education department for the province.... "This is the punishment for going to school," the men told the girls after pouring the acid on them.* [7]

Imagine if the Muslim world felt entitled to take control of Wall Street, impose their will on our cultural practices, and possessed the level of military power to do so. We would most certainly feel invaded. Indeed, we feel invaded when Jihadists kill a few thousands of us, when we have killed, and will continue to kill, many more of Muslims to stabilize the oil fields and our allies in the Middle East that we consider partners in an ordered global market. Make no mistake, I believe that we must fight such evil and that America has a special responsibility and leadership role in this battle. But we must acknowledge that we in fact take this stand and are often willing to exert, if not impose, our will when we witness such behavior. Indeed, our justification for our imposition of military action is often flawed, as most Americans would agree in hindsight regarding our 2003 invasion of Iraq, and perhaps Afghanistan. That "mistake" took perhaps half a million Muslim lives. It is naive of us to think that we can have done so, whatever our justification, without consequences and reaction [7, 8].

On a cultural level, extremist, fundamentalist Islam also feels assaulted both from the West and from within the Islamic world, and this again should not come as a surprise. Many of the cultural impositions of globalism and secularism, as well as the continued tendency for society to become more liberal and less conservative, are perceived as an assault on Christianity by Christians in the U.S. as well. Just as many fundamentalist Christians decry the "war on Christianity," fundamentalist Islam perceives many of the same cultural forces as creating a "war on Islam." As mainstream talk show host Bill O'Reilly, one of the most popular TV personalities of recent time, stated regarding Christian Americans' perception of a war on Christianity:

> *Kenya, Africa—five radical Muslim killers murdered at least 70 people at a college at that country. At least another 75 were wounded. Gunmen burst into a Christian prayer service, proceeded to shoot down the innocent worshipers. That comes after a mid March suicide bombing in Pakistan killing 14 Christians, wounding 70 others. A few weeks before that, Libya—ISIS killers beheading 21 Egyptian Christians. So you can see Christians are being slaughtered all over the place...Here in the U.S.A., verbal attacks against Christians are the headlines. As we reported yesterday, some far-left people aided by a sympathetic media are now smearing Americans who oppose things like abortion and gay marriage. No question it is open season on Christians.* [9]

Even if Saudi Arabia is deeply religiously and culturally fundamentalist Muslim, their Western orientation in the global economy and their own war on those fundamentalist Muslims who threaten their rule make them an enemy as well. Indeed, ISIL's leader al-Baghdadi states in no uncertain terms how he sees Arab governments and Saudi Arabia in particular, depicting them as "guard dogs" of the Jews.

> *O Muslims, the apostate tyrannical rulers who rule your lands in the lands of the Two Holy Sanctuaries (Mecca and Medina), Yemen, Shām (the Levant), Iraq, Egypt, North Africa, Khorasan, the Caucasus, the Indian Subcontinent, Africa, and elsewhere, are the allies of the Jews and Crusaders. Rather, they are their slaves, servants, and guard dogs, and nothing else. The armies that they prepare and arm and which the Jews and Crusaders train are only to crush you, weaken you, enslave you to the Jews and Crusaders, turn you away from your religion and the path of Allah, plunder the goods of your lands, and rob you of your wealth.* (Abu Bakr al-Baghdadi, the leader of ISIS, May 14, 2015 [10])

In fact, radical and Messianic Islam's war with the West is an extension of a tribal war they have fought within Islam for centuries. It is one outgrowth, and a comparably benign one compared to the violence they have perpetrated within Islam. It is absurd not to call al-Qaeda and ISIL Islamic. They are deeply Islamic and represent a centuries-old movement within Islam that is based on the Quran, a tradition of *ijma* (consensus) and based on extensive qiyas (juristic reasoning). When some Islamic scholars or Western politicians claim that the radicals have hijacked Islam, it is like stating the Evangelical Christians have hijacked Christianity. That is, it is a viewpoint of the more liberal toward the fundamentalist. Both liberal, pluralistic and extremist, purist Islam have long represented Islamic thinking and practice. Indeed, Muhammad ibn Saud, the first of the modern Saudi line, joined forced with ibn Abd al-Wahhab, the forefather of ISIL and al-Qaeda's philosophy and tradition in 1744. They have been joined at the hip since, and many scholars would say this marriage created the worldwide spread of extremist tribalism through strategic funding and support by the wealth of Saudi Arabia [11].

6.2   A FIGHT WITHIN ISLAM

Radical, fundamentalist Islam's anger and aggression have existed within this tribal survival prism for centuries. It has only secondarily focused on the West, either in terms of its chronology or its intensity. Rather, it is part of an internal struggle within Islam that is nearly as old as Islam itself. For centuries Muslims have argued, fought, and died over the struggle between pluralism and tribal-based fundamentalism. Indeed, pluralism, an openness to different philosophies, religions, and lifestyles, was first championed within Islam, long before it was found in the Christian West.

Islam's Golden Age of enlightenment, with its championing of literary, religious, and scientific pluralism is traditionally dated from the mid-seventh century to the mid-thirteenth century. It was characterized by religious tolerance, openness to secular thought, scientific advancement, formation of perhaps the world's first universities and hospitals, medical innovation, and the development of advanced mathematics. A culture of traders, the Muslim world absorbed knowledge from others and looked to perfect it. Although Muslims did politically dominate the Muslim world, there was a rare openness to the thinking and contribution of Jews and Christians. Poetry, art, music, literature, and freedom of speech flourished.

Caliph Haroun Al-Rasheed reigned from 786 until 809. He built the leading academy of the sciences and humanities, the *Bayt Al-Hikma*, of the Middle Ages. The Bayt Al-Hikma, following the work of his father, Caliph Mohammad Al-Mahdi (775–785 CE), and grandfather, Caliph Abu Ja'far Al-Mansour (754–775 CE), in their enlightened leadership. As Europe was set in an extended period of darkness, ignorance, and prejudice, and long before any signs of the European Renaissance, the Arab world was flourishing due to its openness to pluralism and scientific method. Books were translated from throughout the educated world, scientists and scholars met and debated, and the wisdom of the Greeks, Romans, Hebrews, and Persians were coveted and respected [12, 13].

There is no agreed single reason for the decline of the Islamic Golden Age. The Islamic world was weakened by invasions of Christian Crusaders from Europe and the Mongols under Genghis Khan in 1206 from the East. European industrial growth also overtook Islam's slow industrialization. Western agricultural advancement, and colonial expansion through sea power, also catapulted the West ahead of the East, including the Middle East. But, the House of Wisdom was also in decline due to the seeds of Muslim fundamentalism under the reign of al-Mutawakkil ala Allah (847–861 CE), who supported a more literal interpretation of the Quran and was uninterested in science and opposed to a liberal humanities. Al-Mutawakkil saw non-Islamic philosophies and teaching as anti-Islamic and began the reversal of the openness of his predecessors. He discriminated against Jews and Christians, destroyed their houses of worship, and excluded them from government [14, 15].

Before one judges this reversal too harshly, the Christian world at the time was steeped in prejudice and ignorance, as well as a xenophobic orientation to anything that was not consistent with New Testament thinking and Catholic orthodoxy. Galileo, after all, was forced by the Roman Inquisition to denounce the belief that the earth moved around the sun more than 700years after the reign of al-Mutawakkil. Six hundred years after al-Mutawakkil's reign, the Spanish Inquisition was active in repression of thought, pluralism, and any hint of challenge to Catholic orthodoxy, persecuting over 100,000 individuals and executing thousands. So, to judge Islam's rising conservatism too harshly would be unfair through the lens of those times, as they were still more open and progressive than their contemporaries in the Christian world. Still al-Mutawakkil's reign represented a turning point from the Islamic Golden Age. As the West moved toward more openness, liberalization, democratization, industrialization, global trade, and internationalism, the Muslim world did not.

At the same time, it would also be a mistake to say that the Islam's liberal and thought advancing contribution ever ended. Rather, there has always been a stream of liberal, open, thinking, a love of philosophy and literature, and a respect for human welfare within the Muslim world. To lose this point is to lose the understanding of the internal struggle that has erupted and expanded in our times.

6.3   WAHHABISM AND ITS FUNDAMENTALIST AND MILITANT INFLUENCE

The modern thread of fundamentalism within Islam was largely codified within what is now called Wahhabism, also referred to as Salafi. Wahhabism is a Sunni religious movement named after the eighteenth-century Islamic leader Muhammad ibn Abd al-Wahhab (1703–1792). It is a conservative, purist, and puritanical movement advocating for a pure Islamic orthodoxy. *It is also the single most important element in the puzzle of understanding radical Islamic terrorism which absolutely emanates from this Islamic movement which is both widespread and well financed.* Salafi teaching is at the heart of al-Qaeda and ISIS philosophies and its advocacy and financing in modern times by Saudi resources has sold it around the world, marketing the basis of Jihad. It divides Sunni Islam, already divided between Shia and Sunni sects. Wahhabism was turned against Islam long before it ever turned an eye to the West. As in many fundamentalist movements, anyone who does not adhere to Wahhabism is apostate (takfir) and subject to execution. It is a return to tribalism and our primitive genetics of "defend and aggress," and emanates, as we have seen in all the instances of tribalism, under the threat of loss and humiliation.

Wahhabism is the most purely tribal religious interpretation pressing on the modern world, and contains all the hallmarks of our evolutionary tribal genetic press. It divides the world between the chosen and the sinful, having deep suspicion of any outsiders. It demands sacrifice and harsh gender differentiation and male privilege. It demands a powerful authoritarian father-leader who is seen as anointed by God and His representative on earth and is dogmatic in its thinking. As we have seen in earlier chapters, the tribal mind defines truth through its own prism, rejecting science, other's interpretation, and often suspending logic. Wahhabism is the personification of these dimensions of our evolutionary roots.

So, al-Qaeda, the Taliban, and ISIL are natural manifestations of the will toward self-rule with a heavy dose of distrust for both the West and any leader who shapes its image in Western, modern cultural ideals. All see themselves as Islamic and all are based on long-standing Islamic fundamentalist traditions that are tribal both in terms of this book's themes and in terms of how they see themselves.

6.4 "It's Okay to Kill Jews": The Crack That Grew to a Flood

Humans' primitive tribal behavioral genetics is expressed in their aggressive, defensive, truth-denying form in extremist Islamic terrorism. They are reflected in White supremacist terrorism, anti-abortion terrorists, violent police behavior toward Blacks, Black gunmen ambushing police, violent over-reaction by Israeli border police against Palestinians, or even bullying behavior in a high school. It is also notable that this primitive tribal expression is always perpetrated by a very small proportion of individuals holding extremist views, enjoined with an angry militancy. However, as illustrated in the iceberg theory of terrorism support that I develop here (see Fig. 6.1), these are all outgrowths of widespread attitudes and beliefs held by millions of individuals.

If we take bullying in a high school as one non-obvious example, we can see that this begins with support promoted by high schools and the greater society that some individuals are more deserving, proper, and esteemed than others. Of course we believe we are against bullying, but

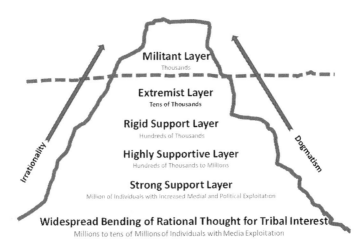

Fig. 6.1 The iceberg theory of terrorism support. (Adapted from Sprinzak [20])

the fact is that much of society and the way we allow our high schools to carry out our own set of competitive, elitist values, is the underpinning that results in bullying as its natural outgrowth. Humans are largely tribal to some degree and our tribal inclinations create social and cultural phenomena that are outgrowths of these tendencies.

Eric Harris and Dylan Klebold murdered 12 students and one teacher at Columbine High School in Colorado in 1999. We should not be surprised that this occurred, but rather that this does not occur more often given the socially supported processes of elitism, exclusionism, and cronyism that so many high schools herald and perpetuate. Star athletes and cheerleaders are featured and winning football teams are supported by mass rallies, with whole towns often parading, while the chess club and the debating team are honored with a small sign on the school's lawn that few notice. Isolated, more awkward, or different teens are ostracized and devalued by the school first and foremost, and by students as a consequence of social processes that exist throughout our society. The U.S. Secret Service found in their study of 37 premeditated school shootings that bullying played a major role in two-thirds of the attacks [16]. Eric Harris and Dylan Klebold were both gifted children and had been subjected to bullying for years. These two individuals were the militant layer that I refer to in the figure. They are a reaction to the often violent shaming and relentless bullying that a small number of students carry out, as many others laugh, still more turn their heads but do not intervene, and a school system and competitive parents create [17, 18].

As described in a *Washington Post* article in July 1999:

"Columbine High School is a culture where initiation rituals meant upper-class wrestlers twisted the nipples of freshman wrestlers until they turned purple and tennis players sent hard volleys to younger teammates' backsides. Sports pages in the yearbook were in color, a national debating team and other clubs in black and white. The homecoming king was a football player on probation for burglary....Increasingly, as parents and students replay images of life at Columbine, they are freeze-framing on injustices suffered at the hands of athletes, wondering aloud why almost no one—not teachers, not administrators, not coaches, not most students, not parents—took the problem seriously....No one thinks the high tolerance for athletic mischief explains away or excuses the two boys' horrific actions. But some parents and students believe a schoolwide indulgence of certain jocks—their criminal convictions, physical abuse, sexual and racial bullying—intensified the killers' feelings of powerlessness and galvanized their fantasies of revenge." [18]

As in the case of bullying in our schools being supported by a broad base of elitist attitudes, it is my stance that extremist Islamic terrorism is an outgrowth of a very broad support in the Muslim world for tolerance for terrorism against Israel, on one hand, and intolerance toward pluralism on the other. This support by millions lays the groundwork for a pyramid of ever-increasing dogmatism and irrationality that becomes more and more extreme among fewer and fewer individuals, culminating in militant extremism.

The vast majority of Muslims in the U.S., 86 percent, believe that suicide bombings are rarely or never justified. However, 7 percent of U.S. Muslims believe that suicide bombings are sometimes justified and 1 percent believe that they are often justified. Most are likely thinking of Israel in answering this question. Forty percent of Palestinians in the territories occupied by Israel believe that suicide bombings and violence against civilians are justifiable. Among Muslims in Afghanistan, 39 percent find this justifiable and in Egypt 29 percent see such murder as justifiable. This translates to tens of millions of Muslims at the lowest level in the iceberg of terrorism support in the figure. It is this layer that creates all the other layers as a natural consequence of the process of tribalism. This lowest layer is the wellspring for the ever increasingly extremist layers that lead to the militant layer in which tribalism plays out at its most primitive, aggressive [19].

Even among Muslims in the U.S., there is a sizable extremist element who have used many of the same tactics of suppression to achieve leadership positions. Following the attacks on the World Trade Center and Pentagon of September 11, 2001, President George W. Bush spoke forcefully that the attacks of September 11 were not the face of Islam from the U.S. capital's most important mosque. Most likely unbeknownst to him, behind him stood several of the leaders of the Wahhabi takeover of American Islam. This group had for years orchestrated a takeover of more pluralist American Islam to the ultra-conservative views of Wahhabism, suppressing broader Islamic traditions. They supported suicide attacks against Israel and often spoke out against U.S. policy. Maher Hathout, a leader of the more liberal Muslim Public Affairs Council (MPAC), was quoted as condemning U.S. actions in Afghanistan as "illegal, immoral, unhuman, unacceptable, stupid and un American."

In stark contrast, when a suicide bomber blew up a Sbarro pizzeria in downtown Jerusalem in August 2001 in which 15 Israelis, including

5 children, were murdered, the Muslim Public Affairs Council declared that Israel was "responsible for this pattern of violence." [21] MPAC claims to be open to peaceful solutions to the Palestinian-Israeli conflict, and most of its members probably are, but the organization routinely sponsors eminent Muslim speakers, such as Mazin Qumisyeh of the West Bank, who claim that American Jews and Israel are responsible for broader "wars on Arab and Muslim countries." Mazin Qumsiyeh published on his website blog that Zionists, not two Muslim brothers, were behind the Boston Marathon bombing [21].

As I have argued, militancy is an outgrowth of the tribal push toward dogmatism and intolerance, which both protect the tribe without equivocation. As pressure to protect the tribe increases, the prism of truth becomes increasingly distorted and only information that supports the tribal narrative is allowed to filter in. Such facts as rocket attacks increasing geometrically against Israel when they fully pulled out of Gaza are ignored in their entirety.

It is true that most Muslims favor democracy and freedom, but 45 percent of Muslims in the Middle East and North Africa do not prefer democracy and 15 percent do not believe that religious freedom is an acceptable course for society. This translates to tens of millions of Muslims who form a fountainhead for extremism, even if the vast majority of these individuals would never themselves harm someone who was not of their faith [22]. And before I am accused of Islamophobia, let me remind the reader that I am arguing that this same tendency toward intolerance and dogmatism is the fountainhead for White supremacy and growing anti-government militia movements in the U.S., built on the general anger, intolerance, and aggressiveness of White working-class men.

Once millions condone the murder of children at a pizzeria in Jerusalem, more radical elements will bring these views to their more primitive tribal conclusions. It is the language of the millions, whether they support hate speech or hate acts, that lays the seeds for the primitive, genetically programmed tribal response by those who translate these messages to their extremes. For there are always a core group of disenfranchised members of the society who more deeply experience a sense of loss and humiliation, and for them the framework of loss, threat, and humiliation must be answered by our deep-brain programmed response to protect and aggress. Terrorism and extremism are the apotheosis of the broader sentiment of hate and prejudice that must resonate for the millions.

6.5   AMERICAN TERRORISM HIGHLIGHTS THE ICEBERG
THEORY OF TERRORISM

We can best understand extremist Islamic terrorism by now stepping back and taking a look at U.S.-based extremist terrorism, as it allows us to disentangle our feelings about terrorism from our many misunderstandings and general unfamiliarity with Islam.

When a single angry male murders an abortion-performing physician, or blows up a federal building in Oklahoma City killing 168 individuals, including 19 children, or slaughter a Black congregation at prayer, their acts are the tribal outgrowth of the violent language of many militant sounding congressional leaders, some presidential candidates, the current president, and millions of ultra-conservative right-wing supporters. Such acts are fueled by the support of millions of Tea Partyists who "understand" even if they do not condone these acts.

Timothy McVeigh, who carried out the Oklahoma City bombing, believed he was fighting the "evil empire" and a government that was out of control, limiting the freedom of true patriots [23]. This occurs when such large swaths of the public depict government as their "enemy," as can be seen in the Pew Research Center findings presented here [24]. As many as 35 percent of Republicans and 12 percent of Democrats view their own government as their enemy (Fig. 6.2).

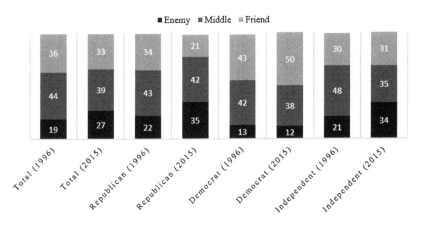

Fig. 6.2 View of government as "enemy" or "friend." (Adapted from Pew Research Center [24])

These millions, where some rationality mixes with a great deal of fantasy and conspiracy politics, give rise to the hundreds of thousands of Americans in White right-wing militias and the Patriot movement. Studies by the Southern Poverty Law Center show a large rise in such groups, focused on anti-immigration, radicalized anti-government, and nativist extremism, and since President Trump's election, they have become more active and emboldened. This movement advocated militant opposition to the U.S. government, and particularly Barack Obama and presidential candidate Hillary Clinton. Although these hate militias had largely evaporated by around 2008, with the election of a Black president and the rise of hate rhetoric, even by public officials, the "second wave of hate militias" flourished. The report by the Southern Poverty Law Center wrote,

A key difference this time is that the federal government—the entity that almost the entire radical right views as its primary enemy—is headed by a black man. That, coupled with high levels of non-white immigration and a decline in the percentage of whites overall in America, has helped to racialize the Patriot movement, which in the past was not primarily motivated by race hate. [25]

In 2008, the Southern Poverty Law Center estimated that there were 42 militia groups. Recently they estimate 276 such groups. Their aggression, paranoid fear of the "other," and self-perpetuated internal propaganda are a reflection of the array of tribal beliefs and practices that is only inches away from the acts of militancy by the few. These are the tens of thousands, created and supported by the hundreds of thousands, whose energy and language are generated and, yes, supported by the millions. It is a widespread belief among millions of Americans on the extreme Right, fomented in the vocal views held by the Republican Presidential Candidate Donald Trump, who became President Trump, that in the end, President Obama is part of the Islamic attack against the U.S. As Trump stated on Fox News following the horrific massacre in Orlando, Florida's gay bar:

Look, we're led by a man that either is not tough, not smart, or he's got something else in mind. And the something else in mind—you know, people can't believe it. People cannot, they cannot believe that President Obama is acting the way he acts and can't even mention the words "radical Islamic terrorism." There's something going on. It's inconceivable. There's something going on. [26]

The natural course of this rhetoric is expressed by extreme Right Terry Jones, in response to the Boston Marathon bombing:

Is it an Islamic attack? It looks like it. The bombing came on Patriots Day. It has all of the earmarkings (sic) of an Islamic attack but will there again be a great coverup by the Great Satan Obama? His Administration, the people he has surrounded himself with, are all some type of closet Muslims, heavily influenced by Islam because of their background. [27]

Since patriots must respond to the war against America that they see perpetrated broadly by all Islam, it follows that it was their duty to treat the president of the United States, Barack Hussein Obama, as their enemy. Militant violence does not fall far behind such a biased, distorted view of "the other" and our tribal pressure to protect, defend, and aggress.

6.6   THE MULTI-BILLION-DOLLAR TEACHING OF JIHADIST TRIBALISM

A key question is why radical, militant tribalism remains fringe and more rhetoric than action in the U.S. and Europe, while it has resulted in violent Jihad in the Middle East and Africa. As in many things, both mundane and pernicious, the answer in large part is "funding" and the semi-official support that underlies that funding. American extremism is actively fought by the FBI and the Bureau of Alcohol, Tobacco, Firearms and Explosives (ATF), as well as private organizations like the anti-Defamation League and the Southern Poverty Law Center. In contrast, Wahhabism and Jihadist movements are supported and substantively funded in the billions of dollars, principally through the wealth of Saudi Arabia.

Strict Wahhabism, and its outgrowth of radical and messianic Jihad, have been financed with a staggering investment of as much as $100 billion. Investment has also come from Qatar, Kuwait, and the United Arab Emirates, but most funding has emanated from Saudi Arabia. Although not orchestrated officially by the Kingdom of Saudi Arabia, the wealth of many of the Saudi princes has gone into this funded spread of Wahhabism and it is clearly coordinated at some level with the Saudi government, or at least influenced by government pressure.

The main mechanisms for the spread of Wahhabism have been the funding of extremist madrassas (religious schools), mainly in poor Muslim countries, and the funding of mosques and Imams (religious leaders) in wealthier nations. To some extent the extremist rhetoric and teachings of the madrassas was toned down following the attacks of September 11, but reports indicate that they largely remain radicalized and extremist in nature. Moreover, the extremist hate teaching at many of these pre-September 11 madrassas set a movement in motion that was world-wide and a powerful tsunami of influence.

For many poor children, the madrassas were the only form of education and parents were left with the choice of no education or extremist indoctrination. In this way, Saudi Arabia spread its Wahhabist message to Pakistan, Indonesia, the Philippines, Malaysia, Thailand, India, and Africa. It was not unusual for children graduating from the madrassas to be channeled to terrorist training camps, and certainly the teachings of the madrassas prepared them well for this next step.

The House of Saud works against the best interests of the West and the Muslim world. Muslim communities worldwide certainly need to eradicate fanatical Wahhabism from their midst, but this will be difficult, if not impossible, to accomplish if the West continues its support of the House of Saud. The monarchy must be modernized and modified—or simply uprooted and replaced. The House of Saud needs a thorough house cleaning. [28]

Nor is this the thinking of anti-Islamic radicals from the West. Then secretary of state Hillary Clinton wrote, *"donors in Saudi Arabia constitute the most significant source of funding to Sunni terrorist groups worldwide... More needs to be done since Saudi Arabia remains a critical financial support base for al-Qaeda, the Taliban, LeT and other terrorist groups."* [29] And it's not just the Saudis: Qatar, Kuwait, and the United Arab Emirates are also implicated in this memo from Secretary Clinton. Other cables released by WikiLeaks outline how Saudi front companies are also used to fund terrorism abroad [29].

The curriculum and books used in the madrasas are created in Saudi Arabia. Their teaching is often virulent, hate-evoking, purist, anti-Semitic and anti-Christian, and militant. It is often highly distorted historically and based more on prejudice and bias than facts. It is anti-science, sexist, and anti-West. It is anti-Muslim, outside of their own purist, fundamentalist approach to Islam.

Insight into the teaching at madrassas is provided by The Center for Religious Freedom of Freedom House which was founded by Eleanor Roosevelt and has been a vigorous proponent and watchdog for the dissemination of democratic values and a leading opponent of infringement of religious freedom and defending human rights against religious intolerance. So, it might appear strange on first blush why they would expose the Saudi dissemination of religious philosophy and teaching. Examining the content of several of the texts leaves no doubt as to the agenda of intolerance, hatred and militant tribalism spread through these schools worldwide and why they have led to a firestorm of militant hate-based radicalism.

The Saudi government has claimed that intolerant and violent material has been removed from public school textbooks. Prince Turki al-Faisla, the Saudi ambassador to the U.S., stated that "any material than can be possibly interpreted as advocating intolerance or extremism" has been eliminated [30]. Instead, Freedom House found the revised textbooks to promote an ideology of hatred that teaches bigotry and actually vilifies tolerance as sinful. The texts teach that Christians, Jews, and non-Wahhabist Muslims are in a united war against Islam and that this must end in the complete destruction of such infidels [31].

A first-grade textbook teaches:

"Every religion other than Islam is false."

- *"Fill in the blanks with the appropriate words (Islam, hellfire): Every religion other than _____ is false. Whoever dies outside of Islam enters _____."*
- *"Give examples of false religions, like Judaism, Christianity, paganism, etc."*
- *"Explain that when someone dies outside of Islam, hellfire is his fate."*

An eighth-grade text has students list the condemnable qualities of Jews and the basis for hatred of Jews as a race that it is one's duty to hate and destroy.

"The student notes some of the Jews' condemnable qualities."

- *"The student is warned against imitating the Jews and Christians' excessive veneration of righteous men."*

(continued)

(continued)
- *"The student gives examples of polytheism among members of this nation."*
- *"They are the people of the Sabbath, whose young people God turned into apes, and whose old people God turned into swine to punish them." "As cited in Ibn Abbas: The apes are Jews, the keepers of the Sabbath; while the swine are the Christian infidels of the communion of Jesus."*
   - *"God told His Prophet, Muhammad, about the Jews, who learned from parts of God's book (the Torah and the Gospels) that God alone is worthy of worship. Despite this, they espouse falsehood through idol-worship, soothsaying, and sorcery. In doing so, they obey the devil. They prefer the people of falsehood to the people of the truth out of envy and hostility. This earns them condemnation and is a warning to us not to do as they did."*
- *"The Jews lost their religion and attacked the religion of Islam, which consists of accepting the oneness of God and the worship of Him alone."*
- *"They are the Jews, whom God has cursed and with whom He is so angry that He will never again be satisfied [with them]."*

By ninth grade, militancy certainly enters the curriculum, advancing the religious requirement to hate Jews and Christians and to fight them.

"The clash between this [Muslim] community (umma) and the Jews and Christians has endured, and it will continue as long as God wills. In this hadith (narrative attributed to the prophet Muhammad) Muhammad gives us an example of the battle between the Muslims and the Jews."

- *"Narrated by Abu Hurayrah: The Prophet said, The hour [of judgment] will not come until the Muslims fight the Jews and kill them. [It will not come] until the Jew hides behind rocks and trees. [It will not come] until the rocks or the trees say, 'O Muslim! O servant of*

(continued)

144 S. E. HOBFOLL

> (continued)
> *God! There is a Jew behind me. Come and kill him.' Except for the gharqad, which is a tree of the Jews."*
> - *"It is part of God's wisdom that the struggle between the Muslim and the Jews should continue until the hour [of judgment]."*

By tenth grade, lesson plans and texts on Islamic culture and Hadith culture (narrative attributed to the prophet Muhammad) advance the "truth" of the Protocols of the Elders of Zion. The Protocols are a long-debunked faked treatise supposedly written by a world-dominating shadow Jewish group that manipulated the world. They have one of the principal tools used to foment anti-Semitism and produce fear of Jews as a powerful group intent on world domination and control of all others. They are a paranoid tribal fantasy, created to justify violent anti-Semitism and to grow children's lifelong hatred of Jews.

> *"Goals of the Zionist Movement*
>
> 1. *Instill a fighting spirit among the Jews, as well as religious and nationalist fanaticism to challenge [other] religions, nations, and peoples.*
> 2. *Establish Jewish control over the world. The starting point for this is the establishment of their government in the promised land, which stretches from the Nile to the Euphrates.*
> 3. *Incite rancor and rivalry among the great powers so that they fight one another, and kindle the fire of war among states so that all states are weakened and their state arises."*
>
> - *The Protocols of the Elders of Zion "were discovered in the 19th century. The Jews have tried to deny them, but there are many proofs of their veracity and their origin among the elders of Zion."*

Nor were these teachings promulgated only in poor Islamic nations. A network of Islamic schools and clubs in Great Britain were exposed, obtained by undercover reporters through the highly respected BBC. Texts stated that Jews "looked like monkeys and pigs," and that non-believers were condemned to "hellfire." The books and curriculum were filled with homophobic and anti-Semitic diatribes, all funded by the Saudi Embassy in London. Texts illustrated where hands and feet should be amputated as punishment for transgression [32].

It is not my thesis that global Jihadism is solely produced at the madrassas. Indeed, the terrorists who perpetrated the September 11 attacks on the World Trade Center and Pentagon were for the most part highly educated. Rather, the madrassas produce the millions that are required to support the pyramid of beliefs that support the few who will act militantly, and may provide an army of foot soldiers to carry out attacks and join ISIL and al-Qaeda in their call for Jihad in places like Syria. They are part of a labyrinth of a particular blend of radical Islamic fundamentalism that is spliced with hatred and distrust for Jews, Christians, the West, and Muslims who do not follow their doctrine. It is important to emphasize that this makes most Muslims their enemy as well.

Although earlier analyses by Peter Bergen argued that a majority of terrorists were college educated, this is no longer the case in the attacks in London in July 2005, Paris in 2016, and Nice in 2016 [33]. Instead, more recent terrorists have been more likely to be uneducated and coming from the poor disenfranchised suburban Banlieue, which are characterized by high rates of unemployment, lack of education, and hotbeds for mostly petty crime. That the movement they created has become a direct threat to the House of Saud and their kingdom is ironic, but also itself dangerous to world stability.

6.7   PICK YOUR FRIENDS, PICK YOUR BATTLES

Given the complexity of Islamic politics, historically and presently, and our penchant to like simple news and simple stories, ignoring deep background analysis, it is tempting for the U.S. and Europe to become isolationist. What I have tried to illustrate in this chapter is that radical and Messianic Islam have been present for hundreds of years, and it is the age of globalism and modern politics that have brought their threat to our homelands. Just as Israel could not entirely eradicate terrorism or the political movements that underlie and fund it, nor can we. However diminished the power of oil, it is still a powerful factor, and disruption in the Middle East threatens our way of life owing to oil, oil money, and oil politics. Clearly, we will continue to have major economic incentives to stay involved.

Whether we have a moral obligation to intercede in other's politics and ways of life is a much more complex question. It has been an American tradition to weigh in when witnessing evil. And, indeed other nations weighed into U.S. politics over the issue of slavery, and the very creation of the U.S.. In the next chapter, I will examine fundamentalist and Jihadist Islam's treatment of women and girls, which I believe challenges more than any other issue our ability to stand by as silent witnesses and not intervene.

The protection of the oil fields, the protection of the growing, nascent liberal movements in the Arab and Muslim world, and the protection of women's rights will influence our own safety. We will have to make complex decisions about such countries as Saudi Arabia and Qatar and how we support them, and whatever we decide will have violent consequences. There is no near-time path to peace in a war that has long simmered and now erupted. That extremism has led to tribal warfare and that tribalism is also alive and well in the West following a rather fallow period after World War II is inescapable. Extremist and Messianic Islam has and will bring the war of terrorism to us as we are in a global world with porous borders and in which even one individual armed with an assault rifle, a rented truck or a hijacked aircraft can murder dozens or even thousands. The extremis of our politics has taken us to a natural consequence of "defend and aggress" tribalism. If we ourselves adopt the tribalist survival tendency to draw lines as black and white, and to act by instinct instead of intellect, we will only further advance and ignite the extremist actions we are witnessing. Perhaps the next chapter's insights into inherent subjugation, violence, and oppression of women fomented by radical and Messianic Islam will force us to examine if we really have the ability to drive our heads into the sand and ignore the plights of millions.

REFERENCES

1. Hamid, S. (2016). *Islamic exceptionalism: How the struggle over Islam is reshaping the world*. New York: St. Martin's Press.
2. Kadi, W., & Shahin, A. A. (2013). Caliphate. In G. Bowering (Ed.), *The Princeton encyclopedia of Islamic political thought* (pp. 81–86). Princeton: Princeton University Press.
3. Mansour, A. S. (2002, December 16). *The roots of democracy in Islam*. Islamic Research Foundation International, Inc. Retrieved August 4, 2016, from http://www.irfi.org/articles/articles_1601_1650/roots_of_democracy_in_islam.html

4. Tignor, R., Adelman, J., Brown, P., Elman, B., Kotkin, S., Prakash, G., et al. (2011). *Worlds together, worlds apart: A history of the world: From the beginnings of humankind to the present.* New York: W.W. Norton & Company.
5. Fromkin, D. (1989). *A peace to end all peace: Creating the modern Middle East, 1914–1922.* New York: Henry Holt & Co.
6. Helmreich, P. R. (1974). *From Paris to Sèvres: The partition of the Ottoman Empire at the peace conference of 1919–1920.* Columbus: Ohio State University Press.
7. Popalzai, M. (2015, July 5). Afghanistan: Men throw acid into girls' faces 'for going to school'. *CNN.* Retrieved July 14, 2016, from http://www.cnn.com/2015/07/04/asia/afghanistan-schoolgirls-acid-attack/
8. Hagopian, A., Flaxman, A., Takaro, T., Al Shatari, S., Rajaratnam, J., Becker, S., et al. (2013). Mortality in Iraq associated with the 2003–2011 war and occupation: Findings from a national cluster sample survey by the University Collaborative Iraq Mortality Study. *PLoS Medicine, 10*(10), e1001533. https://doi.org/10.1371/journal.pmed.1001533.
9. Fox News. (2015, April 3). *Bill O'Reilly: The war on Christianity getting even worse.* Fox News. Retrieved April 10, 2017, from http://www.foxnews.com/transcript/2015/04/03/bill-oreilly-war-on-christianity-getting-even-worse.html
10. Bartal, S. (2017). Jew-hatred in the Islamic State Organization's (ISIS) ideology. *Cultural and Religious Studies, 5*(3), 165–177. https://doi.org/10.17265/2328-2177/2017.03.006.
11. Schwartz, S. S. (2003). *The two faces of Islam: Saudi fundamentalism and its role in terrorism.* New York: Doubleday.
12. Badeau, J. S. (1983). *The genius of Arab civilization: Source of renaissance.* New York: New York University Press.
13. Lyons, J. (2009). *The house of wisdom: How the Arabs transformed western civilization.* Sydney: Bloomsbury Publishing.
14. Kennedy, H. N. (2004). *The prophet and the age of the caliphates: The Islamic near east from the sixth to the eleventh century.* London: Longman.
15. Kraemer, J. L. (1989). *The history of Al-Tabari Vol. 34: Incipient decline: The caliphates of Al-Wathiq, Al-Mutawakkil, and Al-Muntasir A.D. 841–863/A.H. 227–248.* New York: State University of New York Press.
16. Vossekuil, B. (2004, July). *The final report and findings of the safe school initiative: Implications for the prevention of school attacks in the United States.* United States Secret Service and Department of Education. Retrieved April 10, 2017, from https://www2.ed.gov/admins/lead/safety/preventingattacksreport.pdf
17. Boodman, S. G. (2006, May 16). Gifted and tormented. *The Washington Post.* Retrieved October 15, 2014, from http://www.washingtonpost.com/wp-dyn/content/article/2006/05/15/AR2006051501103.html

18. Adams, L., & Russakoff, D. (1999, June 12). Dissecting Columbine's cult of the athlete. *The Washington Post.* Retrieved August 6, 2016, from http://www.washingtonpost.com/wp-srv/national/daily/june99/columbine12.htm
19. Lipka, M. (2017, August 9). Muslims and Islam: Key findings in the U.S. and around the world. *Pew Research Center.* Retrieved August 11, 2017, from http://www.pewresearch.org/fact-tank/2017/02/27/muslims-and-islam-key-findings-in-the-u-s-and-around-the-world/
20. Sprinzak, E. (1985). The Iceberg model of political extremism. In D. Newman (Ed.), *The impact of Gush Emunim—Politics and settlement in the West Bank* (pp. 27–45). Kent: Croom Helm Publishers.
21. Anti-Defamation League. (2013, April 17). Boston bombing prompts extremist conspiracy theories. *Anti-Defamation League.* Retrieved July 18, 2016, from https://www.adl.org/news/article/boston-bombing-prompts-extremist-conspiracy-theories?_ga=1.131270415.1663070028.1488844800
22. Pew Research Center. (2013, April 30). *The world's Muslims: Religion, politics and society.* Pew Research Center's Religion & Public Life Project. Retrieved July 18, 2016, from http://www.pewforum.org/2013/04/30/the-worlds-muslims-religion-politics-society-overview/
23. Michel, L., & Herbeck, D. (2001). *American terrorist: Timothy McVeigh and the Oklahoma City bombing.* New York: Harper Collins.
24. Pew Research Center. (2015, November 23). *Beyond distrust: How Americans view their government.* Pew Research Center for the People and the Press. Retrieved July 19, 2016, from http://www.people-press.org/2015/11/23/2-general-opinions-about-the-federal-government/
25. Southern Poverty Law Center. (2009, July 31). *The second wave: Return of the militias.* Southern Poverty Law Center. Retrieved July 19, 2016, from https://www.splcenter.org/20090801/second-wave-return-militias
26. Graham, D. A. (2016, June 13). Donald Trump implies Obama was involved in the Orlando shooting. *The Atlantic.* Retrieved July 18, 2016, from https://www.theatlantic.com/politics/archive/2016/06/trumps-implication-obama-was-involved-in-the-orlando-shooting/486770/
27. Anti-Defamation League. (2013, April 18). *Extremists and conspiracy theorists react to Boston Marathon terrorist attack.* Anti-Defamation League. Retrieved March 14, 2017, from https://www.adl.org/blog/extremists-and-conspiracy-theorists-react-to-boston-marathon-terrorist-attack
28. Butt, Y. (2015). How Saudi Wahhabism is the fountainhead of Islamist terrorism. *The Huffington Post.* Retrieved August 1, 2016, from http://www.huffingtonpost.com/dr-yousaf-butt-/saudi-wahhabism-islam-terrorism_b_6501916.html
29. The Guardian. (2010, December 5). US embassy cables: Hillary Clinton says Saudi Arabia 'a critical source of terrorist funding'. *The Guardian.* Retrieved August 1, 2016, from https://www.theguardian.com/world/us-embassy-cables-documents/242073

30. Saudi-US Relations Information Service. (2005, November 8). *The global scourge of terrorism*. Saudi-US Relations Information Service. Retrieved April 13, 2017, from http://susris.com/2005/11/08/the-global-scourge-of-terrorism/

31. Center for Religious Freedom. (2006). *Saudi Arabia's curriculum of intolerance*. Center for Religious Freedom. Retrieved September 11, 2017, from https://freedomhouse.org/sites/default/files/CurriculumOfIntolerance.pdf

32. Burns, J. F. (2010, November 22). Lessons of hate at some Islamic schools in Britain. *New York Times*. Retrieved August 1, 2016, from http://www.nytimes.com/2010/11/23/world/europe/23britain.html

33. Bergen, P., & Pandey, S. (2005, June 14). The madrassa myth. *New York Times*. Retrieved April 17, 2017, from http://www.nytimes.com/2005/06/14/opinion/the-madrassa-myth.html

CHAPTER 7

Tribal Enslavement of Women: Women's Bodies as a Battleground

"It is permissible to have sexual intercourse with the female captive. Allah the almighty said: '[Successful are the believers] who guard their chastity, except from their wives or (the captives and slaves) that their right hands possess, for then they are free from blame [Koran 23:5–6]'…" "If she is a virgin, he [her master] can have intercourse with her immediately after taking possession of her. However, if she isn't, her uterus must be purified [first]…" "It is permissible to buy, sell, or give as a gift female captives and slaves, for they are merely property, which can be disposed of [as long as that doesn't cause [the *Muslim* ummah] any harm or damage." "It is permissible to have intercourse with the female slave who hasn't reached puberty if she is fit for intercourse; however if she is not fit for intercourse, then it is enough to enjoy her without intercourse" *[1]*.
I abducted your girls. I will sell them in the market, by Allah. There is a market for selling humans. Allah says I should sell. He commands me to sell. I will sell women. I sell women *[2]*.

The terrorist battle is not about territory; it is about culture and who controls culture. The threat felt by al-Qaeda, ISIL, the Taliban, and even Saudi Arabia from the West and Western influence is centrally about protecting the superior status of men and their control of women. *Humans' strongest behavioral genetic build is to protect the family as it is structured in that society.* Family is more fundamental than territory, and for

© The Author(s) 2018
S. E. Hobfoll, *Tribalism*,
https://doi.org/10.1007/978-3-319-78405-2_7

men their ability to "protect" their women and children, and their "way of life" is intimately linked and even hard-wired to honor. Just as White men have reacted in the West to their sense of threat of their loss of status and power, tenfold has been the reaction of men in the Middle East, parts of Africa and Asia to the threat of what they see as a complete reversal of what they perceive as right, holy, and their duty to protect and preserve. Terrorism is a global battle for "way of life."

This chapter is about this battleground over women's rights and bodies. It will be the hardest to read and it has been the hardest to write, so sad and disturbing are the stories about the abuse of women. Our primitive tribal genetics presses behaviors and thinking associated with survival, honor, territory, and the control of women. We see this clearly as wherever tribalism and our primitive tribal genetics are pronounced, there is a war being fought against the advancement of equal gender rights whose expression is embodied in the subjugation of women. Much of this fight is being conducted with women's bodies as the battleground. The consequence of this at its extremes involves women's treatment as chattel, enslavement, rape, and murder. This is often cast as an anti-Western movement, and even a movement for the "protection" of women, but the battle is most clearly depicted as an inevitable conflict between tribalism and the historical movement toward human rights.

To understand how our tribal behavioral genetics presses toward certain behaviors involving women and gender politics, we should review our understanding of behavioral genetics and underscore some key points. First and foremost, our genetics does not "force" or "determine" that men will subjugate, control, or harm women. Our behavioral genetics for some behaviors, like eating, creates enormous pressure to act in rather specific ways when humans are starving. But our tribal behavioral genetics on gender relations is on a long leash, as illustrated in the great variability in gender-linked behavior.

The Japanese enslaved an estimated 200,000–300,000 Korean, Chinese, Filipino, and some Dutch "comfort women" during World War II for sexual exploitation, repeated rape, and sexual slavery, but did not go raping women when at home in Japan. About three quarters of the "comfort women" died through beatings, physical torture, and maltreatment [3]. Tribal behavior produces certain pressures to act in certain directions, with wide variation in how these might be expressed. Our tribal genetics allows this division between "our own" and "those others," with the harshest treatment of the "other" to be made readily, and to even be institutionalized and rationalized openly. Fifty years later, one courageous woman testified before the U.S. House of Representatives on these Japanese atrocities.

The horrific memories of "opening night" of the brothel have tortured my mind all my life. ... I could hear the screaming coming from the bedrooms. I hid under the table, but was soon found. I fought him. I kicked him with all my might. The Japanese officer became very angry because I would not give myself to him. ...He then threw me on the bed and ripped off all my clothes. He ran his sword all over my naked body, and played with me as a cat would with a mouse. I still tried to fight him, but he thrust himself on top of me, pinning me down under his heavy body. The tears were streaming down my face as he raped me in a most brutal way. I thought he would never stop...I found some of the other girls. We were all crying, and in total shock. In the bathroom I tried to wash away all the dirt and the shame off my body. Just wash it away. But the night was not over yet, there were more Japanese waiting, and this went on all night, it was only the beginning, week after week, month after month... I was systematically beaten and raped day and night. Even the Japanese doctor raped me each time he visited the brothel to examine us for venereal disease. And to humiliate us even more the doors and windows were left open, so the Japanese could watch us being examined. [4]

As I have developed throughout this book, when conditions result in major material, social, and personal resource loss for the group, humans respond with increased "defend and aggress" behaviors. This is further exacerbated when the losses involve humiliation. The danger comes when our genetic tendencies interact with cultural norms and practices that degrade women [5, 6]. In societies where women have gained greater status and equity, loss and humiliation are much less likely to take the form of attempts to subjugate women or harm them through violence or rape. Unfortunately, humans have a tribal tendency to degrade and even dehumanize the "other," and this tribal tendency is reflected in a pressure to allow aggressive tendencies that are in our genetics to be unleashed when the "other" is portrayed as less human or a danger to us. The earlier examples in Chap. 3 on the internment of Japanese citizenship and their exploitation for financial gain of many who benefitted from their expulsion from communities on the West Coast of the U.S. are prime examples of our ability to slip to our more primitive selves as a society.

As such, our tribal behavioral genetics endangers women's status and their safety when conditions are ripe with loss and humiliation in societies where women are culturally viewed as inferior, are controlled by men, or even are seen as needing the "protection" of men as guardians. From an evolutionary viewpoint, we can even predict the course that this will take. Specifically, as loss of status, loss of resources, and loss of honor (humiliation) increase, the following actions against women will occur, those further down the list occurring as more perceived loss of the group is felt.

- Subjugation of women will increase.
- Domestic violence toward women will be sanctioned and seen as men's right.
- Girls and women who are seen as challenging men's status will be violently retaliated against to "preserve the social order" and "protect" women's "modesty."
- Rape will be used as a weapon of war.
- Kidnapping and enslavement of women from the "others" will occur to reconstitute the tribe.

7.1   MEN AS THE SELF-APPOINTED "GUARDIANS" OF WOMEN

Both tribal genetic and social theories of the abuse of women see a patriarchal social structure where men control women legally and socially as the fountainhead of violence toward women [7]. Clearly the actions of Boko Haram and ISIL are outside of mainstream Islam, but women are significantly and profoundly endangered as to their freedom, equality, rights to medical attention, and capacity for free movement in much of the Muslim world where Wahhabi doctrine is dominant. From its onset, Wahhabi doctrine is both territorially aggressive and highly gender stratified, with men designated as the guardians of women.

"Guardian" is legally defined as "*[a] person lawfully invested with the power, and charged with the obligation, of taking care of and managing the property and rights of a person who, because of age, understanding, or self-control, is considered incapable of administering his or her own affairs*" [8].

This is effectively the status of women in Saudi Arabia, based on a verse of the Quran that states that men are the protectors and maintainers of women. Argued as a "law of love" by some, it places the woman as somewhere between child and chattel. The requirement of a male guardian for women actually reduces them to a status less than that of a child in Western countries as it restricts movement, access to health care which most girls have rights to in at least many Western countries if pregnant, and the ability to drive.

Like slaves in the American South, women may not travel without written permission from their male guardian or a male guardian escorting her. In the pre–Civil War south, patrollers protected the pass system where slaves had to show their permission to travel from their master [9]. In Saudi Arabia special police, called Mutaween, enforce laws restricting women's movement without express written permission from their male guardian.

On March 11, 2002, fifteen girls died and 50 were injured when Saudi Mutaween prevented schoolgirls from escaping a burning school in Mecca because they were not wearing headscarves and abayas (black robes) and not being escorted by males. *"One witness said he saw three policemen beating young girls to prevent them from leaving the school because they were not wearing the abaya"*. [10]

The fight to control women is as much a part and central cause of radical, Jihadist, and Messianic Islam's fight with the West and with more liberal Islam as is the issue of control of land, government, financial power, and resources. Extremist Islam, and indeed conservative mainstream Islam, places women as second-class citizens at best and often as no more than chattel. In religion, interpretation is everything and the word of God in any of its testaments has been used for good and evil throughout history by Christian, Jews, and Muslims. But the treatment of women across much of the Muslim world is abhorrent, and despite more liberal Islamic claims that the Quran gives women equal status, the truth is often far from that and has been used as an excuse by extremists to enslave, rape, subjugate, control, and even murder women and young girls.

The use of scripture to subjugate women, often in the name of protecting them, is evidenced in each of the world's major religions. Even today in Israel, the Orthodox Jewish court that controls divorce makes granting of divorce a men's prerogative alone, as can be seen in this newspaper article. Women are locked in marriage until her husband grants a divorce.

JERUSALEM—After four years of marriage, Tamar Tessler filed for divorce, taking her infant daughter and embarking on what she hoped would be a new chapter of her life. Today that daughter is 36 years old—and Tessler is still awaiting the divorce. Her husband long ago moved to America, said the 61-year-old retired nurse. But under Israeli law, she remains trapped in a defunct marriage that her husband won't allow to end. She can't legally remarry, was obligated as his spouse to repay some of his debts, and lost out on tax breaks for single mothers even though she raised their daughter alone.

Tessler is one of hundreds, perhaps thousands, of Israeli women caught in legal and social limbo because of a law that leaves matters of divorce for all Jewish citizens in the hands of a government-funded religious court. The court, consisting of a panel of rabbis, bases its decisions on the customs of Orthodox Judaism. The rulings apply to all Jewish Israelis, whether they are Orthodox, Conservative or Reform, observant or secular. [11]

Our tribal genetics and its evolutionary demands place men, and in particular the ascendant alpha male, as jealously controlling women. Paternity is always suspect, as until modern medical testing there was no way to identify the true father. Men, through their strength, controlled the tribe, and the ascendant male controlled other males. This made women and children dependent on the powerful male for resources and protection.

While other aspects of Israeli society give women equal status, including a female prime minister nearly 50 years ago, and Western and much of Asian society has granted women equal status in law, if not in practice, the same is not the case for much of the Muslim world, as well as some non-Muslim parts of Africa.

For highly traditional Wahhabi society in particular, the global movement for women's rights is a violent assault against their most deeply held convictions. For their world, women are not in the public place, and are under their men's power and control in both a lifestyle and strict legal sense of the word. To preserve this division between men and women is to preserve all that is holy, right, and essential, and they must resist the Western assault on their honor, their family's integrity, and their women's virtue. Women may be praised, adored, beaten, or admonished at their husband's discretion, although the Quran advises men to "punish their wives judiciously" and instructs them to show kindness. They have greater latitude and power over their wives than Western law allows power over children, as domestic abuse is largely both tolerated and protected, whether or not it is lawful. The Quran clearly promotes protection and kindness toward women in dozens, if not hundreds, of verses:

O you who have believed, it is not lawful for you to inherit women by compulsion. And do not make difficulties for them in order to take [back] part of what you gave them unless they commit a clear immorality. And live with them in kindness. For if you dislike them – perhaps you dislike a thing and Allah makes therein much good. (Quran 4:19)

But tradition and practice are inconsistent with this as attested by multiple human rights reports that place the status of women more in line with these Quranic texts:

Men are in charge of women by [right of] what Allah has given one over the other and what they spend [for maintenance] from their wealth. So righteous women are devoutly obedient, guarding in [the husband's] absence what Allah would have them guard. But those [wives] from whom you fear arrogance - [first] advise them; [then if they persist], forsake them in bed; and [finally], strike them. But if they obey you [once more], seek no means against them. Indeed, Allah is ever Exalted and Grand. (Quran 4:34])

Your wives are as fields for you. You may enter your fields from any place you want. Reserve something good for your souls (for the life hereafter). Have fear of God and know that you are going to meet Him. (Muhammad) give the glad news to the believers. (Quran 2:223)

The supposed protection of women in many of these societies is shown for its truth in the dangers that women undergo in such regions. In Pakistan more than 1000 women are murdered in honor killings every year and 90 percent of women are victims of domestic violence in Pakistan. In Afghanistan, women have the greatest health care risks, exposure to domestic violence, economic discrimination, and in many places the greatest inability to attend school of any country in the world, which has hardly changed in the post-Taliban era. This of course extends to other tribal-dominated instances that are not Islamic. Sexual violence in the Congo makes it the most dangerous country for exposure to sexual violence. Not only was rape used as a weapon of war in the mostly Christian Congo, nearly one in four women are victims of sexual violence at the hands of their husbands or partners [12, 13].

To "protect" women and society, a particularly heinous outgrowth of tribalism practices female genital mutilation. As much regional as religious, female genital mutilation is widespread in Gambia, Somalia, Sudan, Indonesia, Malaysia, Mali, Eritrea, Guinea, and Egypt. A U.N. report indicates women's genital mutilation in 29 countries and estimates 125 million women having been genitally mutilated [14]. Women are genitally mutilated, by partial to full removal of the external female genitalia, typically between the ages of 4 and 11 to "protect" them from their "insatiable sexuality" and to ensure women's virginity before marriage and fidelity after marriage [15].

7.2   CONTROL OF WOMEN AND ITS VIOLENT CONSEQUENCES

There are only a handful of well-conducted studies on domestic violence in the Middle East. In a large-scale study in 2002, Natalia Linos and her colleagues found that among over 5000 women in a representative sample of Jordanian women, about 87 percent believed that wife beating was justified in some circumstances [16]. Prevalence of intimate partner violence in Jordan is also widespread. Answering the World Health Organization's domestic violence questionnaire, psychological violence was reported by 73 percent, physical violence by 31 percent, and sexual violence by 19 percent in a sample of 517 Jordanian women [17]. Likewise, a majority (over 60 percent) of a large group of both Palestinian men and women supported wife beating in some situations. The situations in which men and women felt wife beating was justified are listed in Fig. 7.1, and they include "talks back," "behaves in a way he dislikes," and "disobeys husband" [18].

In studies in Pakistan, only 3 percent of women attending a health clinic did NOT report domestic violence in their marriage. Most women reported multiple instances of domestic violence and 25 percent said violence increased when they became pregnant. Nonconsensual sex was

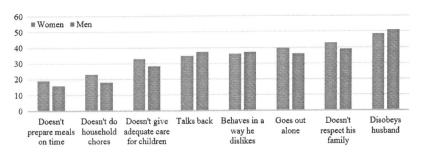

Fig. 7.1   Support for wife beating among married Palestinian refugees. (Adapted from Khawaja et al. [18])

reported by nearly half (47 percent) of women [19]. As in studies elsewhere in the Muslim world, the lead reasons for domestic violence were not caring properly for the husband's family, visiting their own family and friends without husband's permission, being disobedient to the husband, and not having a son [20].

7.3   WOMEN'S EDUCATION AS A DANGER TO MEN'S ASCENDENCY

An educated woman is a dangerous woman in much of the world where tribalism dominates.

> Kabul, Afghanistan (CNN) Attackers on a motorbike threw acid in the faces of three teenage girls on their way to school in Afghanistan's western Herat province on Saturday...The girls, age 16 to 18, are students at one of the biggest girls' schools in Herat city, the provincial capital...Two of the girls were in critical condition after the acid was thrown in their faces... "This is the punishment for going to school," the men told the girls after pouring the acid on them. [21]

> *KANDAHAR, Afghanistan—No students showed up at Mirwais Mena girls' school in the Taliban's spiritual birthplace the morning after it happened. A day earlier, men on motorcycles attacked 15 girls and teachers with acid. The men squirted the acid from water bottles onto three groups of students and teachers walking to school Wednesday, principal Mehmood Qaderi said. Some of the girls have burns only on their school uniforms but others will have scars on their faces. One teenager still cannot open her eyes after being hit in the face with acid.*
> *... multiple teams of assailants [were involved] because the attacks took place at the same time in different neighborhoods*
> *....Arsonists have repeatedly attacked girls' schools and gunmen killed two students walking outside a girls' school in central Logar province last year. UNICEF says there were 236 school-related attacks in Afghanistan in 2007.* [22]

The Taliban's view of women's education was shaped by several principles that combined to their denial of women's education, advancing men's control and power. First, they claimed that all education had become Westernized due to colonial influence, which would give girls thoughts beyond the household. Second, they banned women from the public sphere. Their interpretation on Islamic teaching, not inconsistent with

Saudi Arabia's policies, was that the public sphere is the man's sphere, and the woman's sphere is the home. Schools also lead to mixing, as even if the school is segregated, how can a girl get there without mixing in public? This paralleled banning women from working and even appearing unaccompanied by a male in public. In all this we see the need to protect women's honor, the distrust of women from having sexual contact with men when not married and if not married with other men, and the promulgation of a strong Islamic household, consistent with patriarchal rule.

7.3.1   Rape as a Weapon of War as a Tribal Act

It would be wrong to frame the rape of women as a weapon of war that is particular to extremist Muslim Jihadists, as it has been common around the world where our more primitive selves are expressed where resource loss and threat are high or resource aggression is high. In the Mexican drug wars, for example, women are often kidnapped, raped, and displayed in a disemboweled state to illustrate the proof of cartel dominance in a region. In Columbia, rival gangs have been reported to rape, mutilate, and murder girls and women in order to display their tribal control over towns and villages. The kidnapping and raping of women of rival gangs in Mexico and Columbia are used to intimidate the local population and make clear the claim of dominance. Women's bodies become the symbol of a conquered territory [23, 24].

Rape has been used as a weapon of war for both strategic and opportunistic reasons. Rape is used to take control of women and claim their offspring to revitalize the conquering tribe. It is used to make women impure and of no use to their own people, as tribal cultures often reject women who have been defiled, even murdering them. It is symbolic as it displays control on the deepest levels of human evolutionary drive, the control of others' ability to protect its women and children.

Systematic rape as a strategic weapon of war was widespread in Bosnia, the Bangladeshi battle for independence in 1971, Japanese rapes during the 1937 occupation of Nanking, and in the Republic of Congo. As Brownmiller stated, rape is both an attack on women as women and an attack on the enemy. It "is a message passed between men—vivid proof of victory for one and loss and defeat for the other" [25].

The Rwandan Civil War and genocide is known as one of the most horrific and rapid sequences of genocide in world history. Fought between forces of the government of Rwanda under President Juvénal Habyarimana and the Rwandan Patriotic Front, the war was essentially a battle between Tutsi and more Hutu peoples. During a period of only 100 days in mid-July 1994, members of the Hutu majority government slaughtered an estimated 500,000–1 million Tutsi Rwandans.

The horrors of the Rwandan genocide were particularly sexualized, or perhaps more appropriately said, used sexual violence as a weapon of power. As estimated half a million women were raped. Mass rapes were perpetrated by the Hutu militia, *Interahamwe*, and members of the civilian population who they rallied to carry out these atrocities. The sexual violence was strategically organized and messaged through print and radio directing the use of rape against the Tutsi people. Rape squads were formed with men known to be infected with AIDS with the intent to spread disease among the Tutsi population [26]. Hutu women, as well as men, participated in the rapes, including Hutu women leaders who were later convicted among those who promoted rape as a weapon of genocide. Other atrocities, including genital mutilation with machetes, knives, boiling water, and acid, were common. Women were held as sex slaves for weeks. Young girls were not spared. The rape was so widespread that it is estimated that every female survivor of adolescence or older had been raped.

The justification for the rapes followed the pattern of asserting loss and humiliation and the retrieval of honor. Propaganda was used to argue that Tutsi women dominated employment, were hiding the enemy and using their beauty to sexually seduce and undermine the Hutu. In another twist, propaganda shamed Hutu men, telling them that Tutsi women saw them as inferior. Such thinly veiled propaganda was an excuse to demoralize and destroy the Tutsi women and their people from the time of the rape forward. Their children would be tainted, their status as women stigmatized, and their bodies diseased and deformed [27–29].

Whether in Rwanda, the Congo, or Bosnia, rape is used following deep tribal patterns to destabilize the enemy and to pay this harm forward for generations. Women who are raped are stigmatized and their children are tainted. Returning female survivors are viewed as dishonored and often socially rejected by their husbands, families and communities. The rapes also normalize the more generalized social structure of male dominance in such societies, just as it is an outgrowth of cultures that reflect strong male dominance and women's low status. In an account of the Congo:

Soldiers raped women to mark their territory, to destroy family bonds (women were often ostracized from their families once they were raped), and to show their power and intimidate civilians. They gang-raped women—they used their weapons to tear them apart, causing internal tears resulting in fistula—and they forced the families of the victims to watch gang rapes in progress. [30]

7.4   TRIBAL REPLENISHMENT AND THE DOMINATION BY MALE WARRIORS

There is both clear anthropological evidence and cultural narrative on the forceful abduction and rape of women where the tribe seeks to replenish itself. Our evolutionary history found tribes in situations where there was a shortage of females. This could occur due to disease, death in childbirth, attacks by other tribes, or mere shortage of female births. Polygamy, where practiced, also resulted in a shortage of women. There is enormous genetic pressure for the tribe to reproduce, as it is the essential element of survival of the fittest, and this pressure is represented in an evolutionary history of female abduction for building the tribe. The legend of the rape of the Sabine women is traditionally dated to 750 BCE. It is the story of the first Roman men abducting and raping women from the local Sabine tribes.

Anthropologically, it was common for tribes to kidnap or take hostage nubile women. Indeed, such practices have been documented among several prehistoric people [31]. Neolithic period excavations of slain tribes show an absence of adult females, suggesting that they were abducted. One of the eight forms of Hindu marriage in the Sanskrit literature is the violent seizure of girls after the defeat or killing of her relatives. In the Hebrew *Book of Judges*, when the Tribe of Benjamin was threatened with extinction they slaughtered the men and non-virgin women of a nearby town and took the virgin women as wives. The Goths abducted Christian women to be their wives in the third century. In the Balkan region where Muslims and Christians interfaced during Ottoman rule, abduction of women was common for both sides [32–34].

When you go out to war among your enemies…and you see among the captives a beautiful woman, and you desire to take her…you may go in to her and be her husband…But you shall not sell her for money, nor shall you treat her as a slave, since you have humiliated her. (Deuteronomy: 21:10–14) And

Said Moses, " all the young girls who have not known man by lying with him keep alive for yourselves…" (Numbers: 31)

In this manner, "The defending tribe was attempting not only to protect their territory and their lives, their battle was pitched 'to protect their sexual rights to their wives as well as to protect the sexual integrity of their tribe or ethnic group'" [35].

Ala kachuu, bridal kidnapping, is still common in Kyrgyzstan in Central Asia, a country that has long been dominated by independent tribes and clans. Typically, young men, aided by their families, abduct a woman and the man's female relatives "convince" her to accept the marriage. Studies by Kleinbach Salimjanova found that about half of all Kyrgyz marriages include bridal abduction, and of those, he estimated that two-thirds were nonconsensual [36].

This alteration of the subjugation and harming of women as having a holy religious core that is both ordained and blessed becomes a central, defining aspect of the tribal manifestations that we see in the extremist, militant Islamic movements associated with Wahhabism.

The day was much like any other. For the young Afghan mother, the only difference was that her child was feverish and had been for some time and needed to see a doctor. But simple tasks in Taliban-controlled Afghanistan today are not that easy. The mother was alone and the doctor was across town. She had no male relative to escort her. To ask another man to do so would be to risk severe punishment. To go on her own meant that she would risk flogging.

Because she loved her child, she had no choice. Donning the tent-like burqa as Taliban law required, she set out, cradling her child in her arms. She shouldn't have. As they approached the market, she was spotted by a teenage Taliban guard who tried to stop her. Intent on saving her child, the mother ignored him, hoping that he would ignore her. He didn't. Instead he raised his weapon and shot her repeatedly. Both mother and child fell to the ground. They survived because bystanders in the market intervened to save them. The young Taliban guard was 11, and unrepentant—fully supported by the regime. The woman should not have been out alone.

[*The Taliban's war against women.*] [37]

A young Yazidi woman named Nadia told her story at the hands of ISIL [38]. The ISIL fighters separated the men from the women, and subsequently killed 312, including 6 of Nadia's brothers and stepbrothers.

Nadia was separated by the ISIL fighters along with other young and attractive women. Later mass graves were found with elderly women who were deemed too old to be attractive. Taken with other young women to the city of Mosul, the chosen attractive young women were distributed among the fighters. "They gave us to them," Nadia says. She recounted that women would try to make themselves appear unattractive, but to no avail. "It did not help because in the mornings they would ask us again to wash our face and look pretty." [38]

In the house where she was taken, Nadia saw "[t]here was blood and there were fingerprints of hands with the blood on the walls," where she believed other women had killed themselves.

> Every morning in Mosul, the women would be required to wash. Then, Nadia says, they would be taken to the Shari'a court, where they would be photographed. The photographs would be posted on a wall in the court, along with the phone number of whichever militant or commander currently owned each woman, so that fighters could swap women among themselves. [38]

Nadia escaped at one point, only to be captured again. "That night, he beat me up, forced to undress, and put me in a room with six militants... They continued to commit crimes to my body until I became unconscious" [38].

Nadia felt none of her captors displayed regret or remorse. When a fighter was asked whether Nadia was his wife, she said he replied exuberantly. "'This is not my wife, she is my *sabia*, she is my slave,'" Nadia recalls. "And then he fired shots in the sky, as a sign of happiness" [38].

7.5   THE TRIBE DOMINATES BY ETHNIC CLEANSING

An ultimate use of rape in war is to conduct ethnic cleansing. The book of Exodus tells us that seeing the Hebrew population as a threat, the Pharaoh ordered the Hebrew's male children killed, so that the female children could be married to Egyptian men.

> *Now there arose a new king over Egypt, who knew not Joseph. And he said unto his people: 'Behold, the people of the children of Israel are too many and too mighty for us; come, let us deal wisely with them, lest they multiply, and it come to pass, that, when there befalleth us any war, they also join themselves unto our enemies, and fight against us, and get them up out of the land.'...And the king of Egypt spoke to the Hebrew midwives, of whom the name of the one was Shiphrah, and the name of the other Puah; 1and he said: 'When ye do the office*

of a midwife to the Hebrew women, ye shall look upon the birthstool: if it be a son, then ye shall kill him; but if it be a daughter, then she shall live' (Exodus 1:9–17). [39]

Tribal genetics drives humans to spread their seed and to overwhelm the seed of the "other." Although men from all ethnic groups committed rape during the Bosnian War, rapes were overwhelmingly perpetrated by Bosnian Serb forces of the Army of the Republic by Serb paramilitary units. The strategy was intended to advance ethnic cleansing of Muslim Bosnians. With the rapes, the Serbs aimed to impregnate the Muslim women and to drive their communities from the territory as a consequence of the humiliation and degradation. Rapes have been estimated at between 20,000 and 50,000. Serb forces established rape camps, where women were repeatedly raped until pregnant. Gang rapes were often public events, with families and villages made to watch the atrocities. Kidnapping, prolonged sexual slavery, and murder following rape were commonplace [40, 41].

A woman whose testimony goes by the name of B. told this account. It dispels the myth that only uneducated men participated in the atrocities.

I recognized many of them. [They were] Colleagues, doctors with whom I worked. The first [man] who raped me was a Serbian doctor named Jodi. I had known Jodi for ten years. We worked in the same hospital. I would see him every day in the employees' cafeteria. We spoke generally, "Hi, how are you." He was a very polite, nice man. Another doctor whom I had previously known also raped me; [his name was Obrad F. . . . I wasn't allowed to say anything. Before he raped me he said, "Now you know who we are. You will remember forever." I was so surprised; he was a doctor!

Once I saw the face of a woman I knew; her daughter was with her. Three men were with them inside [the classroom]. I was brought in by one man, and another four men followed. On that occasion, I was raped with a gun by one of the three men already in the room. I didn't recognize him. Others stood watching. Some spat on us. They were raping me, the mother and her daughter at the same time. Sometimes you had to accept ten men, sometimes three. Sometimes when they were away, they wouldn't call me for one or two days. I wanted nothing, not bread, not water, just to be alone. I felt I wanted to die. [40]

7.5.1   Too Terrible for Words

To share such stories of atrocities targeted so clearly at women is as difficult to write as it is to read. This difficulty may also have resulted in a kind of censorship where we know of the atrocities, but not of the details.

Indeed, even the subjugation of women in places like Saudi Arabia, Pakistan, and Afghanistan may be uncomfortable in the telling, because we partner with these nations and so partner with this subjugation. To clarify my thesis, I believe that the subjugation and control of women is a fundamental element in Jihad and Islamic extremist terrorism. Control of women is a fundamental aspect of tribal genetics. We are not forced to subjugate women any more than our genetics forces us to be violent or live in a given nuclear family structure. But our genetics presses us into certain directions, and when cultural norms have enforced these social structures, they deeply resonate with our tribal behavioral genetics. The war against the West and against Westernization is more a war for the control of women than it is a war for any other purpose. It is fundamental to Jihadist terrorism, and quite separate from the terrorism that emanates from liberation movements. It is not Islam, but it is fundamental to a sizable element of Islam, making it a fight among Muslims as well as a fight between East and West.

REFERENCES

1. Botelho, G. (2014, December 13). ISIS: Enslaving, having sex with 'unbelieving' women, girls is OK. *CNN*. Retrieved December 13, 2016, from http://www.cnn.com/2014/12/12/world/meast/isis-justification-female-slaves/
2. Abubakar, A., & Levs, J. (2014, May 6). "I will sell them," Boko Haram leader says of kidnapped Nigerian girls. *CNN*. Retrieved September 12, 2017, from http://www.cnn.com/2014/05/05/world/africa/nigeria-abducted-girls/
3. Hicks, G. L. (1997). *The comfort women: Japan's brutal regime of enforced prostitution in the second world war*. New York: W.W. Norton.
4. O'Herne, J. (2007, February 15). *Hearing on protecting the human rights of 'comfort women'*. Retrieved September 8, 2016, from https://web.archive.org/web/20070228195049/http:/foreignaffairs.house.gov/110/ohe021507.htm
5. Otterbein, K. (1993). A cross-cultural study of rape. In K. Otterbein (Ed.), *Feuding and warfare: Selected works of Keith F. Otterbein (War and society)* (pp. 119–132). New York: Gordon and Breach.
6. Sanday, P. R. (1981). The socio-cultural context of rape: A cross-cultural study. *Journal of Social Issues, 37*(4), 5–27. https://doi.org/10.1111/j.1540-4560.1981.tb01068.x.
7. Kalra, G., & Bhugra, D. (2013). Sexual violence against women: Understanding cross-cultural intersections. *Indian Journal of Psychiatry, 55*(3), 244–249. https://doi.org/10.4103/0019-5545.117139.

8. Gale, T., & Lehman, J. (2008). *West's encyclopedia of American law*. Detroit: The Gale Group.
9. Berkin, C., Miller, C., Cherny, R., & Gormly, J. (2008). *Making America: A history of the United States*. Boston: Cengage Learning.
10. BBC News. (2002, March 15). Saudi police 'stopped' fire rescue. *BBC News*. Retrieved September 8, 2016, from http://news.bbc.co.uk/2/hi/middle_east/1874471.stm
11. Sanders, E. (2013, July 26). Israel divorce law traps women in marriages that died long ago. *Los Angeles Times*. Retrieved August 10, 2016, from http://www.latimes.com/world/middleeast/la-fg-israel-divorce-problems-20130726-story.html
12. Peterman, A., Palermo, T., & Bredenkamp, C. (2011). Estimates and determinants of sexual violence against women in the Democratic Republic of Congo. *American Journal of Public Health, 101*(6), 1060–1067. https://doi.org/10.2105/ajph.2010.30007.
13. Zirulnick, A. (2011, June 16). The five most dangerous countries for women. *The Christian Science Monitor*. Retrieved September 12, 2017, from http://www.csmonitor.com/World/Global-Issues/2011/0616/The-five-most-dangerous-countries-for-women/Somalia
14. UNICEF. (2013). *Female genital mutilation/cutting: A statistical overview and exploration of the dynamics of change*. New York: UNICEF.
15. United Nations Population Fund. (2017, January). *Female genital mutilation (FGM) frequently asked questions*. United Nations Population Fund. Retrieved September 12, 2017, from http://www.unfpa.org/resources/female-genital-mutilation-fgm-frequently-asked-questions#why
16. Linos, N., Khawaja, M., & Al-Nsour, M. (2010). Women's autonomy and support for wife beating: Findings from a population-based survey in Jordan. *Violence and Victims, 25*(3), 409–419. https://doi.org/10.1891/0886-6708.25.3.409.
17. Clark, C. J., Bloom, D. E., Hill, A. G., & Silverman, J. G. (2009). Prevalence estimate of intimate partner violence in Jordan. *Eastern Mediterranean Health Journal, 15*(4), 880–889.
18. Khawaja, M., Linos, N., & El-Roueiheb, Z. (2007). Attitudes of men and women towards wife beating: Findings from Palestinian refugee camps in Jordan. *Journal of Family Violence, 23*(3), 211–218. https://doi.org/10.1007/s10896-007-9146-3.
19. Shaikh, M. (2017). Is domestic violence endemic in Pakistan: Perspective from Pakistani wives. *Pakistan Journal of Medical Sciences, 19*(1), 23–28.
20. Ali, P. A., Naylor, P. B., Croot, E., & O'Cathain, A. (2015). Intimate partner violence in Pakistan: A systematic review. *Trauma, Violence, & Abuse, 16*(3), 299–315. https://doi.org/10.1177/1524838014526065.

21. Popalzai, M. (2015, July 5). Afghanistan: Men throw acid into school girls' faces for 'going to school'. *CNN*. Retrieved September 12, 2017, from http://www.cnn.com/2015/07/04/asia/afghanistan-schoolgirls-acid-attack/

22. Fox News. (2008, November 14). Taliban blamed for acid attack on Afghan schoolgirls. *Fox News*. Retrieved May 8, 2017, from http://www.foxnews.com/story/2008/11/14/taliban-blamed-for-acid-attack-on-afghan-schoolgirls.html

23. Rama, A., & Diaz, L. (2014, March 7). Violence against women 'pandemic' in Mexico. *Reuters*. Retrieved September 12, 2017, from http://www.reuters.com/article/us-mexico-violence-women-idUSBREA2608F20140307

24. Smith-Spark, L. (2004). How did rape become a weapon of war? *BBC News*. Retrieved August 11, 2016, from http://news.bbc.co.uk/2/hi/4078677.stm

25. Brownmiller, S. (1975). *Against our will: Men, women and rape*. New York: Simon and Schuster.

26. Elbe, S. (2002). HIV/AIDS and the changing landscape of war in Africa. *International Security, 27*(2), 159–177. https://doi.org/10.1162/016228802760987851.

27. Aginam, O. (2012, June 27). *Rape and HIV as weapons of war*. United Nations University. Retrieved August 16, 2016, from https://unu.edu/publications/articles/rape-and-hiv-as-weapons-of-war.html

28. Nowrojee, B. (1996, September). Shattered lives: Sexual violence during the Rwandan genocide and its aftermath. *Human Rights Watch*. Retrieved August 16, 2016, from https://www.hrw.org/reports/1996/Rwanda.htm

29. Buss, D. E. (2009). Rethinking 'rape as a weapon of war'. *Feminist Legal Studies, 17*(2), 145–163.

30. Addario, L. (2012, February 7). *What it's like to cover 'unbearable' stories of rape in Congo*. Women's Media Center. Retrieved August 16, 2016, from http://www.womenundersiegeproject.org/blog/entry/what-its-like-to-cover-the-unbearable-stories-of-rape-in-congo

31. Keeley, L. (1996). *War before civilization: The myth of the peaceful savage*. Oxford: Oxford University Press.

32. Eisenhauer, U. (1999). Kulturwandel als Innovationsprozeß: Die fünf großen "W" und die Verbreitung des Mittelneolithikums in Südwestdeutschland. *Archäologische Informationen, 22*(2), 215–239.

33. Barnes, R. (1999). Marriage by capture. *Journal of the Royal Anthropological Institute, 5*(1), 57–73.

34. Simek, R. (2003). *Religion Und Mythologie Der Germanen*. Darmstadt: Wissenschaftliche Buchgesellschaft.

35. Kern, P. (1999). *Ancient siege warfare*. Bloomington: Indiana University Press.

36. Kleinbach, R., & Salimjanova, L. (2007). Kyz ala kachuu and adat: Non-consensual bride kidnapping and tradition in Kyrgyzstan. *Central Asian Survey*, 26(2), 217–233. https://doi.org/10.1080/02634930701517466.
37. Bureau of Democracy, Human Rights and Labor. (2001, November 17). *The Taliban's war against women*. Bureau of Democracy, Human Rights and Labor. Retrieved August 10, 2016, from https://2001-2009.state.gov/g/drl/rls/6185.htm
38. Alter, C. (2015, December 20). A Yezidi woman who escaped ISIS slavery tells her story. *TIME*. Retrieved September 12, 2017, from http://time.com/4152127/isis-yezidi-woman-slavery-united-nations/
39. JPS Tanakh 1917. (n.d.). Exodus 1. *Bible Hub*. Retrieved September 12, 2017, from http://biblehub.com/jps/exodus/1.htm
40. Human Rights Watch Women's Rights Project. (1995). *The Human Rights Watch global report on women's human rights*. Human Rights Watch Women's Rights Project. Retrieved September 12, 2017, from https://www.hrw.org/sites/default/files/reports/general958.pdf
41. Allen, B. (1996). *Rape warfare*. Minneapolis: University of Minnesota Press.

CHAPTER 8

Barricade and Throw Grenades: The Entrenchment of Tribalism and Fear Politics

Those who would give up essential Liberty, to purchase a little temporary Safety, deserve neither Liberty nor Safety.
Benjamin Franklin [1]

If we look at the way tribalism supersedes reason, we might not have predicted Donald Trump to win the presidency in 2016, but we would have fully understood the energy and power behind his campaign and its messaging. The ingredients were all there and he was astute to observe them and highlight them repetitively. Threat from terrorism, both abroad and at home, has been a repeated, shocking element of the news, and terrorism works by having a vastly disproportionate perceived impact than it does an actual impact. Scenes from the Orlando nightclub and the San Bernardino massacres by radicalized Muslims in the U.S. were still fresh in people's minds. The series of Paris and Nice attacks witnessed hundreds brutally murdered as they went about their daily lives, indeed cut down in the midst of joy and celebration at parades and Friday night festivities. Twenty four-hour news and the endlessly streaming internet displayed the blood, gore, and terror in repetitive detail on news channels and the internet. Once again the attacks were perpetrated by radicalized Muslims, living in the West in plain sight, creating an unsettling unpredictability and the reality that we and our children are all vulnerable. The impotence of the police and secret services was constantly underscored, playing into people's sense of defenselessness.

© The Author(s) 2018
S. E. Hobfoll, *Tribalism*,
https://doi.org/10.1007/978-3-319-78405-2_8

171

The Great Recession's fires of doom and gloom further stoked people's fragile grasp on their homes and feeding their families, and to do so with pride in their work. Economic threats, still stinging from the Great Recession and the ongoing Rust Belt's decades-long slow bleed of American industry, were issues on a low boil that created a sea of anxiety for millions of Americans who felt unheard and left behind and ignored by politicians as insignificant. Both Democrats and Republicans were rightly seen as ignoring that 49 million Americans (figures from 2012) live in food-insecure households [2]. A home is a symbol of protection, pride, and security, representing the most basic of humans' evolutionary needs. And millions of Americans were shaken by a recession that saw the loss of over 9 million homes that were foreclosed, surrendered to their lender, or sold in distress [3]. Even those who held on to their homes felt threatened as they watched their neighbors go "under water."

The ever-increasing lopsided distribution of wealth, held more than ever by a small percent of the population, was sounded from the candidates' bully pulpits. In an unprecedented alteration of how American wealth is distributed, 95 percent of the gains since 2009 went to just 1 percent of the top earners [4]. The continued gains by the wealthiest few was a further threat which could only mean that the working and middle class's future would be more bleak, and it was a powerful thread in both Trump's and Bernie Sander's messaging on the two ends of the political spectrum.

The widening wealth gap is undoubtedly the product of a rigged system created through lobbying and systems that favor the powerful. No matter that Trump was a "rigging the system" poster child through his own lobbying, tax evasion, manipulation of bankruptcy law, failure to pay workers, loophole zoning efforts, and bullying use of his wealth, his message was crystal clear.

Tribalism is evoked by threat, and existential threat, terrorist and economic, will be combated powerfully when it looms. With great insight, Trump recognized the depth of many White working-class Americans' fears, so profound that they have been connected to an epidemic of suicides and deaths related to drugs and alcohol abuse. Indeed the Princeton economists Anne Case and her Nobel Prize–winning husband Angus Deaton found that the mortality rate for Whites 45–54 years of age with no more than a high school education increased by 134 deaths per 100,000 from 1999 to 2014 [5]. Deaton noted that only HIV/AIDS has had a comparable impact on death rates in modern times. Further putting this in perspective, this means that 45- to 54-year-old Whites are committing suicide at an appreciably higher rate (in fact 63 percent higher) than active-duty Army soldiers, whose own rise in suicide rates are deeply alarming (23.8 per 100,000 for Army in year 2014 vs. 38.8 for high school or less for Whites in this age group) [6]. I attended a national think tank addressing military suicides at Walter Reed Army Institute of Research in 2015, and the same sense of financial insecurity, and its attendant fears of loss of home, food, and self-respect, was believed by the attending experts to be the central factor for our troops' suicide risk.

Underneath the striking figures for suicide and death from drugs and alcohol were already identified marked increases in mental and physical health declines for Americans as a product of the Great Recession. As suicide and drug-related deaths are still rare events, we must look deeper beneath this tip of the iceberg where we find widespread mental and physical pain and suffering reported by less-educated American Whites [5]. For all other groups, the rates of suicide and drug overdose are improving—suggesting hope even while these others are also under duress. It is no coincidence that working-class, not-so-young Whites were precisely the group most fervently responding to Trump's message.

8.1   People Respond Fervently to Threat of Loss of Culture and Their Way of Life

Tribes, as I have developed, are equally tied to their culture and way of life as they are to material aspects of shelter and sustenance, and recent rapid social change profoundly threatens conservative and working-class Whites, and evangelical Whites in particular. To underscore this point, if one's culture dies, one's tribe has died. Same-sex marriage, unchecked abortions, and bathrooms that anyone can enter were seen as attacks on White, Christian values. And the constant reminder in the news, the knowledge that Whites in the U.S. will be in the minority in the near future, could only mean that White, American, conservative values would be washed away and overtaken in a way that meant death to White, American culture. Liberals (I among them) celebrated the tolling of these death bells for White majority America, which the election was seen as foretelling with the inevitable increase in the proportion of people of color to a near-time majority. I use the term "death" as that is how it is perceived and that is how our tribal genetics respond.

Liberals fail to understand that multiculturalism itself is a threat to those who see their culture being compromised, belittled, and made increasingly insignificant. Multiculturalism is not the only path that a just society can make, nor does it mean the same thing to its proponents and opponents. To its opponents it means the death of the American way of life, a war on Christianity, and the end of religious freedom. People who would take pride in Jackie Robinson breaking the color barrier in major league baseball, or who in fact voted for Barack Obama becoming president, have real fear of immigrants who enter the U.S., not choosing English, and supporting Islamic law. No matter that these threats are exaggerated and even in many cases based on entire un-truths, social media makes them appear true. If fake news and neo-Nazi alt-right opinion is what streams on your Facebook connections, and you believe that mainstream media is purporting falsehoods, then xenophobia becomes a rational and obvious choice that must be made to avoid extinction. Xenophobia is one of the deepest genetic predispositions to those we do not know—the "other"—because in our evolutionary history the "other" was a constant existential threat. In this regard, it is notable that those who supported Trump in the 2016 election come overwhelmingly from areas of the nation that are void of Blacks, immigrants, Mexicans, Muslims, or even liberals. The fears are of imagined others, not actual experiences, and the lack of actual Mexican, Black, or Muslim humans in their lives, means that social media becomes the only source of how threatening the groups are.

Most observers dismissed Trump. They both underestimated his ability to read the public and even more greatly underestimated the bitterness, anger, and conspiracy-generating space that has grown in a broad segment of American politics. Trump is and has always been a businessman of limited integrity and a reality TV star who could not be seen by Americans as having the background or qualifications to be President. Even yielding that some might have seen in Trump some business acumen that could right the economy, the vitriol that came from his speeches, interviews, and tweeting was the stuff of extreme right-wing sentiment that was entirely antithetical to the roots of the Republican Party. Unfortunately, other elements of Republican strategy for arguing in the extreme, claiming a biased press, and language of demagoguery fed into a stream of right-wing conspiratorial thinking. He drew energy from segments of America who have long argued the politics of hatred, propelling Trump's candidacy forward and advancing his presidential agenda. The politics of tribalism and our most primitive instincts have expanded under Trump and will prove difficult to counter for a long time to come. Indeed, had Trump been defeated, tribalism would almost certainly still have led to widespread violence by those who would have felt further disenfranchised and fighting for their way of life, because that is what "patriots" do.

8.2 The Strength of the Tribal "We"

Let us review some of the theses I have developed on tribalism and the genetic predispositions we have as humans. First, when we are faced with loss and threat of loss of things we most value, we react in a manner that accelerates the "defend and aggress" instincts that are imprinted in our genetic tribal makeup. Loss-defend-aggress are genetically linked and once evoked difficult to unhinge and disconnect. We need this for survival, as thoughtfulness and careful consideration take time and also potentially threaten the solidarity of the tribe. At some point, even if the tribe is wrong, its members must fight without question for its survival or the tribe will perish. Although this linkage of loss-defend-aggress was imprinted when we were living in bands of 150 people, faced with harsh environmental challenges to survival from both nature and other warring tribes, they are nevertheless deeply ingrained in how our brains process information and how we react cognitively, emotionally, and in action.

Our tribal instincts also press us to aggregate and form close bonds. Trump was a master at communicating tribal bonding. "**We** are the greatest movement," "No one can stop **us**," "**They** wish to destroy **us** but **we** are too strong," "**We** are the greatest and I am the only leader that can save you," "**We** Americans," "**We** Christians," "**We** patriots," "**They** would do anything to destroy **us**," "**They** began ISIS, **they** are **our** enemies."

[We have] now become a great, great movement, the likes of which our country has never seen before, never ever. [7]

8.3 We Wear the Badge of Deplorables with Honor

The "we" of the largely rural, working-class Whites also becomes solidified as a "we" by the relentless media-communicated assault from the liberal left and African Americans. Working-class White Americans have been stereotyped as a group for their backwardness, racism, "White privilege," misogyny, bigotry, stupidity, and gullibility. Certainly, in the shadow of Trump's supporters are included individuals and groups who are correctly characterized by these epithets. Indeed, I believe we must recognize many of the alt-right as the neo-Nazis that they are, but few who supported Trump are alt-right neo-Nazis. These terms used to describe White working class are not only descriptors. They are intended by those who use them to blame and dishonor working-class Whites, and to assert the superiority of the liberals who use them.

By hurling these insults, the target group naturally becomes defensive and circles their wagons in their own defense. We are genetically primed to exist in tribes with tribal honor. How better to obtain that honor than to reject the messenger and the message? And, if already tarred and feathered, rejected and vilified, there is all the more need to defend and protect and find another path to honor and self-respect.

Most certainly many Whites have racist beliefs, and I really do not know anyone Black or White who does not carry racial prejudices at some level. But, I can also assure you that the great-grandfathers of those who voted for Trump in Pennsylvania, Michigan, and Wisconsin were more likely to have fought and died for liberation of slavery in the Civil War at Gettysburg, Antietam, and Shiloh than the ancestors of liberals from New York or California. Many of the great Union generals of the "war of liberation" hailed from the same Midwest: Ulysses S. Grant—Point Pleasant, Ohio; William Tecumseh Sherman—Lancaster, Ohio; Winfield Scott Hancock—Montgomeryville, Pennsylvania; John Buford—Woodford County, Kentucky.

Rural working-class Whites also disproportionately serve in the U.S. military, protecting all American's freedom [8]. *"America's 1.4 million-strong military seems to resemble the makeup of a two-year commuter or trade school outside Birmingham or Biloxi far more than that of a ghetto or barrio or four-year university in Boston"* [9]. How different if we were to call on their better angels and look for common bonds. How different it would be if we honored the legacy of White working-class America who have led the fight for freedom against tyranny, and indeed racism. Attacking Whites with the broad brush as ignorant racists engenders evolutionarily wired tribal responding. Reaching across boundaries with honor and inclusion breaks down those boundaries and mitigates against the defend and aggress underpinnings of tribal threat and response wiring.

8.4   THE TRIBE DEFINES ITS OWN REALITY: THE TWISTED FABRIC OF UNRELATED THREADS

Earlier I discussed how tribal or cult rationale is characterized by a twisting of logic. If we understand that the emotional and deep-seated areas of our brain are far from the brain areas where logic dominates, we begin to understand this puzzling phenomena which has been readily apparent in right wing media in the U.S. and which came to define the Trump candidacy. I will call it the *twisted fabric of unrelated threads*.

The tribe, defending itself, creates "truths" that fit their emotional responses. If feeling attacked, the others must be attacking us, evil, un-Godly, and deceiving. If the "others" say we are racist, they perhaps are the ones who are the real racists. When they use Wall Street, they are partnering with an evil source that is undermining us. When we use Wall Street, we are partnering with them in ways that somehow must be turning this around. We are for freedom of religion. And when we wish to outlaw Islam, as did a majority of conservatives polled in South Carolina during the 2016 election cycle, it must somehow be because Islam is not a true religion [10].

When a billionaire who has manipulated the system, not paid income tax, and stiffed workers is a champion of the working class, it is because he will use this knowledge to root out the loopholes that allow this. If he was for a war, he merely claims repeatedly he was against it. He finds the generals incompetent, and then disproportionally gives generals key positions. The gymnastics involved in these twists are mind-wrenching, because these inconsistencies emerge from a combination of a gut-level need to defend-and-aggress mixed with the complications of realpolitik. When they must eventually be tied together into a central "mission statement" with corollaries that follow from it they of course lack coherency precisely because they are products of illogical emotions and the dizzying spinning ever-present fabric of strings of incongruities and falsehoods into politics.

Humans not only are good at self-deception; it is an evolutionary necessity as the illogic of the culture and how we live our own lives must be rationalized, not rational. In his book, *The Folly of Fools*, the anthropologist Robert Trivers instructs us that a major thrust of self-deception is to make the group to which we belong appear superior and the "other" to appear inferior [11]. As Trivers states, we do this from a genetic push that does not require such major divides as Sunni and Shia, Christian or Muslim, Israeli or Palestinian. Psychological studies have shown that merely placing one group in blue shirts and another in red shirts, or make one group of students mock-jailers and the other mock-prisoners, and the result will quickly emerge in prejudices, distrust, and denigration of the out-group and elevation of the in-group.

We might also better understand the twisted fabric of unrelated threads when we learn that tribal defensiveness and dreams emanate from the same areas of the deeper brain's emotional centers. Our emotional "thought centers" are deep brain, far from the forebrain where logic exists. Dreams, linked to our defensive system, are often driven by fear and anxiety as two principal axes of emotions. Dreams, like our "defend and aggress" protective system, emanate from a small region in the brain stem called the pons, the primitive part of our brain slightly above the spinal cord. The limbic system in what scientists call the middle brain adds emotions, and these are our centers for fear and our reaction to fear. A walnut-sized amygdala in the midbrain, once thought by Descartes to be the seat of our soul, is now known to be the seat of our fear, and plays a major role in defend and aggress responding. The advanced forebrain then tries to piece together a logic to the emotion-based disconnected images from this primitive brain area, but does so after the fact, trying to make a logical argument out of irrational emotional content [12]. Dreams, like our justification of tribal behavior, are generated in parts of the brain that predate our human ancestors, and little of our advanced forebrain is involved. Putting this together, our primitive self is centered around the survival necessary emotions of fear and anxiety, and our response to these of anger, which is the emotional base of aggression.

Just as in the tribal politics of defend and aggress, the thoughtful, logic generating forebrain is offline during sleep. The logic of our dreams and of our aggressive tribal responding is *post hoc*, after the fact. They are attempts the tie together illogical pieces of an emotional system. Said another way, our tribal responding is primitive and evoked in politics, support of our favorite sports teams, and in our dream states. Logic is an afterthought, literally. We work hard to make it all sound logical, but it is emotionally based and precedes an evolutionary time before our advanced forebrain ever developed.

When loss and threat are clear and apparent there is no need to twist the facts and create conspiratorial narratives. George Lincoln Rockwell, the onetime leader of the American Nazi Party, said, "Ours is not a time when there is a chicken in every pot." So, with the U.S. doing relatively well economically and Republicans actually holding a majority of governorships and both houses of Congress, the only way to create an angry opposition is to dispel truth and create a delusional narrative of anger and disenfranchisement, woven together with the slimmest threads of reality and fact. Toward this end, the alt-right has established an alternate universe of false truths that by being repeated so often, becomes gospel. False stories are promulgated and broadcast on social media and because they are consistent with the angry expression of underlying feelings and the overall false narratives of the tribe, they are the stories that are accepted as truth. So, Obama is a Muslim. Obama is part of a Muslim conspiracy to take over the U.S. The Democrats are enemies of the State. An armed citizenry must be vigilant because the government has already moved its forces into place to take invade and capture within our own borders. All moves by the Democratic, falsely elected government are to be resisted. The media is part of this grand conspiracy. The bank and Wall Street, together with the media and the leaders of the Democratic Party, form a secret cabal that is connected to a shadowy international conspiracy. And if a responsible Republican leadership challenges these myths, then of course they are part of this conspiracy and are no longer to be trusted.

From the beginning Trump, has defined a dystopian U.S. that exaggerates loss and threat of loss in absolutes and extremes. In his "Make America Great Again" he has outlined a litany of loss and threat that is entirely inconsistent with reality and facts. He sees our inner-cities as hellholes of runaway crime and social collapse. He claims the economy is not only in shambles, but is at risk of imminent collapse. He has claimed that Mexican rapists and murderers are pouring across the border. He warns of Muslim immigrants who wish to undermine our system of government and impose Sharia law. Trump stated:

> "Our great civilization, here in America and across the civilized world has come upon a moment of reckoning. We've seen it in the United Kingdom, where they voted to liberate themselves from global government and global trade deal, and global immigration deals that have destroyed their sovereignty and have destroyed many of those nations. But, the central base of world political power is right here in America, and it is our corrupt political establishment that is the greatest power behind the efforts at radical globalization and the disenfranchisement of working people. Their financial resources are virtually unlimited, their political resources are unlimited, their media resources are unmatched, and most importantly, the depths of their immorality is absolutely unlimited." [13]

Only by the language of doom can the false reality that Trumpism and the alt-right have created can enough depth and momentum of fear be generated to foster the end-of-days scenario that evokes our tribal need to defend and aggress. This language came early in Trump's campaign, but it was never his. Rather it was picked up from the extreme right's websites and language and simply broadcast on a national, presidential platform. It often mirrors the early speeches of Adolph Hitler from the time of his rise until he secured power, even if they have removed Nazi terminology from the same White power messaging. In 1967, George Lincoln Rockwell, the leader of the American Nazi party, was already finding better reception of his message when he switched from attacking "Communist Jews" to the more successful, hooded White Power approach. Like Senator Joseph McCarthy, draping his language in patriotism and protection of the American way of life makes this hate messaging more palatable, and even supported by mainstream sympathizers who do not otherwise hold such extreme views.

Whether the hate messaging, anti-immigrant, anti-capitalist, anti-Muslim, anti-academic campaign that mirrors Nazi tactics or those of Senator Joseph McCarthy will translate to fascist policy and political action is an open question. But it is the natural path by which these beginnings follow. They will probably not be anti-Semitic given Trump's daughter is a convert to Judaism and his Jewish son-in-law, Jared Kushner, is a key advisor, and his own history of working with Jews in his long history of business practice. But that is not to say that other scapegoat groups will not be targeted. Nor should any of Trump's messages conjure images of death camps. But targeting millions of Mexicans with illegal status would require police squadrons, containment camps, and the brutalizing of families who have been in the U.S. for decades. Such events could mirror the detainment camps that destroyed the lives of hundreds of thousands of loyal Japanese Americans in the era of World War II and remain a stain on America's history.

8.5   Loss and Threat Messaging in Modern America Borrowed from Perfected Nazi Propaganda

To evoke tribalism requires several key elements. First, we must be under attack. Second, that attack must if lost mean long-term or ultimate destruction. Third, "we" must be different from "those others" in ways that are fundamental in terms of good and evil. Fourth, in the world of modern media access, their messaging must be tainted and lies and only our avenues and sources of information are reliable. Importantly, these threats must be imminent, not far downstream possibilities. In fact, they must already be occurring and we must already be far down this path.

Joseph Goebbels, the architect of Nazi propaganda, underscored the importance of simple repeated messages. He, like Trump, and Russia's Putin have little use for the truth. Rather, you create truths by repeatedly stating the same few, simple points. Even before being nominated by the Republican Party, Trump's ultimate language of destruction was launched. Finally, your movement must be the only path to a bright future that will end the scourge of those who threaten us. Forget nuance, forget truth. Bringing Steve Bannon, a master at White supremacist, at times neo-Nazi propaganda, as a strategy leader for Trump's campaign and as a senior White House advisor in the early Trump administration sharpened Trump's language and, as many fear, the policies that will follow from this language. Trump's messaging comes directly from alt-right, White supremacist, often neo-Nazi, Breitbart News. In many instances, their only defense against it being associated with Nazism is they have removed the word Nazi from the same language and policy. And much of Trump's words are straight from Breitbart News.

> The corrupt establishment knows that we are a great threat to their criminal enterprise. They know that if we win, their power is gone, and it's returned to you, the people, will be. The dark clouds hanging over our government can be lifted and replaced with a bright future.
>
> There is nothing the political establishment will not do—no lie that they won't tell, to hold their prestige and power at your expense. And that's what's been happening.
>
> They've [the corrupt global power structure] stripped away these towns bare and raided the wealth for themselves and taken our jobs away, out of our country, never to return unless I'm elected president. The Clinton machine is at the center of this power structure. [13]
>
> This is the legacy of Hillary Clinton: death, destruction, terrorism, and weakness. [14]

The following excerpt would be scary if it came from an obscure website, but it achieves another magnitude of threat when it comes from Trump's own website. It is a paranoid, extreme narrative that is grandiose, based on longstanding anti-Semitic texts, and the language of government takeover.

- OCTOBER 13, 2016 -
REMARKS ON THE CLINTON CAMPAIGN OF DESTRUCTION
REMARKS AS PREPARED FOR DELIVERY
Our movement is about replacing a failed and corrupt political establishment with a new government controlled by you, the American People.

There is nothing the political establishment will not do, and no lie they will not tell, to hold on to their prestige and power at your expense.

The Washington establishment, and the financial and media corporations that fund it, exists for only one reason: to protect and enrich itself.

The establishment has trillions of dollars at stake in this election. As an example, just one single trade deal they'd like to pass, involves trillions of dollars controlled by many countries, corporations and lobbyists.

For those who control the levers of power in Washington, and for the global special interests they partner with, our campaign represents an existential threat.

This is not simply another 4-year election. **This is a crossroads in the history of our civilization** that will determine whether or not We The People reclaim control over our government.

The political establishment that is trying everything to stop us, is the same group responsible for our disastrous trade deals, massive illegal immigration, and economic and foreign policies that have bled this country dry. The political establishment has brought about the destruction of our factories and our jobs, as they flee to Mexico, China and other countries throughout the world. ...

It's a global power structure that is responsible for the economic decisions that have robbed our working class, stripped our country of its wealth, and put that money into the pockets of a handful of large corporations and political entities...

The Clinton Machine is at the center of this power structure. We've seen this firsthand in the WikiLeaks documents in which Hillary Clinton meets in secret with international banks to plot the destruction of U.S. sovereignty in order to enrich these global financial powers...

The most powerful weapon deployed by the Clintons is the corporate media. Let's be clear on one thing: the corporate media in our country is no longer involved in journalism. They are a political special interest, no different than any lobbyist or other financial entity with an agenda. And their agenda is to elect the Clintons at any cost, at any price, no matter how many lives they destroy.

For them, it is a war—and for them, nothing is out of bounds. This is a struggle for the survival of our nation. This election will determine whether we are a free nation, or whether we have only the illusion of Democracy but are in fact controlled by a small handful of global special interests rigging the system...

This is not just conspiracy but reality, and you and I know it.

The establishment and their media enablers wield control over this nation through means that are well known. Anyone who challenges their control is deemed a sexist, a racist, a xenophobe and morally deformed. They will attack you, they will slander you, they will seek to destroy your career and reputation. And they will lie, lie and lie even more.

The Clintons are criminals. This is well-documented, and the establishment that protects them has engaged in a massive cover-up of widespread criminal activity at the State Department and Clinton Foundation in order to keep the Clintons in power. Never in history have we seen such a cover-up as this, one that includes the destruction of 33,000 emails, 13 phones, laptops, missing boxes of evidence, and on and on.

In this same official Trump website, Trump, unlike the alt-Right adds his own Messianic grandiose, narcissistic sense of self as a kind of Christ figure.

When I declared my candidacy, I knew what bad shape our country was in. I had seen firsthand the corruption and the sickness that has taken over our politics. I knew they would throw every lie they could at me, and my family, and my loved ones.

I knew they would stop at nothing to try to stop me.

But I take all of these slings and arrows for you. I take them for our movement, so that we can have our country back [14]. [Emphasis added in bold]

Such language is messianic and near-apocalyptic. Trump's language as his candidacy progressed was increasingly borrowed from the Protocols of the Elders of Zion, the long-debunked fabricated manifesto of the secret Jewish cabal that rules the world through its control on the media and banks. It is written and spoken in language that we have not seen on the national stage since McCarthyism in the 1950s.

8.6   SCREAMING IN AN ECHO CHAMBER

Whether successful in the election or suffering a defeat, the election would have been an astounding success for right wing extremism. As tribalism progresses our genetics make us increasingly vulnerable to self-deception and assured of the rightness of our cause. Indeed, had Trump not been

184 S. E. HOBFOLL

elected, the circling of the alt-right, White supremacist wagons would have likely been more pronounced and more violent. Both success and failure are interpreted as support for their beliefs within the ultra-high speed spin of the tribe and their interpretation of the social and political meaning of the election.

Tribalism must be insular to protect the group. It does not possess any of the fault lines and fissures of reasoned discourse, and as a belief system is immune to the mirror that reflects its flaws. Seeing that the opposition has valid points to make or may be partially correct endangers the tribe, and so they increasingly scream their epitaphs into the echo chamber of their own beliefs.

Paradoxically, the least committed adherent to Trumpism is Donald Trump, or at least the pre-candidate Trump. From all we know of his life, his speeches and his family, he is not ideological and does not hold the views of those who supported him, or at least did not historically hold those views. He has been pro-life and pro-choice, Democratic leaning and Republican leaning. He has shown himself to be aggressive in his views of the need to protect America from its enemies, but having little knowledge of who those enemies are or what they have done. When questioned, he did not know that Russia had already invaded the Ukraine. He admits to knowing what he does from television, and we know that American television is superficial. Even CNN seldom has experts present their views on any issue, but instead has news "personalities" that give their opinions. At best, a professor of, say, economics, or Russia, or the Middle East, present their views on air, and then in one- to two-minute segments, followed by the endless views of their news regulars.

In terms of tribalism and our genetic predisposition this could mean our entering into an age of the "cult of Trump" which would follow whatever he says on any given issue. Tribes often follow this path when there is a charismatic, authoritarian leader. This would actually be his path of most political power as most Americans that voted for him and most who did not, are not ideological. The largest factors noted by those who voted for Trump was their dissatisfaction with the status quo, feeling unsafe, and their desired need for change. Those in America that are not themselves in politics or holding advanced academic degrees, could hardly outline what conservative or liberal points of view are, and fewer could translate that to foreign policy. The extremes have clarity of their viewpoints, but only the religious right among those groups that support Trump hold sizable numbers.

8.7   Post Defeat Encampment

Rational thought, historical precedence, and common sense would have predicted (and did predict) that with the office of the presidency secured Trump and Trumpism would migrate to normative political discourse, a transformation to more centrist politics, and an acceptance of realpolitik. However, this is not what understanding tribalism and our tribal behavioral genetics would predict, and any such thinking ignores the genetics of tribalism, the needs of the tribe, or the instincts of a tribal leader. Moreover, beyond tribalism, President Trump is the embodiment of the authoritarian narcissistic leader, and as such does not have insight into his own deficiencies or a requirement to listen to others. Instead, the authoritarian narcissistic leader believes that "he is the answer," and believes in his infallibility of judgment.

As Trump stated in his interview with the *New York Times* on November 22, 2016, about the potential for conflict of interest with his international businesses, "The president can't have a conflict of interest." In this way, the authoritarian leader creates "facts" and dismisses any of the legitimate arbiters of facts and knowledge. The press, scientists, and indeed any opposition is misguided, misinformed, or conspiring against him. In many fascist takeovers political leaders shut down the free press or imprisoned those who questioned them. This might be tempting for Trump, but because he is speaking to an audience who already has dismissed any press or science that does not agree with them, the press has already been delegitimized and defined as just another force of the anti-American conspiracy, and part of the secret cabal that has seized power secretly.

Whereas Trump's victory is marginal and historically near the bottom quarter of electoral college victories, and his loss in the popular vote among those who became president is historically the most severe in history (see Fig. 8.1), he repeatedly states that he won by a historical landslide [15]. By repeating this over and over, despite any relationship with the truth, for him and his followers it becomes "truth."

Taking this further, Trump moves to undermine the very basis of the democracy, claiming that his figures are correct because he takes into account his imagined "millions of people" who voted illegally in the election for Clinton. Having claimed before the election that if he lost it would be because of voter fraud and conspiratorial manipulation of the system by an international cabal of bankers, media, and politicians who opposed

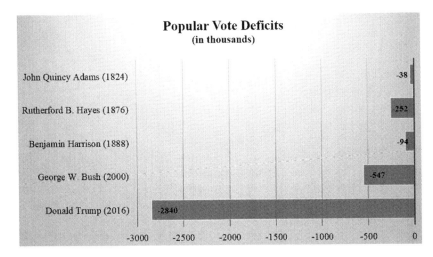

Fig. 8.1 Popular vote deficits by previous presidents. (Adapted from Robert Farley [15])

him, he now states that his win was historically a landslide because he knows the true nature of the vote and fraud. That he does not even attempt to buttress such conspiratorial propaganda with facts and sources is illustrative of the process of "truth is as I speak it."

In a twisted shift of logic, he then denies the actual manipulation of the vote through Russian interference in the election process. No sacred cow is too sacred for a king or dictator.

Even the CIA, a darling of conservatives much more than liberals, is dismissed as misinformed, misguided, and perhaps conspiring against him. When the CIA's investigation points to Russian hackers acting to influence the election in his favor, Trump and his team dismiss the intelligence. They somehow without any intelligence gathering capability know better. They reject fact-finding as the only source of facts is what they say are facts consistent with their emotion-based narrative. They underscore the CIA's past errors on weapons of mass destruction in Saddam Hussein's Iraq. Trump throws doubt on the CIA's conclusions and proposes alternative theories, suggesting it could be anyone hacking the system, and of course offers no evidence for such theories. As the source of "truth," he simply does not need to [16].

Trump's fabrications are not random. Rather, they are distillations of fake news produced by the extreme right to undermine verifiable media sources and to create an alternate reality of information that follows the tribal teachings and dogma of Trumpism and the alt-right. Trump's views are both taken from and adopted by major fake news and conspiracy source points that are increasingly believed. These functions are historically created by fascist and communist leaders via their takeover of the press and information channels, as done in Nazi Germany, Fascist Italy, or today's Russia or North Korea. Instead, the breakdown to truth, promulgated through Fox television and their deconstruction and blending of news and editorial, has gathered momentum that outstrips the channel of its original television ratings-seeking originators and been translated into a massive alteration of the very idea of truth, having become that which the tribe wishes and needs to be truth.

So, Trump undermines the CIA, placing the nation at peril by so doing. But further, in the camp of his extremist supporters, more sinister theories about the CIA are insinuated through the fabrication of fake news and the internet. Alex Jones, an internet conspiracy fabricator of the first order, whom Trump has heralded for his work, set forth the news story that "rogue elements" within the CIA are trying to "assassinate" him before he takes office [17]. Jones's earlier theories which are presented as investigative journalism included that the U.S. government perpetrated the 9/11 attacks, as well as the Columbine, Oklahoma City, Sandy Hook, and Boston Marathon attacks. With over 75 million monthly page views among over 14 million unique monthly, it is no wonder that Trump called Jones to thank him after the election and to promise that he would be especially available to Jones' viewers. Trump's view of Jones is as clear as why he would favor him so, "Your reputation is amazing. I will not let you down" [18].

8.8   TRIBALISM AND THE PATH TO FASCISM

Trumpism will not necessarily migrate to fascism, but the seeds of fascism are planted and propelled by tribalism, as the genetics of tribalism propels it with its own energy. We mistake this argument to be extremist as if fascism is rare and democracy widespread, when fascism is the most common representation of government, and actually mainstream for much of the world. Democracy is fragile, has only a brief history in the world of a few hundred years, and is not well-represented in the world at any time. We also mistake the argument that Trumpism is not fascism because we look at fascist endpoints, whereas fascism always begins by making small inroads. So, where are we on the tribalist path to fascism? The answer is scary, and more downstream on this course than even what has been called the liberal media has outlined. It is instructive to look at what fascism is and how it is orchestrated in its early moments.

Historians and political scientists do not have a single definition of fascism. The central core of fascism is a nationalist, authoritarian system of government. It typically uses romantic symbolism, as in Trump's "Make America Great Again," harking back to a nostalgic view that is code for White Christian America. It is characterized by a call to a "movement," meaning the current system is flawed and needs correction. When we look at fascism around the world and through an historical lens, we see it defined by promotion of violence, heralding of masculinity, and emphasizing charismatic leadership of a single male figure who sees himself as larger than life. Fascism gains momentum by rejecting what it calls "failed systems." Historically, both the politics of conservatism and liberalism are rejected, which appears to leave nothing, until we understand that what is then left is whatever the fascist leadership says is "the new system." This is typically an amalgam of far-right dogma mixed with random notions that are chosen to fit whatever the fascist leadership wants to shape or propose.

The British political theorist Roger Griffin describes this well in his term "palingenetic ultranationalism," meaning a self-defined rebirth. Decline, humiliation, and victimhood, as I have outlined as key elements of the threat response that evokes genetic tribalism, are to be reversed by fascism's sense of cult-like unity of the mass-based movement. Conservative Christian doctrine is historically a key ingredient of Western fascism, according to Griffin, and its main driver is demonizing the decadence of society that the new political system will counter. This is a twisted Christianity, as in fascism the concepts of Christian tolerance and compassion of "love thy neighbor as thyself" are replaced with racism, anti-Semitism, ethnocentrism, and a crowning of the leader as king, in a near-religious sense [19].

Clearly the strength of the American system of government, with its balance of power in the judiciary, congressional, and executive branches, is a powerful countervail to a move toward fascism, but moving in this direction under Trump is clear, powerful, and accelerating. Although the judicial branch is relatively immune to public opinion, the congress is not, and tribalism threatens elected officials with unseating if they do not support the cult of leadership that claims it will end their constituents humiliation, victimhood, and historical decline. As we saw during the period of 1950s McCarthyism, it was more a rallying of a brave free press that challenged this dark fascist period than it was a courageous congress, who were happy to go along with the witch hunts for hidden communists and blacklisting of citizens, especially those in the media, entertainment industry, unions, government positions with views opposing McCarthy, and the free press. In fact, the House Un-American Activities Committee was part of the House of Representatives, and therefore independent of McCarthy, who was in the Senate. Using the powers of the FBI, which is appointed also through the executive branch, the House and Senate fully conspired with McCarthy to subvert the freedom of the American people, all in the name of protecting that freedom.

Lest we forget, the President is also commander of the armed forces, and we are already losing the historical separation between the civilian and military with Trump's appointment of an unprecedented number of former generals to key cabinet position. Indeed, it was for this purpose that the founding fathers heralded the importance of an armed militia at the state level, and why the states originally resisted having a standing army under the direction of the President, this being the true purpose of the Second Amendment, however ironic that seems if the state militias are themselves supportive of the new cult. As James Madison, the main architect of the American Constitution and indeed a strong central government, stated to the Constitutional Convention in June 1787,

A standing military force, with an overgown Executive will not long be safe companions to liberty... The means of defense against foreign danger, have been always the instruments of tyranny at home. [20]

It is instructive that Hamilton, Madison and Washington himself all feared the tying of the executive branch to the military, at the same time that they saw it as necessary for the defense of the nation against foreign enemies. Democracy, as envisioned by the founding fathers, was hoped to be the stronger counterforce to tribalism, which they depicted in their conceptualization of mob rule. But they wrote often of the force of tribalism in the mob, as they did of the tyranny of a too powerful Executive. Trump may never move further on the continuum of fascism and the strength of our system of government may sustain us, but it is naïve to not see that we are at the early stages of that path, with its hallmarks of authoritarian leadership, cult-like call to a "new movement," and a diminishment of the free press and the leadership of both liberal and conservative parties.

Although Trumpism is now being presented as a populist movement that was about jobs and the middle class, it was created on a narrative of hatred, racism, and even anti-Semitic rhetoric, and a heralding of the moralism of "true Christian beliefs" that are the signets of fascism.

In the end it is never how fascist the leader, but how strong the will of the people not to turn to tribalism, and resist our genetic propensity to support that leader for our own security and fear of loss and humiliation. But we would be fools to underestimate the evolutionary-based genetic power of tribalism and its hold once it gains momentum.

REFERENCES

1. Franklin, B. (1755, November 11). *Pennsylvania Assembly: Reply to the Governor.* Benjamin Franklin Papers. Retrieved February 13, 2018, from http://franklinpapers.org/franklin/framedVolumes.jsp?vol=6&page=238a
2. Northwestern Institute for Policy Research. (2014). *The Great Recession: Over but not gone?* Northwestern Institute for Policy Research. Retrieved November 28, 2016, from http://www.ipr.northwestern.edu/about/news/2014/IPR-research-Great-Recession-unemployment-foreclosures-safety-net-fertility-public-opinion.html
3. Kusisto, L. (2015, April 20). Many who lost homes to foreclosure in last decade won't return—NAR. *Wall Street Journal.* Retrieved September 10, 2017, from : https://www.wsj.com/articles/many-who-lost-homes-to-foreclosure-in-last-decade-wont-return-nar-1429548640
4. McCall, L. (2013). *The undeserving rich: Americans beliefs about inequality, opportunity and redistribution.* Cambridge: Cambridge University Press.
5. Case, A., & Deaton, A. (2015). Rising morbidity and mortality in midlife among white non-Hispanic Americans in the 21st century. *Proceedings of the National Academy of Sciences, 112*(49), 15078–15083. https://doi.org/10.1073/pnas.1518393112.
6. Department of Defense. (2015). *Department Of Defense Suicide Event Report Calendar Year* 2014 *Annual Report.* National Center for Telehealth & Technology and Defense Suicide Prevention Office. Retrieved November 28, 2016, from http://www.dspo.mil/Portals/113/Documents/CY%20 2014%20DoDSER%20Annual%20Report%20-%20Final.pdf
7. NPR. (2016, October 13). Transcript: Donald Trump's speech responding to assault accusations. *NPR.* Retrieved May 10, 2017, from http://www.npr.org/2016/10/13/497857068/transcript-donald-trumps-speech-responding-to-assault-accusations
8. U.S. Census Bureau. (2016, December 8). *New Census data show differences between urban and rural populations.* U.S. Census Bureau. Retrieved January

10, 2018, from https://www.census.gov/newsroom/press-releases/2016/cb16-210.html

9. Halbfinger, D. M., & Holmes, S. A. (2003, March 30). A nation at war: The Troops; Military mirrors a working-class America. *NY Times.* Retrieved January 10, 2018, from http://www.nytimes.com/2003/03/30/us/a-nation-at-war-the-troops-military-mirrors-a-working-class-america.html

10. Public Poling Policy. (2016, February 16). *Trump, Clinton continue to lead in SC.* Public Poling Policy. Retrieved March 28, 2017, from http://www.publicpolicypolling.com/pdf/2015/PPP_Release_SC_21616.pdf

11. Trivers, R. (2011). *The folly of fools: The logic of deceit and self-deception in human life.* New York: Basic Books.

12. Ledoux, J. (1998). *The emotional brain: The mysterious Unerpinnings of emoptional life.* New York: Touchstone.

13. Bump, P., & Blake, A. (2016, July 21). Donald Trump's dark speech to the Republican National Convention, annotated. *Washington Post.* Retrieved May 10, 2017, from https://www.washingtonpost.com/news/the-fix/wp/2016/07/21/full-text-donald-trumps-prepared-remarks-accepting-the-republican-nomination/?utm_term=.4aa39100f3ff

14. P2016 Race for the White House. (2016, October 13). *Remarks on the Clinton campaign of destruction.* P2016 Race for the White House. Retrieved May 10, 2017, from http://www.p2016.org/trump/trump101316spfl.html

15. Farley, R. (2016, November 29). Trump landslide? Nope. *FactCheck.* Retrieved March 8, 2017, from http://cf.factcheck.org/2016/11/trump-landslide-nope/

16. Miller, G., Jaffe, G., & Rucker, P. (2017, December 14). Doubting the intelligence, Trump pursues Putin and leave a Russian Threat Unchecked. *The Washington Post.* Retrieved January 10, 2018, from https://www.washingtonpost.com/graphics/2017/world/national-security/donald-trump-pursues-vladimir-putin-russian-election-hacking/?utm_term=.870d62f8870f

17. Hananoki, E. (2016, December 19). Trump ally and news source Alex Jones regularly pushes CIA conspiracy theories. *Media Matters for America.* Retrieved December 21, 2016, from https://www.mediamatters.org/blog/2016/12/19/alex-jones-warns-trump cia trying-assassinate-president-elect/214865

18. Finnegan, W. (2016, June 23). Donald Trump and the 'amazing' Alex Jones. *The New Yorker.* Retrieved September 12, 2017, from http://www.newyorker.com/news/daily-comment/donald-trump-and-the-amazing-alex-jones

19. Eco, U. (1995, June 22). Ur-Fascism. *The New York Review of Books.* Retrieved March 28, 2017, from http://www.nybooks.com/articles/1995/06/22/ur-fascism/

20. Madison, J. (1787, June 29). Madison debates. Retrieved February 13, 2018, from http://avalon.law.yale.edu/18th_century/debates_629.asp

CHAPTER 9

Through a Glass Darkly: Reversing Tribal Intolerance and Aggression

> We have met the enemy and he is us *[1]*. *(Pogo, a prescient cartoon character from our past)*

As we witness tribalism's dark shadow around the world, it is easy to surrender to pessimism. Ethnic division, terrorism, strike and counterstrike, a populism built on intolerance and division, and the oppression of women are all manifestations of tribalism and our tribal genetics. The question we all must ask is, "Are these waves of hatred and fear inevitable, or can they be contained or even reversed?" We often view psychology and the mind on an individual level, but tribalism, once strongly evoked, appears to remain a powerful force for the "collective mind," meaning cognitions that are shared by the group. Tribalism, once evoked through fear conditioning and accelerated by leaders' fear-mongering, carries momentum that is difficult to reverse, so we can discard any simple optimism of "It'll be okay." More scary, if threat and loss increase due to terrorism or if economic losses become more significant, then the drivers of populism and its transition to fascism will only increase because tribalism will become a more powerful counterforce. Our ancestors required these powerful built-in mechanisms of collective consciousness to oppose threat and ensure survival of the group due to the omnipresent dangers of the early human existence. That is how the genetics of tribalism and our evolutionary heritage is expressed

© The Author(s) 2018   193
S. E. Hobfoll, *Tribalism*,
https://doi.org/10.1007/978-3-319-78405-2_9

as individuals and as individuals in tribes. It begins with small steps, but it moves quickly to a gallop.

The answers to the question of ways to reverse populism and the tribal press toward fascism are complex. They must be problem-focused and must address the key elements of fear and loss and create a drive toward an alternative tribal unity that is not hate- and fear-based if we are to counter the buildup of this evolutionary-based defense system. We must appeal to our "better angels," and our direction should be guided by the hard-won gains that have been made in civil rights, women's rights, social justice and advancement of tolerance. The torch on the Statue of Liberty must continue to shine as a beacon to the world. At the same time, we must address and respond to our base instincts as real and part of us. Liberalism champions democracy and tolerance, but can be too cerebral and effete to deal with real threats, and it offers few options that those smitten with tribalism will be attracted to. So, we must build bridges, not walls. And bridges require us to walk across them. Moreover, we will need bridges because we must pass over turbulent, shark-infested waters.

9.1   THE STRUCTURE OF EVOLUTIONARY SOLUTIONS TO TRIBALISM

From an evolutionary tribal perspective, several key ingredients are required to reverse populism's move toward fascism and restore more liberal democracy. From an evolutionary standpoint, the tribe must be made to feel safe, and liberal solutions based on fairness and justice do not have fertile ground to gain traction when threat and loss levels are high. For this reason, we can see historically that the countering of tribal periods has required an integration of seeking social justice in a more tough-minded, and often militant package. Make no mistake about it, Kennedy's new society was coupled with a space program that was aimed at countering Russian domination of warfare through space dominance, and his response to the Cuban missile crisis showed militant muscle flexing, defending our entire hemisphere from Russian interference.

First and Foremost, People Must Feel Safe from Threat and Loss As terrorism's threat will continue, this means seeing an effective, convincing path in the war on terrorism as well as feeling economically secure. As countering jihadist Islamic tribalism will be a much more long-term mission, and may not occur for a century or longer, so deeply rooted is it in Islamic culture and politics in much of the world, safety must come as a counter-force to what will be ongoing threat.

Second, People Must Feel a Sense of Belonging Individualism is not a viable counterforce to tribalism, and certainly not as long as major threats to safety exist. Political organizing translates to involving people in groups, movements, causes, and shared justice through involvement. This sense of involvement for some will take the form of political activity, but for most people it will be a sense of belonging that they will feel in front of their television smart phones, and computer screens.

Third, People Must Associate Pride with Their Group and Shame with the Group They Reject Those who backed Senator Joseph McCarthy during the Red Scare were made to feel shame for their beliefs in backing his hate-ful tactics. Like Trump, McCarthy was initially supported by Republicans because he effectively vilified liberal Democrats. That is until Republican Eisenhower became president and McCarthy went after the U.S. Army as being soft on communism. Like Trump's backing by Evangelical Christians, McCarthy had strong backing from Catholics. Indeed, he was strongly supported by the Kennedy family.

The involvement of Catholics supporting McCarthy raises a pivotal point. Catholics liked McCarthy's standing out as a Catholic at a time when Catholics were not welcomed in national politics. So, they backed him because they gained by his fame. Likewise, many will compromise their freedom, their values, and their rights for personal and financial gains and protection from the "other" who they fear. Hitler would not have won adherents had he not grown the Depression-weakened German economy through effective trade policy, massive infrastructure projects, and record-high military spending. From 1933 to 1936 he nearly tripled employment in construction. Where he could not organize through investment, he nationalized industry and made all workers part of a national union that he controlled. Strikes and labor unrest were outlawed [2]. The West's current fears are not only of terrorism, but of the threat to safety and well-being of economic challenges that workers face, and with this insecurity a sense of shame in their failure that fuels populism and makes fascism attractive. The authoritarian father-leader who will bring economic solutions will answer these tribal pressures, and others less fearful may also support quite fascist policies if it lines their pockets.

We Must Not Underestimate the Power of Tribalism in Our Genetic, Evolutionary Brains, Because to Do So Will Invite a Further Advancing from Populism to Fascism When people feel profoundly unsafe and where leaders emerge to answer their fears of violence, economic loss, and the intrusion of the dangerous "other," our genetics will increase "thinking" from the lower brain where "defend and aggress" dominate. This will produce a ready pathway for simple, powerful solutions that are the hallmark of fascism. Large segments of the public will cling to the authoritarian father-leader who has "the answers." For the U.S. and much of Europe we are not in an advanced stage of fascism and the workings of liberal, or at least non-liberal, democracy are still well fixed. But that does not mean that they are robust—threat creates fragility.

We must not be sanguine because our democratic institutions are still strong. They are weakening and being profoundly challenged. The aggressive disrespect and disdain for the institutions of liberal democracy are a first stage of this process. Authoritarian leaders will work with democratic structures to the extent it meets their agenda, but will challenge them and indeed act to deconstruct them if they do not get their way. And the public will support this because tribalism and its "defend and aggress" primacy will propel this process as democracy is rife with vagaries that are inherent in its open give and take and the involvement of many. Said another way, democracy, liberalism, and conservative thinking are highly philosophical and require thoughtfulness, which is not the part of the brain that is activated or has primacy under threat.

We Must Constantly Reassert Truth and Display It Before the Public As in the reversal of McCarthyism, a valiant, vigilant free press will be the essential counterforce to tyranny. Democracy is a concept that is dependent on rational thought and dedicated action supporting abstract ideas of justice and freedom. With loss and threat omnipresent, power and safety are deeply experienced psycho-emotional states that undermine rational cognitive thought and replace it with "group-think," and "group-speak."

These genetically based processes evoked in tribalism easily reject truth in favor of political agendas that quell fear and create a firm sense of power over threatening forces of "the other." So, this will continue to be an ongoing struggle.

To be clear, President Trump has declared "the other" to be any force that stands in his way. "The other" began with Mexicans and Muslims and moved to Hillary and liberals. But think of how quickly it included Republicans who disagreed, generals who were depicted as know-nothings, and the U.S. intelligence community. Classic conservatism is a rich, complex philosophy that should not be confused with Fox News and certainly not right-wing conspiratorial websites. At this juncture, Trump's only strongly acknowledged linkage outside of his family and a few trusted advisors is Putin and authoritarian Russia. He is no more a friend of conservatism than liberalism, but rather speaks directly to the tribe and its fears.

9.2   COUNTERING THE THREAT OF TERRORISM

In President Roosevelt's famous *Arsenal of Democracy* speech, preparing America for the threat of war that most Americans still fervently hoped to avoid, Roosevelt's words were tribal, powerful, charged, electric, and unequivocal. As he entered living rooms across America in his fireside chats, he warned against the wave of populism that was pushing Americans to avoid getting involved in "someone else's conflict" [3].

Never before since Jamestown and Plymouth Rock has our American civilization been in such danger as now.

The Nazi masters of Germany have made it clear that they intend not only to dominate all life and thought in their own country, but also to enslave the whole of Europe, and then to use the resources of Europe to dominate the rest of the world.

If Great Britain goes down, the Axis powers will control the continents of Europe, Asia, Africa, Australasia, and the high seas—and they will be in a position to bring enormous military and naval resources against this hemisphere. It is no exaggeration to say that all of us in the Americas would be living at the point of a gun—a gun loaded with explosive bullets, economic as well as military.

To counter populism, terrorism, and particularly jihadist Islamic fundamentalist terrorism, must be confronted as evils in the most aggressive terms. The tribalism that is sparking and absorbing the Middle East and elements of Islam will not be short-lived, and we can expect it to continue for decades and perhaps centuries. Attacking terrorism and its root causes will unfortunately be repellent and often antithetical to globalism and multiculturalism. The threat of terrorism is probably the single most potent initiator of the surge of populism, and the ugly tribalism that has emerged under the exaggerated threat that terrorism creates. September 11 marked a turning point in the West's perceived threat from Islamic militancy. The growth of terrorism and its creative use of violence has been the fountainhead of the West's move to ethnocentrism and populism, with no small measure of hatred mixed in with the fear. President Obama's most fundamental errors from a tribalist perspective were his nearly silent war against terrorism, and his attempts to quietly address the devolution of Syria, even as he sometimes employed great force in action. That is, however sound or unsound his policy of action, his use of the bully pulpit to display in plain sight the war against terrorism lacked the rallying cries and saber rattling that presidents at war must undertake to lead the tribe and restore their profound sense of vulnerability.

It will be necessary to enact decisive, clear, highly aggressive, targeted policies that will be effective in fighting terrorism and radicalization—whether at mosques, universities, or through police action—to prevent, fight, and punish the tiny minority who might support or act militantly. Populist leaders have capitalized on our fears and suggested intolerance and exclusion that only increase distrust and are likely to further radicalize new generations of Muslim young people. But the alternative is not to deny the threat, but to make it a major issue with powerful solutions. President Obama's approach was thoughtful and consistent with the need for tolerance, but it was largely inconsistent with people's needs to feel safe from threat.

The policy over the fight against radical Islamic terrorism, and indeed Wahhabism, must be forceful, forthright, clearly delineated, and reported upon regularly. It must be acknowledged as a war, and therefore part of regular press conferences, discussion from the presidential bully pulpit, and multifaceted. Such forcefulness and even militancy are the main language that the deeper brain evoked by tribalism will respond to.

We absolutely should not be entering mosques or places of worship to root out terrorism. At the same time, we must partner with Muslims in teaching against terrorism and to point to radical centers that do otherwise. Current efforts doing just that have to be nurtured, expanded, and made more public. In recent trips lecturing at Yale, Birmingham University in England, and in Paris, I felt I was in parallel worlds, where my lectures against radical Islam were seen as extreme but Islamic radicals' hate speech, particularly if they focused on Israel, was seen as mainstream and to be protected. This drive toward multiculturalism allows a crack in the door that terrorism and radical ideologies exploit, and we cannot allow them to use multiculturalism as a shield.

9.3   THE POWER OF UNITY IN TRIBALISM

The Antidotes to Populist and Fascist Tribalism Must Imitate Aspects of Tribalism to Support Solutions That Evoke the Power of Unity Uniting people in an anti-populism movement must win the hearts and minds of people beyond the current liberal strongholds and their strong individualistic, anti-populist underpinnings. The U.S. and Europe are not as divided as they seem and they are certainly not divided in the ways that a superficial political map would mislead us. Clinton lost by failing to capture some greater percentage of non-urban Michigan, Wisconsin, and Pennsylvania, and by a loss of urban enthusiasm among Black voters [4]. She lost by hardly even visiting these non-urban settings.

Instead of joining with working-class Whites, and "feeling their pain," she disaffected them by including them in the "deplorables," as she called Trump supporters. Bridges to labor and the laborer in particular were eroded rather than strengthened and whole landscapes of America were treated with anathema. Hillary's liberalism neither reached out to the American heartlands nor reached in to the inner-cities. Bernie Sanders' more liberal followers were incapable of stirring African American support because you cannot begin to join with people when you are already campaigning. You must stand with them daily, and join their struggles and White liberals had not connected with African Americans and did not support Black Lives Matter in a way that was convincing to African Americans. So, the antidote here is to meet, caucus, respect, dialogue, and break bread together. I would give no refuge to alt-right White supremacists or outright racists. But polls show that a majority of Americans have common dreams, values, and in fact are moving toward more liberal viewpoints. In fact, there was a magnetic connection on economic revival, fairness of trade practices, and the unholy marriage of politicians with Wall Street among both Trump and Sanders supporters. Virtually all of us see life as precious and recognize that conception is a miracle. Only disturbed individuals support any kind of violence against women. We all wish to see good schools for our children. We cherish our freedom. We want to see our children grow up in safety. We find paying taxes painful, especially where we see waste. We see government as dysfunctional, even if we blame each other for the dysfunction. We don't want to see police killed and we don't want African American children and men to fear the police.

Of course this gathering to discuss and find inclusive solutions will not come easily. It would challenge us to seek pathways that allow states to slow "progress" on liberal solutions, and give greater voice in liberal strongholds to the day-to-day survival of a middle class that fears falling into the lower class, losing their home. We will have to figure out a way to ease coal miners' fears of loss of their livelihood, before we impose clean air standards. People need a stable home and to feed their families in dignity before they will give support for clean air. Said another way, to demand clean air when one's belly is full and rent is secure is elitist when others lack safety and security. Lack of sensitivity to this is the equivalent of "then let them eat cake."

9.4   A New Dawn

Populism, with its xenophobic, protectionist, law-and-order militancy will not be converted to liberal democracy and tolerance with a whimper. Fascism, if it evolves, can only be reversed with eruptive political force. With our genetic, evolutionarily primitive drive fully in gear, historically successful reversals have ridden the powerful wave of a "new dawn." Without the powerful thrust of the "new dawn," slippage back to xenophobia and intolerance and fascist practices are inevitable.

The post-Soviet devolution of communism failed to inspire a new dawn of positive leadership. Instead, power struggles among those already in power developed with the emergence of a billionaire oligarchy that gave way to a new fascism and populist strongman authoritarianism. But we need not look overseas and to our historic enemies for failed new dawns.

With the assassination of Abraham Lincoln in 1865, the proposed new dawn for the reunited America was mismanaged and perpetuated with a period of unprecedented corruption and unscrupulous practices. Lincoln's vice president, Andrew Johnson, hoped to foster Lincoln's vision of reconciliation, but he was weak and lacked the political savvy to outmaneuver those in Congress who were determined to punish the South (i.e., tribalist revenge), rather than help rebuild it. Nor was Johnson motivated to ensure the right to vote to African Americans, a right that was not proffered with their emancipation as we might assume. What followed was nearly one hundred years of Southern poverty, and unmitigated cronyism and corruption. Without the vision and power of federal control, White Southerners reestablished dominance over Blacks through violence, intimidation, and law in a dark era that lasted another ten decades. Rather than a new dawn, the failures of Reconstruction led to a long darkness and a post-Confederate America that lacked prosperity for most and was impoverished, intolerant, and demeaning to millions of African Americans.

9.5   The Solution of Camelot

The most positive recent example of the new dawn is Kennedy's Camelot that followed the dark Red Scare that dominated the Eisenhower years. The new dawn for America was a vision of a lofty, powerful new society characterized by both social justice and safety. And our genetics will not permit us to embark on the former, without a clear sense of the latter. The new dawn must project the evolutionary elements of tribal strength and power, unity, and willingness to answer threat with force, as it calls on a sense of sacrifice to create the new world order.

Kennedy's new dawn was clear:

...a beachhead of cooperation may push back the jungle of suspicion,...a new world of law, where the strong are just, and the weak secure, and the peace preserved.

Now the trumpet summons us again. ... a call to bear the burden of a long twilight struggle, A struggle against common enemies of man, tyranny, poverty, disease, and war itself.... The energy, the faith, the devotion which we bring to this endeavor light our country and all serve it. And the glow from that fire can truly light the world. [5]

But this vision was delivered with a powerful show of force:

Let every nation know, whether it wishes us well or ill, that we shall pay any price, bear any burden, meet any hardship, support any friend, oppose any foe to assure the survival and the success of liberty

....Finally, to those nations who would make themselves our adversary, we offer not a pledge but a request: that both sides begin anew the quest for peace, ...[However] We dare not tempt them with weakness. For only when our arms are sufficient beyond doubt can we be certain beyond doubt that they will never be employed... [5]

Kennedy threatened any would-be foe with a powerful metaphor:

...those who foolishly sought power by riding the back of the tiger ended up inside. [5]

And Kennedy punctuated his vision with the call for unity of the tribe which, as is encoded in our genetic heritage, comes with the expectation of sacrifice to the tribe and its new vision.

In this long history of the world, only a few generations have been granted the role of defending freedom in its hour of maximum danger. I do not shrink from this responsibility, I welcome it. I do not believe that any of us would exchange places with any other people, or any other generation. The energy, the faith, the devotion which we bring to this endeavor light our country and all serve it. And the glow from that fire can truly light the world.

Will you join in that historic effort? ...And so, my fellow Americans: ask not what your country can do for you—ask what you can do for your country. (John F. Kennedy Inauguration speech, January 20, 1961 [5])

9.6   CONCLUSIONS

An understanding of our evolutionary tribal genetics and its power outline the parameters of reversing the current period of intolerance and perhaps its flirtation with fascism. Our renewed approach in the battle against populism, intolerance, and fascism will need to embrace many of the rules of populism's focus on a strong "we" and an identified "enemy," but do so with a positive vision of tolerance and uniting under the banner of liberal democracy. It will need to be a big tent, and cannot exclude those who have not fully embraced any given notions of liberalism, but instead seek the support of those who support a basic set of agreed principles. It must bring honor to those who share the dream. History instructs that it will require a dynamic leader who can inspire the young and be trusted by those older. It will arrive with flag waving and have to carry a clear, and even exaggerated plan to safeguard us from our enemies. It may not need to rattle sabers, but a saber must be clearly visible and held at the ready. It will be as imperfect as Washington, Lincoln, Kennedy, and Obama were as they inspired us with their vision.

For in the end, we need not be ruled by our evolutionary genetics to protect and aggress. Humans have also in their evolutionary capacity to nurture the tribe as nation, and perhaps even as humanity. When safety is felt, people will adopt the risks inherent in altruism and giving to others. When our sense of loss and threat are effectively mitigated, the more evolved aspects of culture can flourish. Working toward the collective good, protection of the weak, charity, and benevolence are not as powerfully represented in our genetics as "aggress and defend," but they are nonetheless there to be nurtured. We share a common garden called earth, and if we can more fairly support policies and practices whereby all can flourish, there is more willingness to compromise and find pathways that promote tolerance and acceptance. Women's rights matter, Black lives matter, and White livelihood matters. We all hold prejudices and yet most are open to accepting others, even if they may do so grudgingly and with caution. Humans have the capacity to override their evolutionary fears and the wiring that elicits aggression.

Although it is only a feeling, and this volume has tried to be more scientific than feeling based, I suspect that the women's movement will be a major driving force for the next new dawn. Our mothers, sisters, wives, and daughters are the only oppressed group that cross all other boundaries of religion, race, ethnicity, and nationality. And women are far less trapped in the genetic-based power of tribalism and have a much stronger drive toward nurturance than men. But change will require a courageous free press, the raising of many voices, and the reaching across many divides. We cannot wait for a Messiah, but we can hope for voices of leadership that restore compassion, tolerance, and a drive toward free and open society, protection of those less able to protect themselves, and a restoration of hope over hatred.

REFERENCES

1. Bush, L. (2014, May 19). *The morphology of a humorous phrase: "We have met the enemy and he is us".* Humor In America. Retrieved February 13, 2018, from https://humorinamerica.wordpress.com/2014/05/19/the-morphology-of-a-humorous-phrase/

2. Braun, H. J. (1990). *The German economy in the twentieth century: The German Reich and the Federal Republic.* New York: Routledge.
3. Roosevelt, F. D. (1940, December 29). Fireside chat. Retrieved October 26, 2017, from http://www.presidency.ucsb.edu/ws/?pid=15917
4. Brownstein, R. (2016, November 17). How the election revealed the divide between city and country. *The Atlantic.* Retrieved January 4, 2017, from https://www.theatlantic.com/politics/archive/2016/11/clinton-trump-city-country-divide/507902/
5. Kennedy, J. F. (1961, January 20). *Inaugural Address.* Washington, DC. Retrieved October 26, 2017, from https://www.jfklibrary.org/Asset-Viewer/BqXIEM9F4024ntFl7SVAjA.aspx

Index[1]

---

[1]Note: Page numbers followed by 'n' refer to notes

© The Author(s) 2018
S. E. Hobfoll, *Tribalism*,
https://doi.org/10.1007/978-3-319-78405-2

205

Made in the USA
Coppell, TX
22 February 2021